P9-AFO-782

Physician Travelers

# Journal of a Voyage

## to

# New South Wales

## John White

Arno Press & The New York Times
New York * 1971

PHYSICIAN TRAVELERS

Editor
ROBERT M. GOLDWYN, M.D.

This book is reprinted from a copy in the
Francis A. Countway Library of Medicine

Library of Congress Catalog Card No. 76-115629
ISBN 0-405-01726-X
ISBN for complete set 0-405-01710-3

Manufactured in the United States of America, 1971

## About the Author

JOHN WHITE HAD BEEN A SHIP SURGEON in the West Indies and in India. In 1788, at the age of thirty, he became Surgeon-General to the First Fleet and later to the settlement at Port Jackson, near Sydney, Australia. His account, published originally in 1790, is an important eyewitness document in the history of New South Wales. White provided considerable information about the voyage from England and the events in the infant colony, which was settled largely by convicts. We read of the dangers that beset the settlement: disease, malnutrition, hostile aborigines. An important part of White's book concerns local plants, trees, flowers, birds, lizards, snakes, fish, spiders, sheels, and mammals. As far as can be determined, White did not have any training in natural history, but he diligently—though haphazardly—collected specimens that were sent back to England, where they were recorded, identified, and illustrated for his book.

We also learn about White's personality through description of his relations with other physicians and settlers and with the female convict who was his housekeeper, then his mistress, and finally the mother of his child. Taking his infant son with him, White returned to England in 1794, after seven years in Australia. He later married and died near Brighton in 1832, aged seventy-four.

R. M. G.

# JOURNAL

*of a*

## Voyage to new South Wales

with Sixty-five Plates of

*Non descript Animals, Birds, Lizards*
*Serpents, curious Cones of Trees and other*

# NATURAL PRODUCTIONS

*By John White Esq.*[re]

Surgeon General to the Settlement.

VIEW IN PORT JACKSON.

## LONDON

*Printed for J. Debrett, Piccadilly*

MDCCXC

# To THOMAS WILSON, Esq.

DEAR SIR,

AS the following Journal was undertaken at your Requeſt, and its principal Object to afford you ſome Amuſement during your Hours of Relaxation, I ſhall eſteem myſelf happy if it anſwers that Purpoſe.

I hope that the Specimens of Natural Hiſtory may tend to the Promotion of your favourite Science, and that, on this Account, it will not be unacceptable to you. By the next Conveyance I truſt I ſhall be enabled to make ſome Additions, that will not be unworthy the Attention of the Naturaliſts.

A

Let

# DEDICATION.

Let my prefent Communications, which the
fudden failing of the Ships from hence, and the
Duties of my Department, have rendered lefs
copious than I intended, at leaft ferve to convince you of my Readinefs at all Times to comply
with your Wifhes; and of the Refpect and Efteem
with which I am,

DEAR SIR,

YOUR VERY OBEDIENT

AND HUMBLE SERVANT,

Sydney Cove,
Port Jackfon, New South Wales,
November 18th, 1788.

JOHN WHITE.

# ADVERTISEMENT.

IT becomes the duty of the Editor, as much as it is his inclination, to return his public and grateful acknowledgments to the Gentlemen, through whofe abilities and liberal communications, in the province of Natural Hiftory, he has been enabled to furmount thofe difficulties that neceffarily attended the defcription of fo great a variety of animals, prefented for the firft time to the obfervation of the Naturalift, and confequently in the clafs of Non-defcripts.

Among thofe Gentlemen he has the honour, particularly, to reckon the names of Dr. Shaw; Dr. Smith, the poffeffor of the celebrated Linnæan Collection; and John Hunter, Efq. who, to a fublime and inventive genius, happily unites a difinterefted and generous zeal for the promotion of natural fcience.

The Public may rely, with the moft perfect confidence, on the care and accuracy with which the Drawings have been copied from nature, by Mifs Stone, Mr. Catton, Mr. Nodder, and other artifts; and the Editor flatters himfelf the Engravings are all executed with equal correctnefs, by, or under the immediate infpection of Mr. Milton. The Birds, &c. from which the drawings were taken are depofited in the Leverian Mufeum.

# A LIST OF SUBSCRIBERS.

## A.

A'COURT, William Pierce Afhe, Efq. M. P.

Addifon, Edward, Efq.

Anderfon, Thomas, Efq.

Anftruther, John, Efq. M. P.

Allen, Jofeph, Efq.

Arthur, Mr.

Adair, James, Efq.

## B.

Burrell, Sir William, Bart.

Barnard, Mr.

Brifac, Mrs. G.

Banks, Sir Jofeph, Bart.

Budgen, John Smith, Efq.

Buck, George, Efq.

Brook, Mr.

Brook, Mr. Richard

Bolt, John, Efq.

Bunbury, Sir Tho. Charles, Bart. M. P.

Bonnor, Mr. William

Bowering, Mr.

Bofville, William, Efq.

Bradfhaw, Auguftus Cavendifh, Efq.

Buckingham Book Club

Bowyer, George, Efq.

Boldero, Charles, Efq.

Binftead, Thomas, Efq.

Blackmore, Mr.

a                    Buckmafter,

# SUBSCRIBERS.

Buckmafter, Jofeph, Efq.
Barwell, Edward, Efq.
Barton, the Rev. Mr.
Brown, Jackfon, Efq.
Bateman, Lord Vifcount
Byrne, William, Efq.
Beckett, Mr. Bookfeller, 4 copies
Barker, George Hollington, Efq.
Baldwin, Mr. Bookfeller, 25 copies
Bew, Mr. ditto, 12 ditto

### C.

Crewe, John, Efq. M. P.
Caldwell, Sir John, Bart.
Cotterell, John, Efq.
Cavendifh, Right Hon. Sir Henry, Bart.
Carpenter, Richard, Efq.
Combe, Dr.
Caflon, William, Efq.
Clake, Rev. James Charles
Church, James Miller, Efq.
Crookfhanks, John, Efq.
Crace, John, Efq.
Carter, Thomas, Efq.
Clarke, Richard, Efq.
Currie, Mark, Efq.
Chafe, John, Efq.
Claridge, Mr.

Chapman, Mr. Henry, two copies.
Calvert, Robert, Efq.
Calvert, Charles, Efq.
Cornewall, Thomas, Efq.
Clark, Mr. Bookfeller, 6 copies
Clarke, Mr. ditto, 3 ditto
Cuthell, Mr. ditto, 3 ditto
Cooper, Mr. ditto, 6 ditto

### D.

Dundas, Sir Thomas, Bart. M.P.
Dawkins, Henry, Efq.
Donegal, the Earl of
Dyer, Mr. George
Dormer, Lady Cottrell
Doo, John, Efq.
Digby, the Rev. Noel
Delgarno, John, Efq.
Dent, John, Efq.
Dilly, Mr. Bookfeller, 6 copies
Deighton, Mr. ditto 6 ditto

### E.

Ellis, George, Efq.
Earle, George, Efq.
Evans, Mr. David
Elliot, William, Efq.
Eardley, Mrs.

Eftridge.

# SUBSCRIBERS.

Eftridge, John, Efq.
Englefield, Sir Henry, Bart.
Eaton, the Rev. Stephen
Elmfley, Mr. Bookfeller, 6 copies
Egerton, Meff. T. and J. ditto, 15 do.
Edwards, Mr. ditto, 9 ditto
Evans, Mr. ditto, 6 ditto
Earle, Mr. 3 copies

## F.

Falkner, Thomas, Efq.
Fullarton, William, Efq.
Fonnereau, Martin, Efq.
Fairbank, Mr.
Fitzhugh, Thomas, Efq.
Faulder, Mr. Bookfeller, 15 copies
Forbes, Mr. Bookfeller, 3 copies
Fofter, Mr. 12 copies
Freeman, John, Efq.

## G.

Gardiner, Sir John Whalley, Bart.
Godfrey, John, Efq.
Gilbert, Captain
Garrow, William, Efq.
Garrow, Jofeph, Efq.
Grierfon, J. Efq.
Gregfon, Mr. C.

Groombridge, Mr.
Goldfmid, Jeremiah, Efq.
Goldfmid, Abraham, Efq.
Goodenough, Rev. Dr.
Gray, Richard, Efq.
Gardner, Mr. Bookfeller, 9 copies

## H.

Harwood, William, Efq.
Hargrave, Francis, Efq.
Holland, Richard, Efq.
Hawke, Lord
Hawkins, Thomas, Efq.
Hookham, Mr. Bookfeller, 12 copies
Hughes, Sir Edward, K. B.
Heydinger, Mr.
Hume, Sir Abraham, Bart.
Holmes, Leonard Troughear, Efq.
Hall, Mr.
Hoare, Charles, Efq.
Halliday, Capt. John Smith
Home, Everard, Efq.
Hibbert, Thomas, Efq.
Hodgfon, John, Efq.
Hibbert, George, Efq.
Hunter, John, Efq.
Heylin, J. Efq.
Howe, Captain
Harlow, Mrs. Bookfeller, 6 copies

Hanbury,

SUBSCRIBERS.

Hanbury, William, Efq.
Harpur, Robert, Efq.
Hafkoll, Mr.

J.

Jenkins, Rev. Mr.
James, Charles, Efq.
Inchiquin, the Earl of, K. P.
Jeffery, Mr. Bookfeller, 6 copies
Jervoife Clarke Jervoife, Efq.
Johnfon, Mr. Bookfeller, 12 copies

K.

Kanmacher, Mr. Frederick
King, Lord
Kelfall, Lieutenant
Kenton, B. Efq.
Kennion, Mr.
Keys, Richard, Efq.
Kerby, Mr. John, Bookfeller, 6 copies
Kerby, Mr. James, ditto, 6 ditto

L.

Lettfom, Dr.
Lewifham, Vifcount
Lucan, Lord

Lomax, Mr. Charles
Lowes, J. Efq.
Lawrence, Richard, Efq. two copies
L. P. Efq.
Lake, Sir James Winter, Bart.
Lofack, Mrs.
London, Rt. Rev. the Lord Bifhop of
Lefter, Mr.
Long, William, Efq.
Ladbroke, Felix, Efq.
Longman, Mr. Bookfeller, 6 copies
Law, Mr. ditto, 9 copies
Lewis, Mr. ditto, 6 ditto

M.

Molefworth, Sir William, Bart.
Monro, Dr. John
Marfham, Hon. Charles
Mellow, A. Efq. two copies
Mundy, Edward Miller, Efq. M. P.
Mollyneux, Sir Francis, Bart.
Murray, Mr. 6 copies
Minfhull, William, Efq.
Minet, Daniel, Efq.
Mollyneux, Mifs
Mackenzie, Alexander, Efq.
Milton, Mr. Thomas

Nefbit,

## N.

Nesbitt, John, Esq. M. P.
Noble, Francis, Esq.
Nassau, Hon. Mr.

## O.

Orford, the Earl of, 2 copies
Orr, Captain
Osbaldeston, George, Esq.
Ormerod, Rev. Mr.
Ogilvy and Speare, Messrs. Book-
    sellers, 3 copies

## P.

Pennant, Thomas, Esq.
Pitt, William, Esq.
Parker, Sir Hyde
Popham, John, Esq.
Peachey, Sir James, Bart.
Peachey, John, Esq.
Price, Charles, Esq.
Popplewell, Mr.
Pratt, John, Esq.
Parkinson, Rev. John
Purling, John, Esq.
Pœliskie, Lewis, Esq.
Poulter, Rev. Mr.

Pratt, Mr. J.
Price, Mr. William.
Powlett, the Rev. Charles
Pigou, W. H. Esq.
Payne and Son, Messrs. Booksellers,
    15 copies
Phillips, Mr. ditto, 6 ditto

## R.

Rushworth, Edward, Esq. M. P.
Rous, Thomas Bates, Esq.
Rainsford, Mr.
Ramus, Mr.
Roberts, John, Esq.
Rebello, D. A. Esq.
Robinson, J. Esq.
Raynsford, Nicolls, Esq.
Rycroft, Sir Nelson, Bart.
Rigg, J. Jun. Esq.
Reppington, Charles Edward, Esq.
Ridley, Sir Mathew White, Baronet,
    M. P.
Richards, the Rev. Mr.
Rowles, Charles Lee, Esq.
Rudge, Samuel, Esq.
Robinsons, Messrs. Booksellers, 60
    copies
Rivington and Sons, ditto, 6 ditto
Robson, Mr. ditto, 6 copies
                    Spencer,

# SUBSCRIBERS.

Spencer, Earl
Sturt, Charles, Efq. M. P.
Songa, A. Efq.
Stimpfon, Captain
Styan, Mr.
Smith, William, Efq.
Swainfon, Ifaac, Efq.
Smith, Mr.
Shuttleworth, Robert, Efq.
Smith, Sir John, Bart.
Sage, Ifaac, Efq.
Spence, George, Efq.
St. John, Lord
Staniforth, William, Efq.
Smith, Mrs. late Mifs Stone
Shaw, Doctor
Smith, Dr.
Sewell, Mr. Bookfeller, 62 copies
Strahan, Mr. ditto, 3 copies
Scatcherd and Whitaker, Meffrs. 6 do.

### T.

Tahourdin, I. S. Efq.
Twigge, Rev. Mr.
Taylor, Michael Angelo, Efq. M. P.
Throckmorton, John, Efq.
Todd, Thomas, Efq.
Tunnard, William, Efq.
Tunftall, Marmaduke, Efq.
Tyrwhit, Emund, Efq.

Trevelyan, Sir John, Bart. M. P.
Turner, John, Efq.
Tahourdin, Captain
Tempeft, John, Efq. M. P.
Tollemache, the Hon. Mr.
Teffeyman, Mr. William, 6 copies
Taylor, Meffrs. J. and J. 3 copies

### U.

Uphill, Mr.
Upjohn, Mr. Peter
Upjohn, Mr.

### W.

Wilfon, Thomas, Efq. 20 copies
Wilfon, Rev. Jofeph
Woodd, Mr. John
Wools, Mr.
Warren, Dr.
Ward, Rev. William
Walfh, John, Efq.
Walford, Thomas, Efq.
Wilfon, Mr. George
Ward, Rev. Mr.
Watfon, Hon. Lewis
Watherfton, Dalhoufie, Efq.
White, Rev. Edward
Watfon, Thomas, Efq.

Winchefter,

## SUBSCRIBERS.

Winchester, the Rt. Rev. the Lord
 Bishop of
Willan, Dr.
Walpole, Lord
Wilson, Lady
Whalley, James, Esq.
Wollaston, Mr.
Wallace, Sir James
Worsley, the Rev. Henry, of Arriton,
 Hants
Worsley, the Rev. H. of Whitcombe
Wynne, Robert Watkyn, Esq. M. P.
White, Mr. Bookseller, 3 copies

Walker, Thomas, Esq.
Weld, Richard, Esq.
Wakeman, Thomas, Esq.
Wright, Mr. Thomas
Walker, Mr. Bookseller, 12 copies
Wilkie, Messrs. ditto, 6 copies
White and Son, ditto, 18 ditto
Walter, Mr. Charing Cross, ditto,
 15 ditto

### Z.

Zimmermann, Mr.

# A
# LIST
## OF
# PLATES.

# A LIST OF PLATES.

# A LIST OF PLATES.

# WHITE's JOURNAL

##### OF A

## VOYAGE

##### TO

## *NEW SOUTH WALES.*


I THIS day left London, charged with difpatches from the Secretary of State's office, and from the Admiralty, relative to the embarkation of that part of the marines and convicts intended for Botany Bay; and on the evening of the feventh, after travelling two days of the moft inceffant rain I ever remember, arrived at Plymouth, where the Charlotte and Friendfhip tranfports were in readinefs to receive them.

General Collins, commander in chief at that port, loft no time in carrying the orders I had brought into execution: fo that on the morning of the ninth, the detachment of marines were on board, with all the baggage. But the


1787.
March 5.

B

next

next day being ufhered in with a very heavy gale of wind, made it impracticable to remove the convicts from on board the Dunkirk prifon-fhip, where they were confined. So violent was the gale, that his Majefty's fhip the Druid, of thirty-two guns, was forced to cut away her main-maft to prevent her driving on fhore.

The weather being moderate the following day, the convicts were put on board the tranfports, and placed in the different apartments allotted for them; all fecured in irons, except the women. In the evening, as there was but little wind, we were towed by the boats belonging to the guardfhips out of the Hamaoze, where the Dunkirk lay, into Plymouth Sound. When this duty was completed, the boats returned; and the wind now frefhening fo as to enable us to clear the land, we proceeded to Spithead, where we arrived the feventeenth, and anchored on the Mother Bank, among the reft of the tranfports and victuallers intended for the fame expedition, under the conduct of his Majefty's fhip the Sirius. As foon as the fhip came to anchor, I vifited all the other tranfports, and was really furprifed to find the convicts on board them fo very healthy. When I got on board the Alexander, I found there a medi-

cal

cal gentleman from Portfmouth, among whofe acquaintance I had not the honour to be numbered. He fcarcely gave me time to get upon the quarter-deck, before he thus addreffed me—" I am very glad you are arrived, Sir; for " your people have got a *malignant* difeafe among them of " a moft dangerous kind; and it will be neceffary, for their " prefervation, to get them immediately relanded!" Surprifed at fuch a falutation, and alarmed at the purport of it, I requefted of my affiftant, Mr. Balmain, an intelligent young man, whom I had appointed to this fhip for the voyage, to let me fee the people who were ill. " Sir," returned Mr. Balmain, taking me afide, " you will not find " things by any means fo bad as this gentleman reprefents " them to be: they are made much worfe by him than " they really are. Unlike a perfon wifhing to adminifter " comfort to thofe who are afflicted, either in body or in " mind, he has publicly declared before the poor creatures " who are ill, that they muft inevitably fall a facrifice to " the malignant diforder with which they are afflicted;— " the malignity of which appears to me to exift only in his " own imagination. I did not, however," continued Mr. Balmain, " think proper to contradict the gentleman; fuppofing,

B 2 " from

" from the confequence he affumed, and the eafe with
" which he had given his opinion, or more properly his
" *directions*, that he was fome perfon appointed by the
" Secretary of State to officiate for you till your arrival.
" When you go among the people you will be better able to
" judge of the propriety of what I have faid." Mr. Balmain
had no fooner concluded than I went between decks, and found
every thing juft as he had reprefented it to be.    There were
feveral in bed with flight inflammatory complaints;  fome
there were who kept their bed to avoid the inconvenience
of the cold, which was at this time very piercing,  and whofe
wretched clothing was but a poor defence againft the
rigour of it; others were confined to their bed through the
effects of long imprifonment, a weakened habit, and low-
nefs of fpirits; which was not a little added to by the declaration of the medical gentleman above mentioned, whom
they concluded to be the principal furgeon to the expedition. However, on my undeceiving them in that point, and
at the fame time confirming what Mr. Balmain had from the
firft told them, viz. *that their complaints were neither malignant nor dangerous*, their fears abated.    To this I added,
that I would immediately give orders for fuch as were in

want

want of clothing, to be supplied with what was needful; a power delegated to me by Captain Phillip, together with the liberty of giving such other directions as I thought would tend to the recovery or preservation of their health. And further, as they had been nearly four months on board, and during that time had been kept upon salt provisions, I would endeavour to get fresh for them while in port. This short conversation had so sudden an effect on those I addressed, and was of so opposite a tendency to that of the gentleman alluded to, that before we got from between decks, I had the pleasure to see several of them put on such clothes as they had, and look a little cheerful. I then pointed out to Lieutenant Johnson, commanding officer of the marines on board, and to the master of the ship, the necessity there was of admitting the convicts upon the deck, one half at a time, during the course of the day; in order that they might breathe a purer air, as nothing would conduce more to the preservation of their health. To this these gentlemen readily assented; adding, that they had no objection to the whole number coming upon deck at once, if I thought it necessary, as they were not apprehensive of any danger from the indulgence. On returning to the quarter-deck, I found my new

medical

medical acquaintance ftill there; and before I could give fome directions to Mr. Balmain, as I was about to do, he thus once more addreffed me—" I fuppofe you are now " convinced of the dangerous difeafe that prevails among " thefe people, and of the neceffity of having them landed, " in order to get rid of it." Not a little hurt at the abfurd part the gentleman had acted, and at his repeated importunity, I replied with fome warmth, " that I was very forry to " differ fo effentially in opinion from him, as to be obliged " to tell him that there was not *the leaft appearance* of " malignity in the difeafe under which the convicts labour- " ed, but that it wholly proceeded from the cold; and was " nearly fimilar to a complaint then prevalent, even among " the better fort of people, in and about Portfmouth." Notwithftanding this, he ftill perfifted fo much in the propriety of their being landed, and the neceffity there was for an application to the Secretary of State upon the occafion, that I could no longer keep my temper; and I freely told him, " that the idea of landing them was as improper as it " was abfurd. And, in order to make him perfectly eafy " on that head, I affured him, that when any difeafe ren- " dered it neceffary to call in medical aid, he might reft

" fatisfied

" fatisfied I would not trouble *him*; but would apply to
" Doctor Lind, Phyfician to the Royal Hofpital at Hafler,
" a gentleman as eminently diftinguifhed for his profef-
" fional abilities as his other amiable qualities: or elfe to
" fome of the furgeons of his Majefty's fhips in Portfmouth
" harbour, or at Spithead, moft of whom I had the plea-
" fure of knowing, and on whofe medical knowledge I was
" certain I could depend." This peremptory declaration
had the defired effect. The gentleman took his leave, to
my great fatisfaction, and thereby gave me an opportunity
of writing by that evening's poft, to inform the Secretary of
State, and Captain Phillip, of the real ftate of the fick; and
at the fame time to urge the neceffity of having frefh provifions ferved to the whole of the convicts while in port, as
well as a little wine for thofe who were ill. Frefh provifions I dwelt moft on, as being not only needful for the
recovery of the fick, but otherwife effential, in order to
prevent any of them commencing fo long and tedious a
voyage as they had before them with a fcorbutic taint; a
confequence that would moft likely attend their living upon
falt food; and which, added to their needful confinement
and great numbers, would, in all probability, prove fatal

to

to them, and thereby defeat the intention of Government.

The return of the post brought me an answer; and likewise an order to the contractor for supplying the marines and convicts daily with fresh beef and vegetables, while in port. A similar order I found had been given long before my arrival; but, by some strange mistake or other, had not been complied with. The salutary effect of this change of diet, with the addition of some wine and other necessaries ordered for the sick, through the humanity of Lord Sydney, manifested itself so suddenly, that in the space of a fortnight, on comparing my list of sick with that of a surgeon belonging to one of the guardships, allowing for the disproportion of numbers, mine did not exceed his. And yet, notwithstanding this, which is a well known fact, the report of a most malignant disease still prevailed: and so industriously was the report promulgated and kept alive by some evil-minded people, who either wished to throw an odium on the humane promoters of the plan, or to give uneasiness to the friends and relations of those engaged in the expedition, that letters from all quarters were pouring in upon us, commiserating our state. The newspapers were daily filled with alarming

accounts

accounts of the fatality that prevailed among us; and the rumour became general, notwithstanding every step was taken to remove these fears, by assurances (which were strictly true) that the whole fleet was in as good a state of health, and as few in it would be found to be ill, at that cold season of the year, as even in the most healthy situation on shore. The clearest testimony that there was more malignity in the report than in the disease, may be deduced from the very inconsiderable number that have died since we left England; which I may safely venture to say is much less than ever was known in so long a voyage (the numbers being proportionate), even though not labouring under the disadvantages we were subject to, and the crowded state we were in.

During the absence of Captain Phillip, I mentioned to Captain Hunter of the Sirius, that I thought whitewashing with quick lime the parts of the ships where the convicts were confined, would be the means of correcting and preventing that unwholesome dampness which usually appeared on the beams and sides of the ships, and was occasioned by the breath of the people. Captain Hunter agreed with me on the propriety of the step: and with that oblig-

C                                                        ing

ing willingnefs which marks his character, made the necef-sary application to commiffioner Martin; who, on his part, as readily ordered the proper materials. The procefs was accordingly foon finifhed; and fully anfwered the purpofe intended.

May 12. His Majefty's fhip the Hyæna joined us this day, and put herfelf under the command of Captain Phillip, who had inftructions to take her with him as far as he fhould think needful. In the evening the Sirius made the fignal to weigh, and attempted to get down to St. Helen's; but the wind fhifting, and feveral of the convoy not getting under way, through fome irregularity in the feamen, fhe was obliged to anchor. When this was done, Captain Phillip fent Lieutenant King on board the fhips which had occafioned the detention, who foon adjufted the difficulties that had arifen; as they were found to proceed more from intoxication than from any nautical caufes.

13th. This morning the Sirius and her convoy weighed again, with an intention of going through St. Helen's; but the wind being fair for the Needles, we run through them, with a pleafant breeze. The Charlotte, Captain Gilbert, on board of which I was, failing very heavy, the

Hyæna

Hyæna took us in tow, until she brought us ahead of the Sirius, and then cast us off.

15th. An accident of a singular nature happened to-day. Corporal Baker of the marines, on laying a loaded musquet down, which he had just taken out of the arms chest, was wounded by it in the inner ankle of the right foot. The bones, after being a good deal shattered, turned the ball; which taking another direction, had still force enough left to go through a harness-cask full of beef, at some distance, and, after that, to kill two geese that were on the other side of it. Extraordinary as this incident may appear, it is no less true. The corporal being a young man, and in a good habit of body, I had the pleasure, contrary to the general expectation, of seeing him return to his duty in three months, with the perfect use of the wounded joint.

20th. A discovery of a futile scheme, formed by the convicts on board the Scarborough, was made by one of that body, who had been recommended to Captain Hunter previous to our sailing. They had laid a plan for making themselves masters of the ship; but being prevented by this discovery, two of the ringleaders were carried on board the Sirius, where they were punished; and afterwards put on

board

board the Prince of Wales tranſport, from which time they behaved very well. Being now near one hundred leagues to the weſtward of Scilly, and all well, Captain Phillip found it no longer neceſſary to keep the Hyæna with him; therefore, having committed his letters to the care of the Hon. Captain De Courcey, he in the courſe of this day ſent her back.

28th. Departed this life, Iſmael Coleman, a convict, who, worn out by lowneſs of ſpirits and debility, brought on by long and cloſe confinement, reſigned his breath without a pang.

30th. In the forenoon paſſed to the ſouthward of Madeira, and ſaw ſome turtle of the hawks-bill kind.

June 2d. Saw and paſſed the Salvages. Theſe iſlands are not laid down in any of the charts we had on board, except a ſmall one, by Hamilton Moore, in the poſſeſſion of the ſecond mate. They lie, by our obſervation, in lat. 30°. 10′. N. long. 15°. 9′. W.

3d. This evening, after ſeeing many ſmall fiſh in our way from the Salvages, we arrived at Teneriffe, and anchored in Santa Cruz road, about a mile to the N. E. of the town of that name, in ſixteen fathom water; ſome of the

ſhips

ships came to in twenty fathom. We were visited the same night, as is the custom of the port, by the harbour master, and gained permission to water, and procure such refreshments as the island afforded. The marines were now served with wine in lieu of spirits; a pound of fresh beef was likewise daily distributed to them as well as to the convicts; together with a pound of rice instead of bread, and such vegetables as could be procured. Of the latter indeed the portion was rather scanty, little besides onions being to be got; and still less of fruit, it being too early in the season.

4th. Captain Phillip, as governor of his Majesty's territories in New South Wales, and commander in chief of the expedition, accompanied by twenty of the principal officers, paid his respects to the Marquis de Brancifort, governor of this and the other Canary islands. We were received by his Excellency with great politeness and cordiality; and after the ceremony of introduction was over, he entered into familiar conversation with Captain Phillip on general topics. In person the Marquis is genteel; he is rather above the middle size, but cannot boast of much *embonpoint*; his countenance is animated; his deportment easy and graceful; and both his appearance and manners

perfectly

perfectly correspond with the idea universally entertained of the dignity of a grandee of Spain. This accomplished nobleman, as I have been informed, is not a Spaniard by birth, but a Sicilian; and descended from some of the princes of that island. On this ancestry and descent, it is visible that he prides himself not a little. The people he is placed over will have it, that he carries himself with too much statelinefs to be long a favourite there; they cannot, however, help acknowledging that he preferves a degree of disinterestednefs, moderation, and justice, in his conduct towards them, that is not to be objected to.

6th. A convict, named James Clark, died of a dropsy; he had been tapped ten days before, and discharged twelve quarts of water.

8th. During the night, while the people were busily employed in taking in water on board the Alexander, a fervice in which some of the convicts assisted, one of them, of the name of Powel, found means to drop himself unperceived into a small boat that lay along-side; and under cover of the night to cast her off without discovery. He then drifted to a Dutch East Indiaman that had just come to an anchor, to the crew of which he told a plausible story,

and

and entreated to be taken on board; but, though they much wanted men, they would have nothing to do with him. Having committed himſelf again to the waves, he was driven by the wind and the current, in the courſe of the night, to a ſmall iſland lying to leeward of the ſhips, where he was the next morning taken. The boat and oars, which he could not conceal, led to a diſcovery; otherwiſe he would probably have effected his eſcape. When brought back by the party ſent after him, Captain Phillip ordered him into irons, in which ſtate he remained for ſome time; but at length, by an artful petition he got written for him, he ſo wrought on the governor's humanity, as to procure a releaſe from his confinement.

As you approach the iſland of Teneriffe, and even when you are near to it, the appearance from the ſea conveys no very favourable idea of its fertility; one rugged, barren hill or mountain terminating in another, until it forms the famous *Peak*. The town of Santa Cruz is large and populous, but very irregular and ill built; ſome of the private houſes, however, are ſpacious, convenient, and well conſtructed. Although this town is not conſidered as the capital, Laguna enjoying that pre-eminence, yet I can-

not

not help thinking it ought to be so; not only from its being more frequented by ships of various nations, and having a greater share of trade than any other port in the Canaries, but on account of its being the residence of the governor-general.

Among other steps for its improvement, the Marquis set on foot a contribution, and from the produce of it has caused to be built an elegant and commodious mole, or pier, about the center of the town. To this pier, water of an excellent quality is conveyed by pipes; so that boats may come along-side, and by applying a hose to the cocks placed there for this purpose, fill the casks without the usual trouble and fatigue. The landing or shipping of goods is likewise, by means of this pier, rendered both convenient and expeditious. In short, I think I may safely recommend this port as a very good one for ships undertaking long voyages to water at, and refresh their crews; more especially in the time of the fruit season.

About four or five miles, inland, from Santa Cruz, stands the city of Laguna; so called from a lake near which it is situated. This lake, during the winter, or in rainy weather, is full of stagnant water, that in a little time

becomes

becomes putrid, and, in very dry hot weather, is totally exhaled. I have before obſerved, that Laguna is conſidered as the capital of the iſland, and added my reaſons for thinking this an ill-judged diſtinction. The road from Santa Cruz to it is a pretty ſteep aſcent, until you approach the town, which is ſituated at the extremity, or rather on a corner, of a plain three or four miles long. This city has two churches, one of them richly ornamented; and ſeveral convents both of friars and nuns. It has likewiſe three hoſpitals; two of which were originally inſtituted for the wiſe, but ineffectual, purpoſe of eradicating the *lues venerea*; a diſeaſe that has long been, and ſtill continues to be, very common in this iſland. I was however informed, that perſons afflicted with other diſorders are now received into theſe two charitable inſtitutions; and that the third is appropriated to the reception of foundlings. Beſides the foregoing, there are ſome other public, as well as private buildings, that tend to improve the appearance of the town. There is very little trade carried on at Laguna, it being rather the retired reſidence of the gentry of the iſland, and of the merchants of Santa Cruz, which is the principal ſeat of commerce. The officers of juſtice likewiſe reſide here;

D

ſuch

such as the corrigedor, lieutenant of the police, &c. and a judge whose business it is to regulate commercial affairs. An office of inquisition, with the proper officers, delegated from, and subject to, the tribunal of the holy office held at Grand Canary, is besides established here.

The present natives of this island seem to have in them very little of the stock from whence they sprung; intermarriages with the Spaniards have nearly obliterated all traces of the original stamina: they are of a middle stature, inclining to be slender, and of a dark complexion, with large animated black eyes. The peasants in general are wretchedly clothed; when they do appear better, they are habited in the Spanish fashion. The men, in a genteeler line, dress very gaily, and are seldom seen without long swords. It is remarked, that few of them walk with dignity and ease; which may be attributed to the long cloaks they usually wear, except on particular occasions.

The women wear veils: those worn by the lower ranks are of black stuff, those of the higher, of black silk; and such among the latter as have any claim to beauty, are far from being over careful in concealing their faces by them. The young ladies, some of whom I saw that were

really

really pretty, wear their fine long black hair plaited, and faftened with a comb, or a ribbon, on the top of the head.

The common people, and in this they refemble the inhabitants of moft of the iflands in the Pacific Ocean lately difcovered, have a ftrong fpice of furacity in them; they are befides lazy; and the moft importunate beggars in the world: I obferved likewife, that the itch was fo common among them, and had attained fuch a degree of virulence, that one would almoft be led to believe it was *epidemic* there.

Some of the women are fo abandoned and fhamelefs, that it would be doing an injuftice to the proftitutes met with in the ftreets of London, to fay they are like them. The females of every degree are faid to be of an amorous conftitution, and addicted to intrigue; for which no houfes could be better adapted than thofe in Teneriffe.

The manufactures carried on here are very few, and the product of them little more than fufficient for their own confumption. They confift of taffeties, gauze, coarfe linens, blankets, a little filk, and curious garters. The principal dependance of the inhabitants is on their wine (their ftaple commodity), oil, corn, and every kind of ftock for fhipping.

D 2 With

With thefe the ifland abounds; and, in their feafon, produces not only the tropical fruits, but the vegetable productions of the European gardens, in the greateft plenty.   Teneriffe enjoys an agreeable and healthful mediocrity of climate.
Indeed I know of none better adapted for the reftoration of
a valetudinarian; as, by going into the mountains, he may
graduate the air, and chufe that ftate of it which beft fuits
his complaint.   But although the inhabitants are thus healthy,
and have fo little occafion for medical aid, they loudly com-
plain of the want of knowledge in the profeffional gentlemen
of the ifland.

The prefent governor has eftablifhed a manufactory of filk
and woollen goods in the fuburbs of Santa Cruz, which is
carried on by poor children, old and infirm people, and by
abandoned females, with a view to reclaiming them: an
inftitution that will ever do honour both to his excellency,
and to thofe who have liberally aided him in fo laudable a
fcheme.

Like the inhabitants of moft catholic countries, the
people of this ifland are very profufe in decorating their
churches, and even their dwelling-houfes, on the feftivals
held in honour of their faints.   This being *Corpus Chrifti*, a
day

day of much folemnity and parade, I went on fhore with
Lieutenant Ball of the Supply to fee the proceffion incident
to the occafion. Before we landed we formed a refolution
to avoid, as much as lay in our power, giving offence even
to the moft zealous devotee. But we found this was not to
be done. When we arrived at the church, from whence the
proceffion commenced, the Hoft was juft making its appearance; a circumftance that is announced by ringing of bells,
and firing of guns. As it paffed by us we fell on our knees,
as we obferved thofe around us to do; but it unfortunately
happening, that the fpot we knelt upon confifted of fand
intermixed with fmall rough pebbles, the pofture we were in
foon became fo exceedingly painful, that, in order to procure a momentary eafe, we only let one knee remain on the
ground. This heretical act did not efcape the obfervation of
one of the holy fathers, all of whom were intent on the exact
performance of every ceremonious etiquette. It procured for
us a frown from him, and treatment that was not of the moft
civil kind; fo that, in order to pacify him, we again dropped
on both knees. He did not, however, pafs on, without exhi-
biting ftrong marks of ill-nature and refentment in his countenance, at this trivial and unintended breach of refpectful
attention

attention to the religious rights of the country. The pro-cession, in which the governor and all the principal inhabi-tants joined, having paſſed through moſt of the ſtreets, returned, with the ſame ſolemnity, to the church it had ſet out from ; which was richly ornamented, and ſplendidly illuminated with large wax tapers, upon the occaſion. During our ſtay here, his excellency the governor entertained Captain Phillip and all the officers belonging to the expedi-tion with a very elegant dinner.

Before we ſailed from the Motherbank, a *ſporatic* diſeaſe had appeared among the marines and convicts. On its firſt appearance it reſembled the mumps, or ſwellings of the chaps; and as that diſtemper ſometimes terminates in a tranſlation of the inflammation to the teſticles, ſo this complaint (after the ſwelling and induration of the jaws had ſubſided, which uſually happened on the ſixth or ſeventh day) never in one inſtance failed to fix on thoſe parts ; and that in ſo very obſtinate a manner, as not to give way to the treatment generally found effectual in ſimilar inflammations. One of the convicts, thus affected, was ſeized with an intermitting fever : between the paroxyſm I gave him an emetic ; which had ſuch a ſudden and wonderful effect on this ſtrange com-plaint,

plaint, that I was induced to repeat it; and I found it effectual in this, as well as in all subsequent cases. As soon as we got to sea, the motion of the ship acted on all those who were affected, to the number of seventeen, in a most surprising and extraordinary manner. Indeed it was so sudden, that it was like a *placebo*. I could never account, with any satisfaction to myself, for the origin of this uncommon disease, though much acquainted with those incident to seamen; nor did I ever see or hear of any that resembled it. The most steady and prudent of the mariners, even those who had their wives on board, were equally affected with those who led more irregular lives. At first I attributed it to the verdigrease that might gather on the copper utensils wherein the provisions were cooked; but I am now fully persuaded that this was not the source from which it proceeded; for at the very time it was most prevalent, and attended with the greatest degree of inveteracy, the coppers were cleaned, and made as bright as they could be, every day, under my own inspection. Another proof, and a very strong one, that it did not proceed from the before-mentioned cause is, that the provisions still continued to be dressed in the same coppers, when the smallest trace of the disease was no

longer

longer to be perceived; which was the cafe after being four or five days at fea.

9th, P. M. the Sirius made the fignal for all officers to repair on board their refpective fhips; an officer was likewife fent to the governor, to inform him that we intended to put to fea in the morning, and, at the fame time, to thank him for the civilities and politenefs he had fhown us. His excellency returned, in anfwer to this meffage, that his beft and moft fincere good wifhes fhould attend us; and that he fhould ever feel a very particular intereft in our fuccefs; which he hoped would anfwer the intention of government, and the expectations of thofe who had fo cheerfully entered as volunteers on fo novel and very uncertain a fervice.

10th.   This morning the fleet got under way with a light breeze, which carried us out of Santa Cruz, but left us two days becalmed between Teneriffe and the Grand Canary. After this a fine breeze fprung up from the north-eaft; and no occurrence worthy of notice happened for fome days. We croffed the tropical line in 18°. 20′. weft longitude, and was nearly preffed on board the Lady Penrhynn tranfport, whofe people did not attend to her fteerage, being deeply engaged in fluicing and ducking all thofe on board who had never croffed it.

17th.

17th. In the morning saw a strange sail to the north-ward, and at night the Sirius made the signal for the convoy to shorten sail.

18th. Early this morning the Sirius threw out the Supply's signal to make sail, and look out ahead. She immediately obeyed, and at eight o'clock made the signal for seeing land; which was repeated by the Sirius to the convoy. At eleven we passed the Isle of Sal, in lat. 16° 38′ N. long. 22° 5′ W., and in the evening Bonavista; two of the Cape de Verd islands, a cluster of islands so called from a cape of that name situated opposite to them on the continent of Africa. We passed the latter island so close, that we saw the breakers which endangered Captain Cook's ship in his last voyage. It blew at the time pretty fresh, and was so hazy, that we could make no other observation, than that the land was high, and the shore (what we could perceive of it through the haze, for the horizon line did not exceed two miles) had a white appearance, as if sand or chalk cliffs. At six in the evening, the Sirius made a signal for the convoy to observe a close order of sailing, and to shorten sail for the night; and at twelve, running under an easy sail,

E

she

she made the signal for the ships to bring to, with their heads to the south-east.

19th. At day break we made sail, the Supply being a-head on the look-out. At eight o'clock she made the signal for seeing land; which proved to be the isle of Mayo, another of the Cape de Verd islands, lying in lat. 15° 10′ N. long. 23° W. The Sirius now made the signal to prepare to anchor; which was followed by one, that the boats from the victuallers and transports may land, as soon as the ships came to an anchor, without asking permission as at Teneriffe. We ran down the east side of the island, close in with the shore, on which we could perceive a high surf, or rather the sea, breaking violently among the rocks. The haze still continued so thick that we could only observe the shore to be rough, craggy, and bold; and that several parts of the island seemed high and mountainous. At twelve, through the haze, saw the island of Saint Jago, the principal of the Cape de Verd islands, lying in lat. 14° 54′ N. long. 23° 29′ W. Half after one, the Sirius leading into Port Praya Bay, on a sudden brought to, as we imagined, to wait for the stern-most ships, which, as they all came up, likewise brought to,

on

on the outfide of the entrance into the bay. After the preparations which had been made for anchoring, and the difpofition fhown by the Sirius to run in, we were not a little
furprifed to fee her, at two o'clock, throw out the fignal for
the convoy to keep nearer the commanding officer; then
make fail and bear away, fteering fouth-weft. At fix in
the evening we loft fight of the ifland, running with a
fmart top-gallant, and fteering fail, breeze at north-eaft. A
fmall Portugueze brig lay at anchor in Port Praya, which
was the only veffel of any kind at that time there. This
bay is rendered memorable by the action that took place
there, on the 16th of April 1781, between Commodore
Johnftone and Monfieur Suffrein; in giving an account of
which, the French admiral (in a letter faid to be written by
him) humoroufly thus obferves: " In leading into the bay,
" I was fome time at a lofs to diftinguifh which was the
" commodore's fhip: but on getting more in, I at length
" faw his pendant blufhing through a foreft of mafts; the
" Romney being fecurely placed in fhore of the merchant
" fhips and fmaller men of war."

The entrance into this bay appeared to be about a mile,
between two bluff points, which makes it fecure from every

E 2                                        wind,

wind, except a foutherly one; and when that prevails, a very high fea tumbles into it. On an eminence, in the center of the bay, ftands a fort, where the Portugueze colours were difplayed. Many people appeared on the batteries, looking at the fhips; which were probably more in number than had been feen there fince the memorable 16th of April. The appearance of the town and the ifland, from the diftant view we had, gave us no very favourable opinion of them. The face of the country feemed to be fterile in the extreme. The lifelefs brown of the Ifle of Mayo, defcribed by Captain Cook, may very well be applied to this ifland; for as far as my eye or glafs could reach, not the fmalleft trace of vegetation or verdure was to be perceived, except at the weft end of the fort, on the left fide of the bay, where a few trees of the cocoa nut or palm kind appeared. But notwithftanding the fterile picture it exhibits when viewed from the fea, geographers, and thofe who have been on fhore, defcribe it to be, in many places, well cultivated and very fertile; producing fugar canes, a little wine, fome cotton, Indian corn, cocoa nuts, and oranges, with all the other tropical fruits in great plenty; and point it out as a place where fhips, bound on long voyages, may be conveniently fupplied

with

with water, and other neceffaries; fuch as fowls, goats, and hogs; all which are to be purchafed at a very eafy rate.

20th. This evening, ftanding to the fouthward with all fail; the wind moderate; the air warm and damp, with haze; the Sirius made the Alexander's fignal, who had dropped confiderably aftern, and reprimanded the mafter for hoifting out a boat without permiffion. The two following days the weather was moderately warm, with fome flafhes of lightning.

23d. The weather became exceedingly dark, warm, and clofe, with heavy rain; a temperature of the atmofphere very common on approaching the equator, and very much to be dreaded, as the health is greatly endangered thereby. Every attention was therefore paid to the people on board the Charlotte, and every exertion ufed to keep her clean and wholefome between decks. My firft care was to keep the men, as far as was confiftent with a regular difcharge of their duty, out of the rain; and I never fuffered the convicts to come upon deck when it rained, as they had neither linen nor clothing fufficient to make themfelves dry and comfortable after getting wet: a line of conduct which cannot be too ftrictly obferved, and enforced, in thofe latitudes.

tudes.    To this, and to the frequent ufe of oil of tar, which
was ufed three times a week, and oftener if found neceffary, I
attribute, in a great degree, the uncommon good health we
enjoyed.    I moft fincerely wifh oil of tar was in more general ufe throughout his Majefty's navy than it is.    If it were,
I am certain that the advantage accruing from it to the health
of feamen, that truly ufeful and valuable clafs of the commu-
nity, and for whofe prefervation too much cannot be done,
would foon manifeft itfelf.    This efficacious remedy won-
derfully refifts putrefaction, deftroys vermin and infects
of every kind; wherever it is applied overcomes all dif-
agreeable fmells;  and is in itfelf both agreeable and wholefome.

In the evening it became calm, with diftant peals of thunder,
and the moft vivid flafhes of lightning I ever remember.    The
weather was now fo immoderately hot, that the female convicts, perfectly overcome with it, frequently fainted away;
and thefe faintings generally terminated in fits.    And yet,
notwithftanding the enervating effects of the atmofpheric
heat, and the inconveniences they fuffered from it; fo predominant was the warmth of their conftitutions, or the depravity of their hearts, that the hatches over the place
where

where they were confined could not be fuffered to lay off, during the night, without a promifcuous intercourfe immediately taking place between them and the feamen and marines. What little wind there was, which was only at intervals, continuing adverfe, and the health of thefe wretches being ftill endangered by the heat, Captain Phillip, though anxious to prevent as much as poffible this intercourfe, gave an order, on my reprefenting the neceffity of it, that a grating fhould be cut, fo as to admit a fmall wind fail being let down among them. In fome of the other fhips, the defire of the women to be with the men was fo uncontrollable, that neither fhame (but indeed of this they had long loft fight), nor the fear of punifhment, could deter them from making their way through the bulk heads to the apartments affigned the feamen.

25th. Still inclinable to calms, in lat. 8° 30' N. long. 22° 36' W. we perceived a ftrong current fetting to the north-weft; fo that on the following day, though by our log we had run thirty miles fouth by eaft, yet by obfervation we found ourfelves in lat. 8° 45'; which fhows the current againft us to be nearly a knot an hour. I vifited the different tranfports, and found the troops and convicts,

from

from the very great attention paid to cleanliſs, and airing the ſhips, in much better health than could be expected in ſuch low latitudes and unfavourable weather.

27th.  Still calm, with loud thunder, and inceſſant heavy rain.

28th.  A gentle breeze ſprung up to the weſtward, and the next day, about eleven in the forenoon, we ſaw a ſtrange ſail ſtanding to the ſouth-weſt.  At twelve ſhe tacked, ſtood towards us, and hoiſted Portugueze colours.  The Sirius ſpoke her; after which we all made ſail again, ſteering ſouth-eaſt by eaſt.

July 2d.  The wind continuing ſoutherly, in latitude 6° 36′ N. and being ſtill ſo far to the eaſtward as 20° 23′ W. longitude, the Sirius made the ſignal for the convoy to tack; and ſtood to the weſtward.  This day we ſaw ſome re-markable flights of flying fiſh; they were ſo very numerous as to reſemble flights of ſmall birds.  The poor creatures were ſo cloſely purſued, on all ſides, by their common ene-my, bonitoes, albacores, and ſkip-jacks, that their wings availed them little.  The ſucceeding night was a continua-tion of heavy rain.  Every evening, while we continued be-tween nine and ſix degrees of north latitude, we were baffled

with

with calms, and adverfe winds. For feven days together I obferved that each day generally clofed with heavy rains, and fome fqualls of wind, which were always remarked to be from the northward.

5th. The wind fouth-weft by fouth, the fleet tacked by fignal and ftood to the eaftward. In the evening, a more numerous fhoal of porpoifes than ever remembered to be feen by the oldeft feaman on board, prefented themfelves to our view. They were, as we conjectured, in purfuit of fome wounded fifh; and fo very intent were they on the object of their chace, that they paffed through the fleet, and clofe to fome of the fhips, without fhowing any difpofition to avoid them. The failors and mariners compared them to a numerous pack of hounds, fcouring through watery ground; and indeed, when the rays of the fun beamed upon them, I know not what they refembled more. The weather being moderate, I went round the fhips, and was really furprifed, confidering the damp and unfavourable weather we had had, to find the people look fo well, and to be in fo good a ftate of health.

6th. In lat. 5° 38′ N. long. 21° 39′ W. the wind S. S. W. we tacked by fignal, and in the courfe of the day fpoke

F                                              a floop

a floop bound to the coaft of Africa, belonging to the houfe of Mether in London; had been out four months, and was then ftanding to the weftward.

The wind continuing adverfe, and the fleet making little progrefs in their voyage, Captain Phillip put the officers, feamen, marines, and convicts to an allowance of three pints of water per day (not including a quart allowed each man a day for boiling peafe and oatmeal); a quantity fcarcely fufficient to fupply that wafte of animal fpirits the body muft neceffarily undergo, in the torrid zone, from a conftant and violent perfpiration, and a diet confifting of falt provifions. Neceffity, however, has no law in this inftance as well as in every other; and I am fully perfuaded the commander acted upon this occafion from the beft of motives, and for the good of the whole. Were it by any means poffible, people fubject to long voyages fhould never be put to a fhort allowance of water; for I am fatisfied that a liberal ufe of it (when freed from the foul air, and made fweet by a machine now in ufe on board his Majefty's navy) will tend to prevent a fcorbutic habit, as much, if not more, than any thing we are acquainted with. My own experience in the navy has convinced me, that when fcor-

butic

butic patients are reftrained in the ufe of water (which I believe is never the cafe but through abfolute neceffity), and they have nothing to live on but the fhip's provifion, the furgeon's neceffaries being ill-chofen and very inadequate to the wife and falutary purpofes for which government intended them, all the antifeptics and antifcorbutics we know of will avail very little in a difeafe fo much to be guarded againft, and dreaded, by feamen. In one of his Majefty's fhips, I was liberally fupplied with that powerful antifcorbutic, effence of malt; we had alfo four krout; and befides thefe, every remedy that could be comprifed in the fmall compafs of a medicine cheft; yet, when neceffity forced us to a fhort allowance of water, although, aware of the confequence, I freely adminiftered the effence, &c. as a prefervative, the fcurvy made its appearance with fuch hafty and rapid ftrides, that all attempts to check it proved fruitlefs, until good fortune threw a fhip in our way, who fpared us a fufficient quantity of water to ferve the fick with as much as they could ufe, and to increafe the fhip's allowance to the feamen. This fortunate and very feafonable fupply, added to the free ufe of the effence of malt, &c. which I had before

ftrictly

strictly adhered to, made in a few days so sudden a change for the better in the poor fellows, who had been covered with ulcers and livid blotches, that every person on board was surprised at it : and, in a fortnight after, when we got into port, there was not a man in the ship, though, at the time we received the water, the gums of some of them were formed into such a fungus as nearly to envelope the teeth, but what had every appearance of health.

7th. Dark, cloudy, unpleasant, sultry weather; the wind south by east. We saw many fish, and caught two bonitoes. The boatswain struck, with a pair of grains, out of the cabin window, a most beautiful fish, about ten pounds weight. In shape it a good deal resembled a salmon, with this difference, that its tail was more forked. It was in colour of a lovely yellow; and when first taken out of the water, it had two beautiful stripes of green on each side, which, some minutes after, changed to a delightful blue, and so continued. In the internal formation of this fish I observed nothing particular, except that its heart was larger, and its respirations contracted and dilated longer, than I had ever seen before in any aquatic animal, a tortoise not excepted. As we were at a loss

what

what appellation to give it, having never met with a fish of this species, and it being a non-descript, the sailors gave it the name of the Yellow Tail.

8th. The wind still S. by E. in lat. 4° 36′ N. long. 23° W. we saw a large vessel standing to the northward under a press of sail. Her colours, though at a considerable distance, were judged to be Imperial. Again saw fish of various kinds in chase of the flying fish, whose enemies seem to be innumerable. In order to avoid being devoured by their pursuers, they frequently sought for shelter in the ships; but much oftener flew with such force against their sides as to drop lifeless into the water. We caught three fine bonitoes, and thereby rid the poor flying fish, whose wings seemed to excite the enmity of all the larger finny race, of three formidable enemies.

9th and 10th. Caught a great number of fish, as did the Alexander, who was near us. At night, in the wake of the ship the sea appeared quite luminous; a phænomenon we attributed to the spawn of the fish which surrounded us on all sides.

14th. About five in the evening we crossed the equator, without any wish or inclination being shewn by the seamen

to

to obferve the ceremony ufually practifed in paffing under it. The longitude was 26° 37′ W. the wind at eaft, the weather moderate and clear.    In lat. 1° 24′ S. long. 26° 22′ W. the boatfwain caught fixteen fine bonitoes, which proved a very feafonable and acceptable fupply.    At night the fea, all around the fhip, exhibited a moft delightful fight.    This appearance was occafioned by the gambols of an incredible number of various kinds of fifh, who fported about us, and whofe fudden turnings caufed an emanation, which refembled flafhes of lightning darting in quick fucceffion.    What I before fpoke of as the fpawn, I am now fully convinced were rather the fifh themfelves, turning up their white bellies at fome little diftance below the furface of the water, and thefe fudden evolutions were what gave the fea the luminous appearance obferved on it before.    I can the more readily affirm this to be the caufe, as, one evening, when we had immenfe quantities about us, I carefully attended to them till it became dark, and was fully fatisfied, from the obfervations I was then able to make, that it was the fifh, and not the fpawn, which occafioned the appearance ;  for there was not an officer or perfon on board but what was able very plainly to perceive their frolicfome turn-

ings

ings and windings. Indeed, some of them came so near the surface, that we frequently attempted to strike them with a pair of grains.

18th. Being informed that several of the mariners and convicts on board the Alexander were suddenly taken ill, I immediately visited that ship, and found that the illness complained of was wholly occasioned by the bilge water, which had by some means or other risen to so great a height, that the pannels of the cabin, and the buttons on the clothes of the officers, were turned nearly black, by the noxious effluvia. When the hatches were taken off, the stench was so powerful, that it was scarcely possible to stand over them. How it could have got to this height is very strange; for I well know, that Captain Phillip gave strict orders (which orders I myself delivered) to the masters of the transports to pump the ships out daily, in order to keep them sweet and wholesome; and it was added, that if the ships did not make water enough for that purpose, they were to employ the convicts in throwing water into the well, and pumping it out again, until it became clear and untinged. The people's health, however, being endangered by the circumstance, I found a representation upon the subject to Captain Phillip

Phillip needful; and accordingly went on board the Sirius for that purpofe. Captain Phillip, who upon every occafion fhowed great humanity and attention to the people, with the moft obliging readinefs fent Mr. King, one of his lieutenants, on board the Alexander with me, in order to examine into the ftate of the fhip; charging him, at the fame time, with the moft pofitive and pointed inftructions to the mafter of the fhip inftantly to fet about fweetening and purifying her. This commiffion Mr. King executed with great propriety and expedition; and by the directions he gave, fuch effectual means were made ufe of, that the evil was foon corrected: and not long after all the people, who, fuffering from the effects of it, were under Mr. Balmain, my affiftant's, care, got quite rid of the complaint. I now returned to the Sirius, and folicited an increafe of water; which Captain Phillip with equal readinefs complied with; and as we had by this time got into a regular fouth-eaft trade wind, our allowance ferved tolerably well; every man having three quarts a day.

22d. The weather moderate and cloudy, in lat 9° 6′ S. long. 26° 4′ W. we faw a noddy and two pintado birds. At night, the commanding officer of marines having received

ceived information that three men had made their way, through the hole cut for the admiffion of the windfail, into the apartment of the female convicts, againft an exprefs order iffued for that purpofe, he apprehended them, and put them in confinement for trial.

23d. The weather being dark and cloudy, with heavy rain and ftrong breezes, the Sirius carried away her main-topfail-yard, in the flings; which, however, in a little time fhe got replaced. In the evening we faw fome grampufes fporting about.

26th. In latitude 15° 18′ fouth, the Sirius made the fignal for the longitude by lunar obfervation, which was found to be 29° 34′ W. Strong breezes and cloudy weather. The Borrowdale victualler carried away her foretop-gallant-maft. This evening we obferved fome flying fifh, very different from thofe we had before feen. They had wings on both the head and tail, and when in the act of flying, were faid by our people to refemble a double-headed fhot. About fix o'clock the Alexander brought to, and hoifted out a boat in order to pick up a man who had fallen over board from the fpanker boom; but, as he funk before the boat could reach him, the attempt proved ineffectual.

G

27th.

27th. The Sirius made the fignal to clofe, and keep nearer the commanding officer. The weather rainy and unfettled, with ftrong breezes, and a heavy fwell from the eaftward.

28th. Frefh breezes and cloudy weather. At ten in the morning the Sirius made the Supply's fignal to come within hail, and defired the commanding officer to acquaint the different tranfports, that in the track we then were, lat. 18° 9′ S. long. 28° 2′ W. there were fome funken rocks, for which we were directed to keep a good look-out. This fignal was followed by one, for the fhips to take their proper ftations in the order of failing; and for the Lady Penrhyn, who was confiderably to windward, and aftern withal, to come into the wake of the Sirius. After thefe orders were complied with, we bore away, fteering S. by W. the wind E. S. E.

30th. The Supply hailed us, and acquainted me, that a female convict, on board the Prince of Wales, had met with an accident which endangered her life. It being then nearly dark, and the fhips making quick way through the water, it was judged imprudent to hoift a boat out. Lieutenant Ball, of the Supply, therefore promifed to fend a boat early

in

in the morning, in order that I might go and ſee her : but it was then too late, as ſhe died in the night. Her death was occaſioned by a boat, which rolled from the booms, and jammed her in a moſt ſhocking manner againſt the ſide of the ſhip.

Auguſt 1ſt. In latitude 22° 39′ S. Captain Phillip for the firſt time diſplayed his broad pendant; and in the evening made the ſignal for the longitude; which, being conſiderably aſtern, we could not diſcern.

2d. Early in the morning paſſed and ſpoke a Portugueze brig ſteering the ſame courſe with us, which was to the coaſt of Brazil. She ſailed ſo very dull, that we paſſed her as if ſhe lay at anchor, although we had not a faſt ſailing ſhip in the fleet. At eight in the morning ſaw a ganet, which are ſeldom ſeen out of ſoundings. Being now in expectation of ſoon ſeeing land, the commodore made the Supply's ſignal to look out ahead; and the Alexander's and Prince of Wales's to take their ſtation in the order of ſailing, being too far ahead. At three in the afternoon the Supply made the ſignal for ſeeing land, which was repeated by the commodore to the convoy. At nine at night, being well in with Cape Frio, we ſhortened ſail, running at an

eaſy

eafy rate until morning; when the wind was little and variable.

3d.  This evening, finding it impoffible to get hold of anchorage, the commodore difpatched Lieutenant King in the Supply, which failed well in light winds, to the viceroy, with information that he was, with his convoy, arrived near the mouth of the harbour.  He then made the fignal for the fhips to bring to, with their heads to the fouthward, about fix miles from the fhore, Rio de Janeiro Sugar Loaf bearing weft half north, diftant about fix leagues.  In the courfe of the day we faw many whales playing about.

4th.  This morning, ftanding in for the harbour, the wind headed us; which obliged us to tack, and ftand out to fea a little, in order to prevent our falling to leeward of the port, which it would have been no eafy matter to have regained.

5th.  Still calm.  This morning a boat came alongfide, in which were three Portugueze and fix flaves; from whom we purchafed fome oranges, plantains, and bread.  In trafficking with thefe people, we difcovered, that one Thomas Barret, a convict, had, with great ingenuity and addrefs, paffed fome quarter dollars which he, affifted by two others, had

coined

coined out of old buckles, buttons belonging to the marines, and pewter fpoons, during their paffage from Teneriffe. The impreffion, milling, character, in a word, the whole was fo inimitably executed, that had their metal been a little better, the fraud, I am convinced, would have paffed undetected. A ftrict and careful fearch was made for the apparatus wherewith this was done, but in vain; not the fmalleft trace or veftige of any thing of the kind was to be found among them. How they managed this bufinefs without difcovery, or how they could effect it at all, is a matter of inexpreffible furprife to me; as they never were fuffered to come near a fire; and a centinel was conftantly placed over their hatchway, which, one would imagine, rendered it impoffible for either fire or fufed metal to be conveyed into their apartments. Befides, hardly ten minutes ever elapfed, without an officer of fome degree or other going down among them. The adroitnefs, therefore, with which they muft have managed, in order to complete a bufinefs that required fo complicated a procefs, gave me a high opinion of their ingenuity, cunning, caution, and addrefs; and I could not help wifhing that thefe qualities had been employed to more laudable purpofes. The officers of marines, the mafter of

the

the ſhip, and myſelf, fully explained to the injured Portu-gueze, what villians they were who had impoſed upon them. We were not without apprehenſions that they might entertain an unfavourable opinion of Engliſhmen in ge-neral from the conduct of theſe raſcals; we therefore thought it neceſſary to acquaint them, that the perpetrators of the fraud were felons doomed to tranſportation by the laws of their country, for having committed ſimilar offences there.

About one o'clock a gentle breeze from the eaſt carried us within about a mile of the bar; where, at nine o'clock, we anchored in ſixteen fathom water. The calms had baffled the Supply ſo much, that ſhe had only dropped her anchor a little while before us.

6th. Early this morning, it being quite calm, the com-modore diſpatched an officer to the viceroy, who met with a courteous reception, and about eleven o'clock returned with the boat nearly full of fruit and vegetables, ſent as preſents to the commodore from ſome of his old friends and acquaintance. Some years ago Captain Phillip was on this coaſt, commander of a Portugueze man of war. During that time he performed ſeveral gallant acts, which, aided by

his

his other amiable qualities, rendered him extremely popular here, and recommended him to the notice of the court of Liſbon. Shortly after, his own country having a claim to his ſervices, on the breaking out of a war, he declined a command offered him by the Portugueze, and returned to the Engliſh navy; where he ſerved ſome time as lieutenant (a rank he had held before he had engaged in the ſervice of Portugal) on board the Alexander, under the command of that brave and exemplary character, Lord Longford.

About two o'clock we got under way, with a gentle ſea-breeze, which ran us into the harbour. In paſſing Santa Cruz fort, the commodore ſaluted it with thirteen guns, which was returned with an equal number. This day a Portugueze ſhip ſailed for Liſbon, which gave us an opportunity of writing ſhort letters to our friends in England.

8th. In the forenoon, the commodore, attended by moſt of the officers on the expedition, paid the viceroy a viſit of ceremony. On our landing, we were received by an officer and a friar, who conducted us to the palace. As we paſſed the guard on duty there, the colours were laid at the feet of the commodore; than which nothing could have been a higher token of reſpect. We then proceeded up ſtairs into

a large

a large anti-chamber, crowded with officers, ſoldiers, and do-
meſtics.  Here we were received by ſeveral officers belonging
to the houſehold, and the ſurgeon-general to the army, who
ſpoke good Engliſh, having acquired his profeſſional knowledge in London.  A few minutes after our arrival, a curtain,
which hung over the door of the preſence-chamber, was
drawn aſide ; and on our entrance we were individually introduced to the viceroy by the commodore.  The ceremony
being ended, and a ſhort converſation having taken place,
we were uſhered into another ſpacious room, where we all
ſat down.  I could not help remarking that the viceroy
placed himſelf in ſuch a manner as to have his back turned
on moſt of the officers.  I was told afterwards that he apo-
logized for this ; but I did not hear him, though very near.
Neither the room we were now in, nor that into which we
were firſt introduced, exhibited any marks of magnificence
or elegance.  I acknowledge, that for my own part I was
exceedingly diſappointed.  From the parade without, ſuch
as the number of guards, &c. I was led to ſuppoſe that we
ſhould find every thing within the palace proportionably
magnificent and princely.  But this was by no means the
caſe.  The only furniture I ſaw in the room we were in,

except

except chairs, were ſix card tables, and portraits of two of the ſovereigns of Portugal ; one of which was that of King Sebaſtian the Firſt, the other of her. preſent majeſty ; the former placed in the centre, the latter at the upper end of the room. The viceroy appeared to be of a middle age, ſomewhere between forty and fifty, ſtout and corpulent, with a ſtrong caſt or defect in both his eyes. He ſeemed to be a perſon of few words, but at the ſame time civil and attentive. I could not, however, help obſerving the very great differ-ence there was between his excellency's manner and addreſs, and that of the elegant and accompliſhed Marquis de Bran-cifort.

9th. The contract being ſettled, the commiſſary ſup-plied the troops and convicts with rice (in lieu of bread), with freſh beef, vegetables, and oranges ; which ſoon re-moved every ſymptom of the ſcurvy prevalent among them.

11th. The commodore ordered ſix female convicts, who had behaved well, to be removed from the Friendſhip into the Charlotte ; and at the ſame time an equal number, whoſe conduct was more exceptionable, to be returned to the Friendſhip in their ſtead. The commodore's view was (a matter not eaſily accompliſhed) to ſeparate thoſe whoſe de-

H cent

cent behaviour entitled them to ſome favour from thoſe who were totally abandoned and obdurate.

13th.    Cornelius Connell, a private in the marines, was, according to the ſentence of a court martial, puniſhed with a hundred laſhes, for having an improper intercourſe with ſome of the female convicts, contrary to orders.    Thomas Jones was alſo ſentenced to receive three hundred laſhes, for attempting to make a centinel betray his truſt, in ſuffering him to go among the women; but in conſideration of the good character he bore previous to this circumſtance, the court recommended him to the clemency of the commanding officer; and, in conſequence thereof, he was forgiven. John Jones and James Reiley, privates, accuſed of ſimilar offences to that of Connell's, were acquitted for want of evidence, there being no witneſſes to ſupport the charge except convicts, whoſe teſtimony could not be admitted.

15th.    This being a day of great parade and gaiety with the Portugueze, the inhabitants of Rio de Janeiro, arrayed in their beſt and richeſt attire, as their cuſtom is on regale days, began to ſhow themſelves, during the forenoon, between the city and the church of St. Gloria, which is about a mile diſtant, and ſituated on a riſing ground near the ſea.

Perſons

Perſons of all ranks, as well in carriages as equeſtrians and pedeſtrians, joined in the crowd; but what was the purpoſe of this cavalcade, or to what circumſtances it owed its origin, I am ſtill at a loſs to know. Gloria church, which is rather neat than rich, was decorated with various flowers (in the diſpoſal of which ſome taſte was diſplayed), and moſt brilliantly illuminated. I obſerved that the multitude generally ſtopped here, in ſucceſſion, and employed themſelves in ſome religious ceremonies, ſuch as praying and ſinging hymns, before they returned to the city. This kind of parade was continued the whole day; the better ſort of people, however, made their appearance only in the afternoon. Returning with the reſt of the crowd, after it was dark, to the town, I perceived a ſmall church, in one of the bye ſtreets, richly ornamented and elegantly illuminated. As I ſaw men, women, and children, ſtruggling for entrance, I joined in the throng out of mere curioſity, and with no little difficulty made my way in; but all the ſatisfaction I reaped from being thus ſqueezed and joſtled was, ſeeing ſuch as could gain admiſſion fall on their knees, and praying with more fervor, to appearance, than real devotion. On one ſide of the church ſtood a ſhabby ill-looking fellow,

H 2                              ſelling

ſelling to the multitude conſecrated beads ; as did another, on the outſide of the door. I own I could not help reſembling them to mountebanks vending and diſtributing their noſtrums. There were many more of theſe religious hawkers in the ſtreets ; from ſome of whom, as I ſaw it was the cuſtom, I purchaſed a few of their beads. At a little diſtance from the door of the church was erected a ſtage, on which was placed a band of vocal and inſtrumental performers, who exerted themſelves with might and main to pleaſe the ſurrounding audience. I cannot, however, ſay that they ſucceeded in pleaſing me. About ten o'clock a diſplay of fireworks and rockets, of which the Portugueze ſeem to be very fond, concluded the entertainments of the day. Some intrigues, I have reaſon to believe, followed. I was led to this concluſion from ſeeing many well-dreſſed women in the crowd quite unattended ; and this was the only time, during my ſtay in the country, that I ever ſaw any circumſtances which could warrant my forming ſuch an opinion. I know it has been aſſerted by ſome writers, that the women of Rio de Janeiro are not uncenſurable in this point. They have affirmed, that as ſoon as it became dark, the generality of them expoſed themſelves at their doors

and

and windows, diſtinguiſhing, by preſents of noſegays and flowers, thoſe on whom they had no objection to beſtow their favours; a diſtinction in which ſtrangers ſhared as well as their acquaintance. That this might have been the caſe I will not take upon me to deny; and, impreſſed with the idea, on my firſt arrival, I conſidered every woman as a proper object of gallantry; but a month's reſidence among them convinced me that this imputed turn for intrigue is chiefly confined to the lower claſs, and that, in general, the higher ranks are as undeſerving of the imputation as the females of any other country.

The popularity of our commodore with the viceroy and principal inhabitants here, procured for the officers the liberty of going wherever they pleaſed. It has always been the cuſtom, for a ſoldier to follow every foreign officer that landed at this port; and it was ſcarcely ever diſpenſed with. It was, however, unknown to us; and this unaccuſtomed liberty gave us an opportunity of inſpecting more minutely into the manners and diſpoſition of the women as well as the men.

21ſt. This being the Prince of Brazil's birth-day, the commodore, with moſt of his officers, went to court, to

compliment

compliment the viceroy on the occafion.  As foon as we landed, we were received by an officer, who conducted us to the prefence-chamber; where his excellency ftood under a canopy of ftate, receiving the compliments of the officers of the garrifon, the principal inhabitants, and fuch foreigners as were in the place.  After having paid our refpects, we withdrew, as did every other perfon, except the principal officers of ftate, fome general and law officers, and thofe of the governor's houfehold.  The Sirius and one of the forts fired royal falutes.  The court was brilliant, if a place where a female does not appear can be faid to be brilliant; but this, I was informed, is always the cafe here.  Thofe gentlemen who appeared in the circle were richly and elegantly dreffed.  The officers of the army and of the militia were particularly fo, and that in a ftile and fafhion which did no fmall credit to their tafte.  The viceroy wore a fcarlet coat trimmed with very broad rich gold lace; and his hair, according to his ufual mode of wearing it, in a remarkable long queue, with very little powder; an article of drefs to which I obferved the Portugueze were not very partial; while, on the contrary, they were profufe in the ufe of pomatum.  The day ended without any other demonftrations of joy.  As the

Portugueze

Portugueze feemed fond of fireworks and illuminations, and never fail to exhibit them on every religious feftival, we were not a little difappointed in finding them omitted on the birth-day of their prince.

31ft. James Baker, a private marine, received two hundred lafhes, agreeable to the fentence of a court-martial, for endeavouring to get paffed on fhore, by means of one of the feamen, a fpurious dollar, knowing it to be fo; and one he had undoubtedly got from fome of the convicts, as it was of a fimilar bafe metal to thofe which they had coined during the paffage, and had attempted to put off on our firft arrival at this port.

September 1ft. Having now procured every thing at Rio de Janeiro that we ftood in need of, and thoroughly recovered and refrefhed our people, the commodore, with fuch officers of the fleet as could be fpared from duty, waited on the viceroy to take leave, and to return our acknowledgments for the indulgence and attention fhown us; which, I think we may fay, we experienced in a greater extent and latitude than any foreigners had ever before done. On our landing, the fame officer who had attended us upon every other public occafion, conducted us to the prefence-chamber. As we
passed,

paffed, every military and public honour was paid to the commodore; the colours were laid at his feet, as they hitherto had been whenever he landed in his public character; a token of refpect that is never beftowed on any perfon but the governor himfelf. When we arrived at the palace, an officer of the houfehold, who was waiting to receive us, conducted us through a moft delightful recefs, hung round with bird-cages, whofe inhabitants feemed to vie with each other, both in the melody of their notes and the beauty of their plumage. The paffage we walked through was adorned on each fide with odoriferous flowers, and aromatic fhrubs; which, while they charmed the eye, fpread a delightful fragrance around. This paffage led to a private room, on the outfide of the door of which we were received by the viceroy, who ftood uncovered, and noticed each perfon feparately in the moft friendly and polite manner. His excellency preceded us into the room, and having requefted all of us to be feated, placed himfelf by the commodore, in a pofition that fronted us. In return for our thanks and acknowledgments, he faid, " it gave him " infinite pleafure and fatisfaction to find that the place had " afforded us the fupplies we ftood in need of:" to this he

added,

added, " that the attention of the inhabitants, which we
" were good enough to notice, was much fhort of his wifhes."
We then arofe and took our leave ; but not before his excellency had expreffed a defire of hearing from the commodore, with an account of his fuccefs in the eftablifhment of
the new colony.  He concluded with faying, " that he
" hoped, nay did not doubt, from the charaƈter the En-
" glifh bore for generofity of difpofition, but that thofe who
" had fo cheerfully engaged in a fervice, ftrange and uncer-
" tain in itfelf, would meet with an adequate reward—a
" recompence that every one muft allow they juftly merited."
The room in which the governor received us was that
wherein he ufually fat in his retired moments.  It was furnifhed and painted in a neat and elegant ftile ; the roof
difplaying well-executed reprefentations of all the tropical
fruits, and the moft beautiful birds of the country.  The
walls were hung round with prints, chiefly on religious
fubjeƈts.

Rio de Janeiro is faid to derive its name from being difcovered on St. Januarius's day.  It is the capital of the
Portugueze fettlements in South America, and is fituated on

I                              the

the weſt ſide of a river, or, more properly (in my opinion), of a bay. Except that part which fronts the water, the city is ſurrounded by high mountains, of the moſt romantic form the imagination can faſhion to itſelf any idea of. The plan on which it is built has ſome claim to merit. The principal ſtreet, called Strait Street, runs from the viceroy's palace, which is near the ſouth-eaſt end of the town, to the north-weſt extremity, where it is terminated by a large convent belonging to the Benedictine friars, ſituated on an eminence. The ſtreet is broad, well built, and has in it a great number of handſome ſhops. All the others are much inferior to this, being in general only wide enough to admit two carriages to paſs each other in the centre. The pavement for foot-paſſengers (except in Strait Street, which is without any) is ſo very unſociably narrow, that two perſons cannot walk with convenience together. The houſes are commonly two, and ſometimes three ſtories high; of which, even though inhabited by the moſt wealthy and reſpectable families, the lower part is always appropriated to ſhops, and to the uſe of the ſervants and ſlaves (who are here extremely numerous), the family rather chuſing to reſide in the upper

I

part,

part, that they might live in a lefs confined air. To every houfe there is a balcony, with lattice-work before it; and the fame before all the windows.

The churches are very numerous, elegant, and richly decorated; fome of them are built and ornamented in a modern ftile, and that in a manner which proclaims the genius, tafte, and judgment of the architects and artifts. Two or three of the handfomeft are at this time either unfinifhed or repairing; and they appear to go on but very flowly, notwithftanding large fums are conftantly collecting for their completion. As they are erected or repaired by charitable contributions, public proceffions are frequently made for that purpofe; and the mendicant friars, belonging to them, likewife exert themfelves in their line. At thefe proceffions, which are not unfrequent, perfons of every age and defcription affift. They ufually take place after it is dark, when thofe who join in it are dreffed in a kind of cloak adapted to religious purpofes, and carry a lanthorn fixed at the end of a pole of a convenient length: fo that upon thefe occafions you fometimes fee three or four hundred moving lights in the ftreets at the fame time; which has an uncommon and a pleafing effect. Confiderable fums

I 2

are

are collected by this mode. At the corner of every street, about ten feet from the ground, is placed the image of a saint, which is the object of the common people's adoration.

The town is well supplied with water from the neighbouring mountains; which is conveyed over a deep valley by an aqueduct formed of arches of a stupendous height, and from thence distributed by pipes to many parts of the city. The principal fountain is close to the sea, in a kind of square, near the palace; where ships water at a good wharf, nearly in the same manner as at Teneriffe, and with equal expedition and convenience. On the opposite side of the fountain are cocks, from which the people in the neighbourhood are supplied. This convenient and capital watering place is so near the palace, that when disputes or contentions arise between the boats crews of different ships, the slaves, &c. they are suppressed and adjusted by the soldiers on guard; who, in the Portugueze service, have great power, and often treat the people with no little severity.

While we staid at this place, we made several short excursions into the country; but did not go near the mines, as we knew the attempt would not only prove hazardous, but ineffectual: and as the liberty and indulgence granted

us was on the commodore's account, we never extended our
trips beyond a few miles, left our doing fo fhould appear
fufpicious, and reflect difcredit on him; we confidering him
in fome degree refponfible for our conduct.   As far as we
did go, we experienced the fame polite and attentive behaviour we met with from the inhabitants of the city.   Never
was more diftinguifhed urbanity fhown to ftrangers, than
was fhown to us by every rank.

From its complicated ftate, I could learn but few particulars relative to the government of Brazil.   The viceroy is
invefted with great power and authority, fubject in fome
cafes to an appeal to the court of Lifbon; but, like a wife
and prudent ruler, he feldom exerts it, unlefs in inftances
where found judgment and true policy render it expedient
and neceffary.   He is a man of little parade, and appears
not to be very fond of pomp and grandeur, except on public
days, when it is not to be difpenfed with.   When he goes
abroad for amufement, or to take the air, his guard confifts
only of feven dragoons; but on public occafions he makes
his appearance in a grander ftile.   I once faw him go in
ftate to one of the courts of juftice; and, though it was
fituated not a hundred yards from his palace, he was attended

tended by a troop of horfe. His ftate carriage is tolerably neat, but by no means elegant or fuperb; it was drawn by four horfes irregularly mottled.

Carriages are pretty common at this place; there is fcarcely a family of refpectability without one. They are moftly of the chaife kind, and drawn in general by mules, which are found to anfwer better than horfes, being more indefatigable and furer footed; confequently better calculated to afcend their fteep hills and mountains.

The military force of Brazil confifts of a troop of horfe, which ferve as guards for the viceroy, twelve regiments of regulars from Europe, and fix raifed in the country: thefe laft enlift men of a mixed colour, which the former are by no means fuffered to do. Befides the foregoing, there are twelve regiments of militia always embodied. This whole force, regulars and militia, except thofe on out-pofts and other needful duties, appear early in the morning, on every firft day of the month, before the palace, where they undergo a general mufter, and review of arms and neceffaries. The private men, although they are confidered as perfons of great confequence by the populace, are, on the other hand, equally fubmiffive and obedient to their officers. This ftrict

discipline

difcipline and regularity, as the city is in a great meafure under military orders, renders the inhabitants extremely civil and polite to the officers, who, in return, ftudy to be on the moft agreeable and happy terms with them.

A captain's guard (independent of the cavalry, who are always in readinefs to attend the viceroy) is mounted every day at the palace. Whenever Commodore Phillip paffed, which he did as feldom as poffible, the guard was turned out, with colours, &c. and, as I before obferved, the fame mark of honour paid to him as to the governor. To obviate this trouble and ceremony, he moft frequently landed and embarked at the north-weft fide of the town, where his boat conftantly waited for him.

On both fides of the river which forms the bay or harbour, the country is picturefque and beautiful to a degree, abounding with the moft luxuriant flowers and aromatic fhrubs. Birds of a lovely and rich plumage are feen hopping from tree to tree in great numbers; together with an endlefs variety of infects, whofe exquifite beauty and gaudy colours exceed all defcription. There is little appearance of cultivation in the parts we vifited; the land feemed chiefly pafturage. The cattle here are fmall, and when killed do

not

not produce such beef as is to be met with in England : it is not, however, by any means so bad as represented by some travellers to be ; on the contrary, I have seen and eat here tolerably good, sweet, and well-tasted beef. I never saw any mutton : they have indeed a few sheep, but they are small, thin, and lean. The gardens furnish most sorts of European productions, such as cabbages, lettuce, parsley, leeks, white radishes, beans, pease, kidney beans, turnips, water melons, excellent pumpkins, and pine-apples of a small and indifferent kind. The country likewise produces, in the most unbounded degree, limes, acid and sweet lemons, oranges of an immense size and exquisite flavour, plantains, bananas, yams, cocoa-nuts, cashoo apples and nuts, and some mangos. For the use of the slaves and poorer sort of people, the capado is cultivated in great plenty ; but this cannot be done through a want of corn for bread, as I never saw finer flour than at this place, which is plentiful, and remarkably cheap.

Brazil, particularly towards the northern parts, furnishes a number of excellent drugs. In the shops of the druggists and apothecaries of Rio de Janeiro, of which there are many, hippo, oil of castor, balsam capiva, with most of the valu-

able

able gums, and all of an excellent quality, are to be found; but they are fold at a much dearer rate than could poffibly have been conceived or expected in a country of which they are the natural produce.

The riches of this country, arifing from the mines, are certainly very great. To go near, or to get a fight of thefe inexhauftible treafuries, is impoffible, as every pafs leading to them is ftrongly guarded; and even a perfon taken on the road, unlefs he be able to give a clear and unequivocal account of himfelf and his bufinefs, is imprifoned, and perhaps compelled ever after to work in thofe fubterraneous cavities, which avarice, or an ill-timed and fatal curiofity, may have prompted him to approach. Thefe circumftances made a trial to fee them without permiffion (and that permiffion I underftand has never been granted the moft favoured foreigners) too dangerous to be attempted.

In addition to the above fource of wealth, the country produces excellent tobacco, and likewife fugar canes, from which the inhabitants make good fugar, and draw a fpirit called *aquadente*. This fpirit, by proper management, and being kept till it is of a proper age, becomes tolerable rum. As it is fold very cheap, the commodore purchafed a

K                    hundred

hundred pipes of it for the use of the garrison when arrived at New South Wales. Precious and valuable stones are also found here. Indeed they are so very plenty, that a certain quantity only is suffered to be collected annually. At the jewellers and lapidaries, of which occupation there are many in Rio, I saw some valuable diamonds, and a great number of excellent topazes, with many other sorts of stones of inferior value. Several topazes were purchased by myself and others; but we chose to buy them wrought, in order to avoid imposition, which is not unfrequent when the stones are sold in a rough state. One of the principal streets of this city is nearly occupied by jewellers and the workers of these stones; and I observed that persons of a similar profession generally resided in the same street.

The manufactures here are very few, and those by no means extensive. All kinds of European goods sell at an immoderate price, notwithstanding the shops are well stored with them.

The Brazil, or native Indians, are very adroit at making elegant cotton hammocks of various dyes and forms. It was formerly the custom for the principal people of Rio to be carried about in these hammocks; but that fashion is succeeded by the use of sedan chairs, which are now very com-

mon

mon among them; but they are of a more clumfy form than thofe ufed in England. The chair is fufpended from an aukward piece of wood, borne on the fhoulders of two flaves, and elevated fufficiently to be clear of the inequalities of the ftreet. In carrying, the foremoft flave takes the pavement, and the other the ftreet, one keeping a little before the other; fo that the chair is moved forward in a fidelong direction, and very unlike the procedure of the London chairmen. Thefe fellows, who get on at a great rate, never take the wall of the foot-paffengers, nor incommode them in the fmalleft degree.

The inhabitants in general are a pleafant, cheerful people, inclining more to corpulency than thofe of Portugal; and, as far as we could judge, very favourably inclined to the Englifh. The men are ftrait and well-proportioned. They do not accuftom themfelves to high living, nor indulge much in the juice of the grape.

The women, when young, are remarkably thin, pale, and delicately fhaped; but, after marriage, they generally incline to be lufty, without lofing that conftitutional pale, or rather fallow appearance. They have regular and better teeth than are ufually obfervable in warm climates, where

fweet

sweet productions are plentiful. They have likewise the most lovely, piercing, dark eyes; in the captivating use of which they are by no means unskilled. Upon the whole, the women of this country are very engaging; and rendered more so by their free, easy, and unrestrained manner. Both sexes are extremely fond of suffering their hair, which is black, to grow to a prodigious length. The ladies wear it plaited, and tied up in a kind of club, or large lump; a mode of hair-dressing that does not seem to correspond with their delicate and feminine appearance. Custom, however, reconciles us to the most *outré* fashions; and what we thought unbecoming, the Portugueze considered as highly ornamental. I was one day at a gentleman's house, to whom I expressed my wonder at the prodigious quantity of hair worn by the ladies; adding, that I did not conceive it possible for it to be all of their own growth. The gentleman assured me that it was; and, in order to convince me that it was so, he called his wife, and untied her hair, which, notwithstanding it was in plaits, dragged at least two inches upon the floor as she walked along. I offered my service to tie it up again; which was politely accepted, and considered as a compliment by both. It has been said that

the

the Portugueze are a jealous people; a difpofition I never could perceive among any of thofe with whom I had the pleafure of forming an acquaintance; on the contrary, they feemed fenfible of, and pleafed with, every kind of attention paid to their wives or daughters.

The current coin here is the fame as that in Portugal, but filver as well as gold is coined at this place, where they have an eftablifhed mint. The pieces of gold are of various fizes, and have marked on them the number of thoufand rees they are worth. The moft common coin is a 4000 ree piece, which paffes for £. 1. 2. 6, though not fo heavy as an Englifh guinea. The filver pieces, called petacks, value two fhillings, are alfo marked with the number of rees they are worth. You get ten of thefe in exchange for a guinea; and for a Spanifh dollar two petacks, five vintins and a half, which is about four fhillings and eight-pence. Here, as in Portugal, they have five, ten, and twenty thoufand ree pieces. A ree is a nominal coin; twenty make a vintin, value about three half-pence; eight vintins make one fhilling; a petack is worth two fhillings, and of thefe there are fome double pieces, value four fhillings fterling.

One morning, as I attended Mr. Il de Fonfo, furgeon ge-

I                                                      neral

neral to the army, and a man of ingenuity and abilities in his profeffion, to a large public hofpital, a foldier was brought in with a wound in his left fide. The inftrument had penetrated the abdomen, without injuring the inteftines; and from its form and nature the wound muft have been inflicted with the point of a knife, or a ftiletto. The patient, after being dreffed, acquainted us, that the preceding night he had had fome words with another man about a woman; who, notwithftanding blows had not paffed, ftabbed him with fome fharp inftrument, of what kind he could not fee, as it was then dark, and afterwards made his efcape. This account led me to believe that affaffinations were not unfrequent in Brazil; but Mr. Il de Fonfo affured me to the contrary; telling me that fuch inftances feldom happened, except among the negroes, whofe vindictive and treacherous difpofitions led them wonderful lengths to gratify their revenge, whenever night and a convenient opportunity confpired, at once to aid and to conceal their horrid acts.

While we remained here, the weather being cool and favourable, I prevailed on the furgeon who was about to amputate a limb, to allow me to take it off according to

Allenfon's

Allenſon's method. During the operation I could plainly ſee, that he and his pupils did not ſeem much pleaſed with it; and he afterwards told me it was impoſſible it could ever anſwer. A very ſhort ſpace of time, however, made them of a different opinion; and in eighteen days after, when we ſailed, I had the ſatisfaction to leave the patient with his ſtump nearly cicatrized, to the no ſmall joy of the ſurgeon, who ſaid, that if the man had died, he ſhould have been heavily cenſured for making him the ſubject of experiments. The circumſtance of a man's leg being cut off, and almoſt healed in as many days as it generally takes weeks, ſoon became known, and added very much to the eſtimation in which the people of this place held Engliſh ſurgeons. Whenever I viſited the hoſpital afterwards, the objects of pity with which it was filled, uſed to crowd around me in ſuch a manner, and in ſuch numbers, for my advice, that I found it difficult to get from them. And they now would readily have ſubmitted to any operation I ſhould have propoſed; but as I ſaw the ſurgeon did not much approve of my interference, I gave up all ideas of it.

The harbour of Rio de Janeiro lies in 22° 54′ ſouth latitude, and 43° 19′ weſt longitude, about eighteen or twenty

leagues

leagues to the weſtward of Cape Frio. The entrance is good, and cannot be miſtaken, on account of a remarkable hill, reſembling a ſugar loaf, that is on the left hand ſide; and ſome iſlands before it, one of which is oblong, and does not, at ſome diſtance, look unlike a thatched houſe : they lie from the mouth of the harbour S. by W. about two leagues. Ships going in may run on either ſide. The bar, over which we carried ſeven fathom water, is not more than three-fourths of a mile acroſs, and well defended by forts. The ſtrongeſt is called Santa Cruz, built on a rock, on the ſtarboard ſide as you run in, from which every ſhot fired at ſhips paſſing muſt take effect. The other, named Fort Lozia, is ſmaller, and built on an iſland or rock, on the larboard ſide, a little higher up, and lying contiguous to the main land. The tide in the harbour rarely ebbs and flows more than ſeven feet; however, ſhips, if poſſible, never anchor in this narrow paſs between the forts, as the bottom is foul, and the tide runs with conſiderable rapidity. All danger in going in, or running out, may be avoided by keeping the mid channel, or a little bordering on the ſtarboard ſhore. After Santa Cruz fort is paſſed, the courſe is nearly N. by W. and N. N. W.; but, as I before obſerved, the eye is the beſt pilot.

pilot. When you get within a mile of a strong fortified island which lies before the town (only separated by a narrow pass), called the Isle of Cobras, you are then in the great road; where we anchored in fifteen fathom water; or, should you have occasion to get nearer the town, you may run round this island, on the north side, and anchor above it, before the convent of Benedictine friars at the N. W. end of the city, before spoken of.

The city and harbour are strongly defended and fortified, but with very little judgment or regularity. The hills are very high, and so is the coast, which has such strange, romantic, and almost inaccessible terminations, that nature of her own accord, without the aid of military skill, seems disposed to defend them. Taking every thing into the account, I think it one of the best harbours I have ever seen; and, upon the whole, better calculated to supply the wants of people who have long been at sea, and stand in need of refreshment, than any part of the world, every thing being so remarkably cheap. Beef may be purchased at seven farthings per pound; hogs, turkeys, and ducks, both English and Muscovy, were equally reasonable. Fowls were dearer, but still sold at a lower rate than in England. Fish

L                                                    was

was not very plentiful, but I was told, that at other seasons they have a most excellent market for that article. Their market for vegetables, however, abounded with fruit, roots, and garden stuff, of every kind, notwithstanding it was not the best season for fruit, it then being too early in the spring to expect abundance. Oranges, which we had in the greatest plenty, cost only five-pence the hundred.

On a hill, about half a mile S. E. of the city, stands a convent, named Convento de Santa Theresa; the nuns of which, amounting to about forty, are not allowed to unveil when they come to the grate: and on a plain between this convent and the city, stands another, called Convento A. de Juda, a very large building, governed by an abbess and several nuns, all under the direction of a bishop. Here about seventy young ladies are placed to be educated, who are subject to all the restrictions of a monastic life, only they are permitted to be frequently at the grate, and that unveiled. But what is singular, the nuns of this convent, when they arrive at a proper age, are allowed either to take a husband, or to take the veil, just as their inclination leads. They are not however suffered to quit the convent on any other terms than that of marriage; to which the consent and approba-

tion

tion of the bishop is always neceffary. If they do not get a hufband early in life, it is common for them to take the veil. Many of thefe young ladies were very agreeable both in perfon and difpofition; and by frequently converfing with them at the grate, we formed as tender an intercourfe with them as the bolts and bars between us would admit of. Myfelf, and two other gentlemen belonging to the fleet, fingled out three of thofe who appeared to be the moft free and lively, to whom we attached ourfelves during our ftay, making them fuch prefents as we thought would prove moft acceptable, and receiving more valuable ones in return. Thefe little attentions were viewed by them in fo favourable a light, that when we took a laft farewel they gave us many evident proofs of their concern and regret. Indeed every circumftance while we continued at this charming place (except there being no inns or coffee-houfes, where a ftranger could refrefh himfelf, or be accommodated when he chofe to ftay a night or two on fhore) confpired to make us pleafed and delighted with it; and I can truly fay, that I left it with reluctance, which I believe was the cafe with many of my companions.

September 3d. The commodore fent Mr. Moreton, the

L 2　　　　　　　　　　master

1787.
September.

master of the Sirius, and two of his midshipmen, who had been put on the invalid list, aboard an English ship returning from the Southern whale fishery to England, which, being leaky, had been forced into Rio. As this ship was to sail in a few days, it furnished us with an opportunity of writing to our friends. About two in the afternoon the commodore made the signal for all officers to repair on board their respective ships, and for the transports to hoist in their boats.

4th. At six the fleet weighed with a light land breeze. On the commodore's approaching Santa Cruz Fort, he was saluted from the batteries with twenty-one guns; which he returned from the Sirius with an equal number. About ten o'clock we got clear of the land, steering to the eastward with a gentle breeze. Thomas Brown, a convict, was punished with a dozen lashes, for behaving insolently to one of the officers of the ship. This was the first that had received any punishment, since their embarkation on board the Charlotte.

5th. Wind variable and cloudy; Rio Sugar-loaf still in sight, about eight or nine leagues distant.

6th. The officers, ship's company, marines, and convicts,

were, by fignal from the Sirius, put to an allowance of three quarts of water per day, including that ufually allowed for cooking their provifions.   In the courfe of the day a fteady breeze fprung up at N. E.   About fix in the evening, the Fifhburne victualler carried away her fore-top-gallant yard, which fhe foon got replaced with another.

7th and 8th.   The weather continued dark and cloudy, with fome heavy fhowers of rain.   On the evening of the 8th, between the hours of three and four, Mary Broad, a convict, was delivered of a fine girl.

9th and 10th.   Fine, clear, dry weather.   The commodore made a fignal for the convoy to clofe, being fcattered about at a confiderable diftance from him.

11th, 12th, and 13th.   Frefh breezes, with fudden fqualls and heavy rain.   The four fucceeding days, light airs, and hazy, with fome fhowers, and a damp moift air.   On the evening of the 17th, our longitude being, by fignal from the commodore, 31° 34′ W. we caught a fhark fix feet long, of which the people made a good mefs.

18th.   Heavy rain, with dark and cold weather.   Saw feveral albatroffes and pintado birds.

19th.   William Brown, a very well behaved convict, in

bringing

bringing some clothing from the bowsprit end, where he had hung them to dry, fell overboard. As soon as the alarm was given of a man being overboard, the ship was instantly hove to, and a boat hoisted out, but to no purpose. Lieutenant Ball of the Supply, a most active officer, knowing from our proceedings (as we were at the time steering with a fair wind, and going near six knots an hour) that some accident must have happened, bore down; but notwithstanding every exertion, the poor fellow sunk before either the Supply or our boat could reach him. The people on the forecastle, who saw him fall, say, that the ship went directly over him, which, as she had quick way through the water, must make it impossible for him to keep on the surface long enough to be taken up, after having received the stroke from so heavy a body.

23d. From the 19th, the weather had been cold, dry, and pleasant; it now became wet, squally, and unsettled; the wind westerly, with a high sea; albatrosses, pintado birds, and some small hawks, hovering round the ship.

30th. The weather became more moderate and pleasant, the wind variable, inclining to calms.

October 1st. Light airs, with haze and rain. Saw a

great

great number of different birds; we were then in latitude 34° 42' S. longitude 1° 10' E. of the meridian of London.

13th.   The Sirius made the signal for seeing land; and at seven in the evening we came to, in Table Bay, at the Cape of Good Hope, in seventeen fathom water, abreast of Cape Town, distant about a mile or a mile and half.   As soon as the Sirius anchored, the commodore and commissary went on shore, and took up their residence in lodgings at the house of Mrs. De Witt.   They were soon followed by such officers as could be spared from the duty of the fleet, all wishing to prepare themselves, by the comforts and refreshments to be enjoyed on shore, for the last and longest stage of their voyage.

14th.   The contract for provisions being settled with Messrs. De Witts and Caston, the troops, men, women, and children, were served with a pound and half of soft bread, and an equal quantity of beef or mutton daily; and with wine in lieu of spirits.   The convicts, men, women, and children, had the same allowance as the troops, except wine.

16th.   Commodore Phillip, attended by most of the officers of the fleet, paid a complimentary visit to his excel-

lency

lency Mynheer Van Graaf, the Dutch governor, by whom we were received with extreme civility and politenefs. A few hours after we had taken leave, he called on the commodore at his lodgings, to return his vifit; and the next day returned the vifit of fuch officers, refiding on fhore, as had paid their refpects to him.

Notwithftanding this ftudied politenefs, feveral days elapfed before the commodore could obtain a categorical anfwer to the requifition he had made for the fupplies he ftood in need of for the expedition: and had it not been for the judicious perfeverance Commodore Phillip obferved, in urging his particular fituation, and the uncommon exigency of the fervice he was engaged in; it was believed the governor, fifcal, and council, would have fheltered their refufal under the pretence that a great fcarcity had prevailed in the Cape colony the preceding feafon, particularly of wheat and corn, which were the articles we ftood moft in want of. This idea they wifhed to imprefs us with; but, as juft obferved, the commodore's fagacity and induftrious zeal for the fervice fubdued and got over the fupinenefs fhown by the governor, &c. and procured permiffion for the contractor to fupply us with as much ftock, corn, and other neceffaries, as we could ftow.

ſtow. It is, however, much to be lamented that the quantity we could find room for fell very ſhort of what we ought to have taken in; as the only ſpare room we had, was what had been occaſioned by the conſumption of proviſions, &c. ſince we left Rio de Janeiro, and the removal of twenty female convicts from the Friendſhip into the Charlotte, the Lady Penrhyn, and the Prince of Wales.

After the ſupplies had been granted, his excellency Governor Graaf invited the commodore, and many of the officers of the expedition, to a very handſome dinner at his town reſidence. The houſe at which we were entertained, is delightfully ſituated, nearly in the centre of an extenſive garden, the property of the Dutch Eaſt India company, uſefully planted, and at the ſame time elegantly laid out. The governor's family make what uſe they pleaſe of the produce of the garden, which is various and abundant; but the original intention of the company in appropriating ſo extenſive a piece of ground to this purpoſe was, that their hoſpital, which is generally pretty full when their ſhips arrive after long voyages, may be well ſupplied with fruits and vegetables, and likewiſe that their ſhips may receive a ſimilar ſupply.

M                                          This

This garden is as public as St. James's park; and, for its handsome, pleasant, and well-shaded walks, is much frequented by persons of every description, but particularly by the fashionable and gay. There are many other agreeable walks about Cape Town, but none to be compared with these. At the upper end of the principal of them is a small space walled in for the purpose of confining some large ostriches, and a few deer. A little to the right of this is a small menagery, in which the company have half a dozen wild animals, and about the same number of curious birds.

As you approach the Cape of Good Hope, a very remarkable mountain may, in clear weather, be discovered at a considerable distance; it is called the Table Land, from its flat surface, which resembles that piece of furniture. Mr. Dawes, lieutenant of marines on board the Sirius, an ingenious and accurate observer, who has undertaken during the voyage the astronomical observations; accompanied by Messrs. Fowell and Waterhouse, midshipmen of the Sirius; Lieutenant De Witt, of the Dutch navy; and myself, went to the top of this mountain; an undertaking which we found to be of a far more serious nature than we at first were aware of. For my own part, I suffered so much from heat
and

and thirſt, that had not the fear of ſhame urged me on, my companions being determined to accompliſh it at all events, I ſhould moſt certainly have given it up, before I reached the top. During this ſultry and fatiguing expedition, I found great benefit, towards alleviating my thirſt, by keeping a ſmall pebble in my mouth; and ſometimes by chewing ruſhes, which we met with in our way. But, when we had reached the ſummit, the delightful and extenſive proſpect we there enjoyed, the weather being uncommonly fine, fully atoned for the trouble, fatigue, and every ſuffering, we had undergone. From this elevation we could overlook all the country about the Cape.

As ſoon as we got to the top, our firſt buſineſs was to look out for water; but all we could find was ſome ſtagnant rain, which lay in the hollow of the ſtones. Our thirſt, however, was ſo intolerable, that the diſcovery even of this gave us inexpreſſible pleaſure; and, notwithſtanding we all perſpired moſt violently, and were ſenſible of the danger and impropriety of drinking a quantity of bad water in ſuch a ſituation, yet we could not refrain. As for my own part, it was utterly out of my power to liſten at that time to the dictates of prudence; and I believe it was equally difficult

M 2

to

to my companions, if I might judge from the avidity with which they drank out of the little pools, lying on the ground at full length, that being the only posture in which it was to be obtained.

The regularity of the streets of the town, which interfect each other at right angles; the buildings, gardens, castle, and forts; with twenty-three ships then at anchor in the bay; all which appeared directly underneath us; was a sight beautiful and pleasing beyond description. The perpendicular height of this land is 1857 feet from the surface of the water. On the top of it we gathered several species of heath, some wild celery, a few shrubs, and some non-descript plants; we found also some little stones of a fine polish and singular whitenefs.

In our descent, which proved nearly as difficult and troublesome as going up, we saw some runaway negroes, round a fire, on the clift of a stupendous rock, where it was entirely out of the power of their owners to get at them. To look at their situation, one would think it beyond the utmost stretch of human ingenuity to devise a way to reach it. Here they remain all day in perfect security, and during the night make frequent excursions to the town and the parts

adjacent,

adjacent, committing great depredations on the inhabitants. The whole subsistence of these fugitives depends on this precarious method: and even this method would prove insufficient, were it not for the assistance they receive from those who were once their fellow slaves. Nor is it always that they succeed in the depredatory trips, which necessity thus urges them to take; they are often betrayed by their quondam friends; and when this happens, as the Dutch are not famed for their lenity in punishing crimes, they are made horrid examples of. But neither the fear of punishment, nor hunger, thirst, cold, and wretchedness, to which they are often unavailably exposed, can deter them from making Table Land their place of refuge from what they consider to be greater evils. Scarcely a day passes but a smoke may be seen from some of these inaccessible retreats.

In the mild or summer season, which commences in September, and continues till March, the Table Land is sometimes suddenly capped with a white cloud, by some called the *spreading of the Table-cloth*. When this cloud seems to roll down the steep face of the mountain, it is an unerring indication of an approaching gale of wind from the south-east;

eaſt; which generally blows with great violence, and ſome-times continues a day or more, but in common is of ſhort duration. On the firſt appearance of this cloud, the ſhips in Table Bay begin to prepare for it, by ſtriking yards and top-maſts, and making every thing as ſnug as poſſible.

A little to the weſtward of the Table Land, divided by a ſmall valley, ſtands, on the right hand ſide of Table Bay, a round hill, called the Sugar Loaf; and by many the Lion's Head, as there is a continuance from it contiguous to the ſea, called the Lion's Rump; and when you take a general view of the whole, it very much reſembles that animal with his head erect. The Sugar Loaf or Lion's Head, and the Lion's Rump, have each a flag-ſtaff on them, by which the approach of ſhips is made known to the governor, par-ticularizing their number, nation, and the quarter from which they come. To the eaſtward, ſeparated by a ſmall chaſm from the Table Land, ſtands Charles's Mount, well known by the appellation of the Devil's Tower; and ſo called from the violent guſts of wind ſuppoſed to iſſue from it, when it partakes of the cap that covers the Table Land; though theſe guſts are nothing more than a degree of force the wind acquires in coming through the chaſm. When

I                              this

this phænomenon appears in the morning, which is by no means so frequent as in the evening, the sailors have a saying, as the Devil's Tower is almost contiguous to the Table Land, that the old gentleman is going to breakfast; if in the middle of the day, that he is going to dinner; and if in the evening, that the cloth is spread for supper.

The foregoing high lands form a kind of amphitheatre about the Table Valley, where the Cape Town stands. From the shipping the town appears pleasantly situated, but at the same time small; a deception that arises from its being built in a valley with such stupendous mountains directly behind it. On landing, however, you are surprised, and agreeably disappointed, to find it not only extensive, but well built, and in a good stile; the streets spacious, and intersecting each other at right angles with great precision. This exactness in the formation of the streets, when viewed from the Table Land, is observed to be very great. The houses in general are built of stone, cemented together with a glutinous kind of earth which serves as mortar, and afterwards neatly plastered, and whitewashed, with lime. As to their height, they do not in common exceed two stories, on account of the violence of the wind, which at some seasons of the year

blows

blows with great ſtrength and fury; indeed ſometimes ſo violently as to ſhake the houſes to the very foundation. For the ſame reaſon, thatch has been uſually preferred to tiles or ſhingles; but the bad effects that have proceeded from this mode when fires happen, has induced the inhabitants in all their new buildings to give the preference to ſlates and tiles. The lower parts of the houſes, according to the cuſtom of the Dutch nation, are not only uncommonly neat and clean in appearance, but they are really ſo; and the furniture is rather rich than elegant. But this is by no means the caſe with the bed-rooms or upper apartments; which are more barely and worſe furniſhed than any I ever beheld: and the ſtreets ſeem to be much upon a par with them, they being rough, uneven, and unpaved. I was, however, upon the whole, extremely well pleaſed with the town. Many of the houſes have a ſpace flagged before the door, and others have trees planted before them, which form a pleaſant ſhade, and give pleaſing novelty to the ſtreets.

The only landing place is at the eaſt end of the town, where there is a wooden quay running ſome paces into the ſea, with ſeveral cranes on it, for the convenience of loading and unloading the ſcoots that come along ſide. To

this

this place excellent water is conveyed by pipes, which makes the watering of ſhips both eaſy and expeditious.

Cloſe to this quay, on the left hand, ſtands the caſtle and principal fortreſs; a ſtrong extenſive work, having excellent accommodations for the troops, and for many of the civil officers belonging to the company. Within the gates, the company have their principal ſtores; which are ſpacious as well as convenient. This fort covers and defends the eaſt part of the town and harbour, as Amſterdam fort does the weſt part. The latter, which has been built ſince commodore Johnſtone's expedition, and whereon both French and Dutch judgment have been united to render it effectual and ſtrong, is admirably planned and calculated to annoy and haraſs ſhips coming into the bay. Some ſmaller detached fortifications extend along the coaſt, both to the eaſt and weſt, and make landing, which was not the caſe before the late war, hazardous and difficult. In a word, Cape Town is at this time fortified with ſtrength, regularity, and judgment.

There are two churches here; one large, plain, and unadorned, for the Calviniſts, the prevailing ſect; and a ſmaller one for the Lutherans.

The hoſpital, which is large and extenſive, is ſituated

N                                                                at at the upper end of the town, clofe to the company's garden. It is an honour to that commercial body, and no fmall ornament to the town. The only objection that can be made to it as a building, is its fituation: had it been erected on an eminence, and a little detached from the town, which might eafily have been done, no fault could have been found with it. As it is, the convalefcents have free accefs to the company's gardens, where they reap the benefit of a wholefome pure air, perfumed with the exhalations of a great variety of rich fruit trees, aromatic fhrubs, and odorous plants and flowers; and likewife have the ufe of every production of it, as before obferved; advantages that compenfate, in a great meafure, for the flat fituation of the hofpital.

The inhabitants are all exceedingly fond of gardens, which they keep in moft excellent order. The doing this is very little trouble to them, the climate and foil being moft benign and friendly to vegetation. Among the many which afforded me delight, I muft not forget that belonging to Colonel Gordon, commander in chief of the Dutch troops at the Cape; where not only the tafte and ingenuity of the gardener, but the fkill and knowledge of the botanift, are at once manifeft. The colonel is a man of fcience, of an active and well-cultivated genius, and who

appropriates

appropriates thofe hours he can fpare from his military duties (in which he is faid to excel), to a perufal of the book of nature, and refearches after ufeful knowledge. Thefe purfuits tend not only to his amufement, but to his honour; and they will, doubtlefs, at fome time or other, further conduce to the advancement of natural hiftory, and to the honour of his country; as it is faid he intends to publifh the obfervations and remarks which have been the refult of his refearches. Thofe he has made on the Hotten-tots, Caffres, and the countries they inhabit, will doubt-lefsly be valuable; he having made himfelf better acquainted with the fubject, and penetrated farther into the interior parts, than any traveller or naturalift that has hitherto vifited the Cape. It is to be lamented, that he has fo long withheld from the world the gratification and improvement, which moft affuredly muft be derived from the obfervations of a perfon fo well and fo extenfively informed. His polite attention and civility, during our ftay at the Cape, claim our moft grateful acknowledgments.

Befides their hofpital, the Dutch Eaft India company have feveral other public buildings, which tend to improve the appearance of the town. The two principal of thefe

are,

are, the ftables, and a houfe for their flaves.   The former is
a handfome range of buildings, capable of containing an
incredible number of horfes.  Thofe they have at  the Cape
are fmall, fpirited, and full of life.   The latter is a building
of confiderable extent,  where the flaves,  both  male and
female, have feparate apartments, in a very comfortable ftile,
to refide in after  the fatigues and toil of the day;  which
undoubtedly is great, but by no means equal, in my opinion,
to that endured by the flaves  in  our  own  colonies.   However fevere and cruel the Dutch may be confidered in other
refpects, they certainly treat their flaves with great humanity
and kindnefs;  which, I am forry to fay, I fcarcely ever faw
done in the Weft Indies, during a refidence there of three years.
On the contrary, I  have frequently been witnefs to the in-
fliction of the moft brutal, cruel, and wanton punifhments on
thefe poor creatures, who  are the fource and immediate fup-
port of the fplendour of the Creoles.  The bare retrofpect of
the cruelties I have feen exercifed there, excites a kind of hor-
ror that chills my blood.   At the Cape, there are feveral
officers placed over the flaves, who have commodious apartments, and treat them humanely.

The firft week  after our arrival at this place, the militia,
consisting

confifting both of horfe and foot, were embodied, and held their annual meeting: I fay annual, as that is the ufual period; but this was the firft time of their affembling fince the conclufion of the war in 1783. The Cape militia differ from the Englifh, in not receiving pay, or wearing regimentals. In fact they fhould rather be called volunteers, who turn out for the protection of their own property, and are not fubject to ftrict military difcipline. Moft of them wore blue coats, with white metal buttons, aukwardly long, and in the cut and fhape of which uniformity had not been attended to. Neither was it vifible in the other parts of their drefs or accoutrements; fome wore powder, others none; fo that, upon the whole, they made a very unmilitary appearance. The officers are chofen annually from among themfelves. Some of thefe, indeed, I obferved to be very well dreffed. Neglect, non-attendance, and every other breach of their military rules, is punifhed by fine or forfeiture, and not corporally. At this burlefque on the profeffion of a foldier, I could not help obferving, that many of them had either got intoxicated that morning, or were not recovered from their overnight's debauch; notwithftanding which they marched to the field, and went through their evolutions

with

with a steadiness and regularity that was really astonishing, considering the state they were in: but it is said, and I believe with some truth, that a Dutchman, when half drunk, is more capable of performing every kind of business, than if he were perfectly sober. After these annual exhibitions, the members of the corps meet their wives, daughters, &c. (who take care to be present, that they may be witnesses of their military skill and atchievements) at some friend's house, where they crown the night in dancing, of which they are uncommonly fond. To dancing are added substantial suppers, and potent libations; in which they indulge not only upon this, but on all other occasions. A Dutch supper to me, at first, was a matter of wonder, as I could never see any kind of difference, either in the quality or quantity, between them and their dinners, which were always abundant, and consisting chiefly of heavy food.

The inhabitants of the Cape, though in their persons large, stout, and athletic, have not all that phlegm about them which is the characteristic of Dutchmen in general. The physical influence of climate may in some degree account for this; for it is well known that in all

southern

southern latitudes the temper and difpofition of the people are more gay, and that they are more inclined to luxury and amufements of every kind, than the inhabitants of the northern hemifphere.

The ladies at the Cape are lively, good natured, familiar, and gay. They refemble the women of England more than any foreigners I have ever feen. Englifh fafhions prevail among them (the female part of the governor's family excepted, who imitate the French), notwithftanding their intercourfe with France is now by far greater than with England. The habits and cuftoms of the women of this place are extremely contrafted to thofe of the inhabitants of Rio de Janeiro. Among the latter a great deal of referve and modefty is apparent between the fexes in public. Thofe who are difpofed to fay tender and civil things to a lady, muft do it by ftealth, or breathe their foft fighs through the lattice-work of a window, or the grates of a convent. But at the Cape, if you wifh to be a favourite with the fair, as the cuftom is, you muft in your own defence (if I may ufe the expreffion) *grapple* the lady, and paw her in a manner that does not partake in the leaft of gentlenefs. Such a rough and uncouth

I                                     conduct,

conduct, together with a kiss ravished now and then in the most public manner and situations, is not only pleasing to the fair one, but even to her parents, if present; and is considered by all parties as an act of the greatest gallantry and gaiety. In fact, the Dutch ladies here, from a peculiar gay turn, admit of liberties that may be thought reprehensible in England; but perhaps as seldom overstep the bounds of virtue, as the women of other countries.

During my residence on shore, whenever I heard of any Hottentots being in town, I made a point of endeavouring to get a sight of them, in order to see whether their manners and appearance corresponded with the description given of them by travellers; such as being besmeared with grease, and decorated with the stinking entrails of animals; on which they likewise, when pressed by hunger, are said to feed.

I saw many of the men, without being able to make any other remarks on them, than that they were thin, of rather a low stature, but formed for activity: and further, that their hair, which was short and woolly, as well as their whole bodies, was bedaubed with some unctuous or greasy substance, which was very offensive.

They

They were of a dark brown colour, had a flat nose, thick lips, large full eyes, and were ornamented with ivory rings, and wore narrow strips of the skin of some animal, devoid of its hair, around their neck, legs, and arms. The only female of that nation I could get a sight of, was during a little excursion in the environs of Cape Town: walking one evening with a Dutch gentleman, to see a garden about a mile from the town, I accidentally met one of these ladies, who was equally as offensive as the male I had met.

The heavy draft work about the Cape is mostly performed by oxen; which are here brought to an uncommon degree of usefulness and docility. It is not uncommon to see fourteen, sixteen, and sometimes eighteen, in one of their teams; when the roads are heavy, they sometimes, though rarely, yoke twenty; all which the Hottentots, Malayes, and Cape slaves, have in the most perfect subjection and obedience. One of these fellows places himself on the fore part of the waggon, or, when loaded, on the top of the load, and with a tremendous long whip, which, from its size, he is obliged to hold in both his hands, manages these creatures with inexpressible addreſs. I have often

O                                    seen

seen the driver, when he has found expedition needful, make them keep whatever pace he thought proper; either trot or gallop (a gait performed or kept up with difficulty by European oxen), and that with as much ease as if he was driving horses. This immense whip, the only thing with which they guide the team, the drivers use so dexterously, that they make them turn a corner with the utmost nicety; hitting even the leading pair, in whatever part they please. The blows thus given must inflict intolerable pain, or these slow animals could never be brought to go with the velocity they do at the Cape. These sooty charioteers likewise manage horses with the same dexterity. To see one of them driving three, four, five, and sometimes six pair, in hand, with one of these long whips, as I have often done with great surprise, would make the most complete master of the whip in England cut a despicable figure. Carriages are not very numerous at the Cape, as the inhabitants in general travel in covered waggons, which better suit the roughness of the country. The governor and some few of the principal people keep coaches, which are a good deal in the English stile, and always drawn by six horses. The only chariot

I saw

I saw there belonged to the governor; I however heard there were some others.

November 11th. Having got on board such animals, provisions, &c. as we could stow, the commodore, with all the officers that had lodgings on shore, embarked. Previous to the commodore's embarkation he gave a public dinner to some of the gentlemen of the town and the officers of his fleet. The Dutch governor was to have been of the party, but by some unforeseen event was detained in the country, where he had been for some days before. Commodore Phillip had his band of music on shore upon the occasion, and the day was spent with great cheerfulness and conviviality.

13th. About half past one o'clock we sailed from the Cape of Good Hope. A small American ship had arrived during the forenoon, bound on a trading voyage to China, with several passengers on board. We learnt from her, that the Hartwell East Indiaman had been lost, by bordering too close on the island of Bonavista, in order to land some recruits, who had mutinied, and occasioned great disorder and confusion in the ship. It gave us pleasure to hear from

O 2                                    the

the carpenter of the Hartwell, who was on board the American ship, that no lives were loft by the accident. The principal part of the crew, we found, had got to Madeira, on their return to England. Abreaft of Penguin Ifland, about three o'clock, we paffed a large Dutch fhip from Holland, bound to the Cape, with troops on board. A little before it was dark, we fpoke the Kent whaler, from London, who had been four months out. She with ourfelves was endeavouring to get to the eaftward. On our firft difcovering her, as fhe feemed defirous of joining or fpeaking to the fleet, we were in hopes of her being from England, probably to us; or at leaft that we might get letters by her; but our fufpenfe on thefe points, a fufpenfe only to be conceived by perfons on long voyages, was foon put an end to by hearing fhe had been fo many months out. A few days before we left the Cape, fome of the officers of the expedition received letters from England by the Ranger Eaft India packet, Captain Buchanan, who had put in to water, and ftop a leak; both of which being foon accomplifhed, fhe proceeded on her voyage.

14th. This morning Catherine Pryor, one of the con-

victs,

victs, was delivered of a male child. The officers, seamen, troops, and convicts, were put to an allowance of three quarts of water a day.

17th. The wind variable, inclining to the southward and eastward, with hazy weather, an epidemic dysentry appeared among the convicts, which very soon made its way among the marines, and prevailed with violence and obstinacy until about Christmas, when it was got under by an unremitting attention to cleanliness, and every other method proper and essential for the removal and prevention of contagion. It gives me pleasure to be able to add, that we only lost one person by this disease, violent and dangerous as it was; and that was Daniel Cresswell, one of the troops intended for the garrison; who was seized on the 19th of November, and died the 30th of the same month, the eleventh day of his illness. From the commencement of his disorder, he was in the most acute agonizing pain I ever was witness to; nor was it in the power of medicine to procure him the shortest interval of ease. His case being a very singular one, I have transmitted it, with some others, to a medical friend in London, with permission to make what use of them he may think proper. The wind kept to the southward and

eastward

eaftward until the 21ft, without veering a point in our favour, which carried us far out of our way to the weftward; but that day it fhifted.

23d. We fpoke the Prince of Wales, who informed us, that the preceding night one of the feamen had fallen from the top-fail yard, and was drowned. Indeed it was fo dark, and the fhip went fo faft through the water, that all efforts to fave him, had any been made, would have proved fruitlefs. This day and the following running to eaftward, with the wind to the fouthward and weftward, we faw many aquatic birds.

25th. The commodore removed into the Supply armed tender, and took with him Lieutenant King of the Sirius, and Mr. Dawes of the marines, whom I had before occafion to mention as having undertaken the aftronomical obfervations during the voyage. Having likewife felected fome artificers from among the convicts, he went on, taking the Alexander, Scarborough, and Friendfhip with him, being faft failing veffels; leaving the heavy failers, both tranfports and victuallers, under the direction of Captain Hunter of the Sirius. Major Rofs, commanding officer of the troops, removed into the Scarborough, as did the adjutant.

26th. We

26th. We had not loft fight of the Supply and other fhips, though they were confiderably ahead. Between nine and ten at night the wind came to the S. S. E. which made us tack and ftand to the S. W. In the morning could fee nothing of the *flying fquadron*, as the feamen termed them. The wind continued all this day at E. S. E. with pleafant clear weather.

28th. The wind fhifted to the E. N. E.; the weather hazy, with fmall rain and ftrong breezes. The Sirius made a fignal for the convoy to clofe.

30th. The wind variable, with fome heavy fhowers, and in the intervals clear weather.

December 1ft and 2d. The wind from W. S. W. to S. W. by W. in lat. 40° fouth, long. 35° 10' eaft; the weather moderate, cold, clear, and pleafant. We faw birds of different kinds.

3d. In the evening, and on the fucceeding day, the wind to northward and weftward; frefh gales, dark, wet, unpleafant weather, with a high fea. The Sirius, for fear of feparation, as the weather did not look kindly, made the fignal for the convoy to keep nearer the commanding officer.

5th. In

5th.   In the morning almoſt calm, with a heavy ſwell ; in the evening a ſmall breeze ſprung up at the N. E. which next day ſhifted to the weſtward.

16th.   In lat. 41° 7′ ſouth, long. 74° 54′ eaſt, clear weather, with a ſmall breeze at N. N. W. we ſaw ſome large whales, ſeveral birds, moſtly of the peteral kind, a ſeal, and ſome rock weed.

17th.   Dark, cold, and gloomy.   Had ſome gulls and whales round the ſhip.

20th.   Wind variable, inclining to the ſouth.   I viſited the Prince of Wales, where I found ſome of the female convicts with evident ſymptoms of the ſcurvy, brought on by the damp and cold weather we had lately experienced.   The two ſucceeding days the wind to the weſtward, though at times variable, with dark, wet, gloomy weather ; in lat. 41° 18′ ſouth, long. 90° 7′ eaſt.   We ſaw and paſſed ſome ſea weed.   On thoſe days the ſcurvy began to ſhow itſelf in the Charlotte, moſtly among thoſe who had the dyſentery to a violent degree ;   but I was pretty well able to keep it under, by a liberal uſe of the eſſence of malt, and ſome good wine, which ought not to be claſſed among the

moſt

moſt indifferent antiſcorbutics.   For the latter we were indebted to the humanity of Lord Sydney and Mr. Nepean,
principal and under ſecretaries of ſtate.

24th.   The weather ſtill dark and gloomy.   Had ſeveral
birds round the ſhip of the albatroſs and peteral kind;
with what appeared to me to be ſomething of the ſea-hawk
ſpecies.

27th.   Dark hazy weather, with ſome light ſqualls.   We
paſſed more ſea weed; ſome gulls, and many of the before-
mentioned birds, about the ſhip.

30th and 31ſt.   Strong breezes, with unſettled-looking
weather; birds ſtill about us, and likewiſe ſome whales.

January 1ſt, 1788.   The new year was introduced
with a pretty heavy gale of wind from the northward and
weſtward, which was the firſt we had encountered ſince
we left England.   It began a little before 12 o'clock the
preceding night, and continued till ſeven this evening.
The Sirius was the whole day under her ſtay-ſails; and the
convoy under their fore-ſail and ſtay-ſails.

2d and 3d.   Smart gales, with dark gloomy weather.
Some ſeals and oceanic birds about the ſhip.

4th. Cloudy weather, in latitude 44° 2′ S. The Sirius

P                                    made

made the signal for the longitude by lunar observation, which was found to be 135° 30′ East. In the evening some birds, called Mother Cary's Chickens, were round the ship.

5th. The weather cold and clear, the wind N. W. Passed some sea weed. In the morning the third mate thought he saw some divers; but as they were not seen by any other person, not much attention was paid to the report. At night we had some squalls, with light showers of rain.

7th. Early in the morning the Lady Penrhyn made the signal for seeing land; but it only proved to be a fog-bank; a circumstance that often deceives the anxious mariner. About two o'clock in the afternoon the Prince of Wales, being the headmost ship, made the same signal. The Charlotte being next in succession, the signal was scarcely displayed, before we also discovered it very plainly through the haze; and repeated the signal, which was answered by the Sirius. By our last lunar observation this land appears to be well laid down in Maskelyne's Tables, and in the journals of the celebrated Cook: but to the surprise of every one on board, we found a small chart, published by Steele, and which was held in little estimation, to be not only accurate as to the situation, but also to give a to-

lerable

lerable appearance and defcription of Van Dieman's Land : indeed fuch as may prove extremely ufeful to fhips coming this way, and fully fufficient to enable them to avoid all danger if the weather be clear. For my own part, I fee no hazard that attends making this land by day (fuch an attempt by night would be very incautious and abfurd), as nature has been very particular in pointing out where it lies, by rocks which jutt out of the fea, like fo many beacons. I believe a convoy was never conducted with more care, or made the land with greater accuracy and certainty, than this. Indeed, ability and experienced nautical knowledge were never more fully evinced on all occafions than by Captain Hunter; who, I may venture to pronounce, without much rifk of having my veracity called in queftion, one of the moft affiduous and accurate obfervers, and able navigators, the prefent day furnifhes. His appointment to this expedition by Lord Howe is ftrongly marked with that prudence and wifdom which are known to govern his Lord-fhip's conduct. Captain Hunter has a pretty turn for draw-ing, which will enable him, no doubt, to give fuch a defcription of this coaft as will do credit to himfelf, and be of fingular advantage, as well to thofe whofe lot it may

P 2                                              be

to vifit, hereafter, this extenfive coaft, as to navigation at large. The affiftance of Lieutenant Bradley, firft of the Sirius, (who likewife is an officer of more than common abilities), as a navigator in conducting a convoy in a track fo little known, muft have been pleafing to Captain Hunter.

As we run in with the land, which is pretty high, we were furprifed to fee, at this feafon of the year, fome fmall patches of fnow. The haze being difperfed, by a gentle breeze at N. N. W. we could obferve, and hear, as we were not more than fix or feven miles from the fhore, the furf beating high and loudly againft fome uneven rocks which jutted out, in ftrange projections, into the fea. This part of the coaft, as far as we could fee, is bold, irregular, and craggy; and very few trees, or appearance of verdure, to be feen. At four in the afternoon, being about fix or eight miles to the eaftward of the eaftwardmoft rock, called the Mewftone (there being feveral others which we diftinctly faw), bearing N. N. W. we difcovered to the weftward of them fome eminences, which probably might be iflands; or, if not, fome land running a confiderable way into the fea. For my own part I am inclined

to

to believe the latter to be the cafe; though the diftance was too great to hazard a conclufive opinion upon it, as a large fmoke was feen clofe to the innermoft height.

About feven, fteering to the eaftward, along fhore, nearly at the diftance of four miles, being well in with the weftward-moft point of a very large bay, called Storm Bay, laid down in lat. 44° 3′ S. and long. 146° E. we difcovered Swilly bearing S. E. ½ S. and a little to the eaftward of it a fmall rock rifing out of the fea, diftinguifhed by the name of the Eddyftone, from its refemblance to the Eddyftone light-houfe off Plymouth, which was very perceptible at the diftance we were then from it. Our being clofe in with the land, prevented us from feeing either of thefe before, as they lie at leaft fix or feven leagues out to fea. From the S. W. cape, which lies in lat. 43° 39′ S. and long. 145° 50′ E. to the S. E. cape, which is admitted to be Tafman's South Cape, is about the diftance of fifteen or fixteen leagues. As we got to the eaftward, we faw many trees, moftly of a dwarf or ftunted kind, with a whitifh bark, and perfectly leaflefs. This part of the country ftill continued to be a rough, rugged, uneven tract, with very little appearance of fertility.

Some

Some small patches of verdure were discovered about Storm Bay, and the trees seemed to increase in number and size. Between eight and nine at night, we saw a large fire on the east point of land which forms this bay, made by the natives; none of whom could we see during the day, though close in with the shore: nor did we perceive any other indication of its being inhabited, but this fire, and the smoke mentioned to be seen on our first falling in with the land. The distance between the smoke and the fire was eight leagues, a space that would surely have exhibited some other proofs of populosity had it been thickly peopled.

About 10 o'clock, off Storm Bay, the weather moderately pleasant, the ship was taken aback. The Lady Penrhyn was then under our lee quarter, which obliged us to tack; after which we immediately wore, brought the ship to the wind on the other tack, and stood to sea with the rest of the ships. The wind was then at N. E. which just enabled us to weather Swilly and the Eddystone. As we got to sea the wind increased moderately.

8th. The wind and weather variable; could perceive nothing of the land. I went on board the Fishburne, to see

the

the boatswain, who, on the first night of the new year, having probably drank more grog than he ought, and the ship labouring much, had fallen from the top-sail yard; by which he bruised himself in a dreadful manner. The man being highly scorbutic, the parts soon mortified, and he died about half an hour after I got on board. The master of the ship showed evident marks of great concern for this *invaluable* man, as he termed him. He declared to me, that sooner than venture again on so long a voyage without a surgeon, he would put to sea with less than half his complement of men; for he was strongly of opinion, that if the poor fellow had received immediate assistance he would have recovered. I should have seen him sooner, but was prevented by my own indifferent state of health. How owners of ships can think of sending them through such a variety of climates, and a voyage of so great a length, without a surgeon, is to me a matter of surprise. The Lady Penrhyn, owned by Alderman Curtis, was the only merchant ship in our fleet that had a surgeon. What the others will do on their return, Heaven only knows; but this I well know, that they would never have reached

I

thus

thus far but for the fuccour given them by myfelf and my affiftants.

9th. Wind variable, and weather hazy, damp and dark; with fome vivid flafhes of lightning, fucceeded by diftant peals of loud thunder. On the morning of this day died Edward Thomfon, a convict, worn out with a melancholy and long confinement. Had he lived, I think he would have proved a deferving member of fociety, as he feemed fenfible of the impropriety and imprudence of his former life, and ftudious to atone for it.

10th. The wind variable, and weather dark and gloomy, with a very troublefome high fea. About two o'clock P. M. we had one of the moft fudden gufts of wind I ever remember to have known. In an inftant it fplit our main-fail; and but for the activity fhewn by the failors, in letting fly the fheets, and lowering the top-fails, the mafts muft have gone over the fide. The Prince of Wales, who was clofe to us, had her main yard carried away in the flings. Fortunately for us the fquall was of fhort duration, otherwife the fhips muft have fuffered confiderably from the uncommon crofs fea that was running; which

we

we had found to be the cafe ever fince we reached this coaft.

11th. and 12th. The wind variable, inclining to the southward and weftward, and ftill an unpleafant crofs troublefome fea. We faw a whale, feveral feals, and many large oceanous birds, which we frequently fired at, without their betraying the fmalleft fymptom of fear either at the report, or at the balls, which frequently dropped clofe to them. A conclufion may be drawn from hence, that they had never been haraffed with fire arms before; if they had, they would undoubtedly have fhown fome fear; a fenfation they feemed to be totally unacquainted with. In all our firings we did not kill one of them.

19th. In the evening we faw the land over Red Point, bearing W. by N. the extremes of the land from S. S. W. to N. We were then about three leagues from the fhore; and finding it unlikely to get in that night, Captain Hunter made the fignal for the convoy to come within hail; when he acquainted them, that the entrance into Botany Bay bore N. N. W.: adding, that for the night he intended to ftand off and on, and early in the morning make fail for the bay.

Q

20th. At

20th. At four in the morning the Sirius and convoy made fail, and at eight o'clock anchored in eight fathom water; Cape Banks E. S. E. Point Solander S. S. E. and the entrance of the bay, between thefe two lands, W. S. W. We found here the Supply tender, which had arrived the 18th, and the Alexander, Scarborough, and Friendfhip tranfports, who had only arrived the day before. To fee all the fhips fafe in their deftined port, without ever having, by any accident, been one hour feparated; and all the people in as good health as could be expected or hoped for, after fo long a voyage, was a fight truly pleafirg, and at which every heart muft rejoice. As we failed into the bay, fome of the natives were on the fhore, looking with feeming attention at fuch large moving bodies coming amongft them. In the evening the boats were permitted to land on the north fide, in order to get water and grafs for the little ftock we had remaining. An officer's guard was placed there to prevent the feamen from ftraggling, or having any improper inter-courfe with the natives. Captain Hunter, after anchoring, waited on the governor, on board the Supply; who, with feveral other officers, landed. As they rowed along the fhore, fome of the natives followed the boat; but on her

putting

putting in for the fhore, they ran into the woods. Some of the gentlemen, however, before they returned on board, obtained an interview with them; during which they fhowed fome diftruft, but, upon the whole, were civilly inclined. The boats fent to haul the feine returned, having had tolerable fuccefs. The fifh they caught were bream, mullet, large rays, befides many other fmaller fpecies.

21ft. The governor, Captain Hunter, and the two mafters of the men of war, with a party of marines, fet off this morning, in two rigged long boats, to examine Port Jackfon, a harbour lying a little to the northward, which was difcovered by Captain Cook.

23d. The party returned this evening, full of praifes on the extent and excellence of the harbour, as well as the fuperiority of the ground, water, and fituation, to that of Botany Bay; which, I own, does not, in my opinion, by any means merit the commendations beftowed on it by the much-lamented Cook, and others, whofe names and judgments are no lefs admired and efteemed. During his excellency's abfence the lieutenant governor had iffued his orders to land all the artificers that could be found among the convicts, and a party of others, to clear the ground for the in-

Q 2

tended

tended town, to dig fawpits, and to perform every thing that was effential towards the works purpofed to be carried on. Although the fpot fixed on for the town was the moft eligible that could be chofen, yet I think it would never have anfwered; the ground around it being fandy, poor, and fwampy, and but very indifferently fupplied with water. The fine meadows talked of in Captain Cook's voyage, I could never fee, though I took fome pains to find them out; nor have I ever heard of a perfon that has feen any parts refembling them. While the people were employed on fhore, the natives came feveral times among them, and behaved with a kind of cautious friendfhip. One evening, while the feine was hauling, fome of them were prefent, and expreffed great furprife at what they faw; giving a fhout expreffive of aftonifhment and joy, when they perceived the quantity that was caught. No fooner were the fifh out of the water, than they began to lay hold of them, as if they had a right to them, or that they were their own; upon which the officer of the boat, I think very properly, reftrained them; giving, however, to each of them a part. They did not at firft feem very well pleafed with this mode of procedure, but on obferving

with

with what juſtice the fiſh was diſtributed, they appeared content.

While we remained at Botany Bay, as I was one morning on board the Supply, we ſaw twenty-nine of the natives on the beach, looking towards the ſhipping; upon which Lieutenants Ball and King, Mr. Dawes, and my-ſelf, went on ſhore, landing at the place where they were. They were friendly and pacific, though each of them was arm-ed with a ſpear or long dart, and had a ſtick, with a ſhell at the end, uſed by them in throwing their weapons. Beſides theſe, ſome few had ſhields made of the bark of the cork tree, of a plain appearance, but ſufficient to ward off or turn their own weapons, ſome of which were pointed and barbed with the bones of fiſh, faſtened on with ſome kind of adheſive gum. One of the moſt friendly, and who appeared to be the moſt confident, on ſigns being made to him, ſtuck the end of his ſhield in the ſand, but could not be prevailed upon to throw his ſpear at it. Finding he declined it, I fired a piſtol ball through it. The exploſion frightened him, as well as his companions, a little; but they ſoon got over it, and on my putting the piſtol into my pocket, he took up the ſhield, and appeared to be much

I                                        ſurpriſed

surprifed at finding it perforated. He then, by figns and geftures, feemed to afk if the piftol would make a hole through him; and on being made fenfible that it would, he fhowed not the fmalleft figns of fear; on the contrary he endeavoured, as we conftrued his motions, to imprefs us with an idea of the fuperiority of his own arms, which he applied to his breaft, and by ftaggering, and a fhow of falling, feemed to wifh us to underftand that the force and effect of them was mortal, and not to be refifted. How-ever, I am well convinced that they know and dread the fuperiority of our arms, notwithftanding this fhow of indif-ference; as they, on all occafions, have difcovered a diflike to a mufquet: and fo very foon did they make themfelves acquainted with the nature of our military drefs, that, from the firft, they carefully avoided a foldier, or any perfon wearing a red coat, which they feem to have marked as a fighting vefture. Many of their warriors, or diftinguifhed men, we obferved to be painted in ftripes, acrofs the breaft and back, which at fome little diftance appears not unlike our foldiers crofs belts.

24th. The boats were employed in getting water and grafs for the live ftock; as the governor, finding Port Jack-

fon

ſon more ſuited to his wiſhes, had determined to remove to that place, and form the ſettlement there. While theſe preparations were making, every perſon in the fleet were ſurpriſed to ſee, in this part of the world, two large ſhips plying hard in the offing to get into the bay. It was ſeen, in the evening, that they had French colours flying; but the wind blowing pretty ſtrong out of the bay, they were unable to get in; and the weather becoming thick and hazy, we ſoon loſt ſight of them.

25th. Nothing of the ſtrange ſhips to be ſeen. The governor, with a detachment of marines, ſailed in the Supply tender for Port Jackſon; leaving inſtructions with Captain Hunter to follow him with all the tranſports and victuallers, as ſoon as the wind and weather would permit.

26th. We again deſcried the French ſhips ſtanding in for the bay, with a leading wind; upon which Captain Hunter ſent his firſt lieutenant on board the commanding officer's ſhip, which was diſtinguiſhed by a broad pendant, to aſſiſt them in coming in. Soon after the lieutenants were returned to the Sirius, Captain Clonnard, the French commodore's captain (who during the late war commanded

3                                                    the

the Artois, taken by the Bienfaisant, Captain Macbride), waited on Captain Hunter, and informed him, that the ships were
the Astrolabe and the Boussale, which sailed from France in
the year 1786, under the command of Messieurs de la
Perouse, and De Langle. He further acquainted him, that
having touched at Navigator's Isles, they had had the misfortune to lose Captain De Langle, the second in command,
with ten other officers, and two boats crews, all of whom
were cut off by the natives of those islands, who appeared to
be numerous and warlike. This accident induced them to
put into this port, in order to build some boats, which they
had in frames. It also had afforded room for the promotion
of Monsieur Clonnard, who, on their leaving France, was
only the commodore's first lieutenant.

At ten o'clock the Sirius, with all the ships, weighed, and
in the evening anchored in Port Jackson, with a few
trifling damages done to some of them, who had run foul of
each other in working out of Botany Bay. Port Jackson I
believe to be, without exception, the finest and most extensive harbour in the universe, and at the same time the
most secure; being safe from all the winds that blow. It
is divided into a great number of coves, to which his

excellency

excellency has given different names. That on which the town is to be built, is called Sydney Cove. It is one of the smallest in the harbour, but the most convenient, as ships of the greatest burden can with ease go into it, and heave out close to the shore. Trincomalé, acknowledged to be one of the best harbours in the world, is by no means to be compared to it. In a word, Port Jackson would afford sufficient and safe anchorage for all the navies of Europe. The Supply had arrived the day before, and the governor, with every person that could be spared from the ship, were on shore, clearing the ground for the encampment. In the evening, when all the ships had anchored, the English colours were displayed; and at the foot of the flag-staff his Majesty's health, and success to the settlement, was drank by the governor, many of the principal officers, and private men, who were present upon the occasion.

27th. A number of convicts from the different transports were landed to assist in clearing the ground for the encampment. His excellency marked the outlines, and as much as possible to prevent irregularity, and to keep the convicts from straggling, the provost marshal, aided by the patrole, had orders to take into custody all convicts that

R should

fhould be found without the lines, and to leave them in charge of the main or quarter guard. The boats fent this day to fifh were fuccefsful. Some of the natives came into the little bay or cove where the feine was hauled, and behaved very friendly. Indeed they carried their civility fo far, although a people that appeared to be averfe to work, as to affift in dragging it afhore. For this kind office they were liberally rewarded with fifh, which feemed to pleafe them, and give general fatisfaction.

29th.   A convenient place for the cattle being found, the few that remained were landed. The frame and materials for the governor's houfe, conftructed by Smith in St. George's Fields, were likewife fent on fhore, and fome preparations made for erecting it. This day Captain Hunter and Lieutenant Bradley began to take a furvey of the harbour. In the courfe of the laft week, all the marines, their wives and children, together with all the convicts, male and female, were landed. The laboratory and fick tents were erected, and, I am forry to fay, were foon filled with patients afflicted with the true camp dyfentery and the fcurvy. More pitiable objects were perhaps never feen. Not a comfort or convenience could be got for them, befides the very few we

had

had with us. His excellency feeing the ftate thefe poor ob-jects were in, ordered a piece of ground to be inclofed, for the purpofe of raifing vegetables for them. The feeds that were fown upon this occafion, on firft appearing above ground, looked promifing and well, but foon after withered away; which was not indeed extraordinary, as they were not fown at a proper feafon of the year. The fick have increafed fince our landing to fuch a degree, that a fpot for a general hofpital has been marked out, and arti-ficers already employed on it. A proper fpot, contiguous to the hofpital, has been chofen, to raife fuch vegetables as can be produced at this feafon of the year; and where a permanent garden for the ufe of the hofpital is to be eftablifhed.

February 1ft. We had the moft tremendous thunder and lightning, with heavy rain, I ever remember to have feen.

2d. This morning five fheep, belonging to the lieutenant-governor and quarter-mafter, were killed by the lightning under a tree, at the foot of which a fhed had been built for them. The branches and trunk of the tree were fhivered and rent in a very extraordinary manner.

R 2                                   5th. A

5th. A ftorehoufe has been begun, for the purpofe of receiving the ftores and provifions of the three tranfports bound to China. On a mufter of the convicts this morning, fome were found to be miffing, and fuppofed to have gone to Botany Bay, in hopes of being received on board the French fhips; which are faid to be fhort of hands, and made more fo by the lofs they had recently fuftained, as before mentioned.

7th. The governor's commiffion, and that for eftablifh-ing a criminal court of judicature, admiralty court, &c. were read. After this was done the troops under arms fired three volleys; when his excellency thanked the foldiers for their fteady and good conduct; which Major Rofs caufed to be inferted in the general order book. The governor then addreffed the convicts in a fhort fpeech, extremely well adapted to the people he had to govern, and who were then before him. Among many circumftances that would tend to their future happinefs and comfort, he recommended marriage; affuring them that an indifcriminate and illegal intercourfe would be punifhed with the greateft feverity and rigour. Honefty, obedience, and induftry, he told them, would make their fituation comfortable; whereas

a contrary

a contrary line of conduct would subject them to ignominy, severities, and punishment. When the ceremony was concluded, his excellency, attended by all the officers of the colony, withdrew to a tent pitched for the occasion, where a cold dinner was laid out; and after the cloth was removed, many loyal and public toasts were drank.

8th. A party of the gentlemen of the garrison set out by land to pay a visit to the French at Botany Bay; from whom they met with the most hospitable, polite, and friendly reception and treatment. Many of the convicts who had been missing had been at Botany Bay. They had offered themselves to the French navigators on any terms, but not one of them had been received. This refusal obliged them to return; and when they came back they were real objects of pity. Conscious of the punishment that awaited so imprudent and improper an experiment, they had stayed out as long as the cravings of nature would permit, and were nearly half starved. A woman named Ann Smith, and a man, have never since been heard of. They are supposed to have missed their way as they returned, and to have perished for want. As the French commodore had given his honour that he would not admit any of them on board,

I

board, it cannot be thought he would take them. The convict, it is true, was a Frenchman, named Peter Paris, and it is possible, on that account, he might have been concealed through pity, by his countrymen, and carried off without the knowledge of the commanding officer. At the very time the party from hence were gone by land to Botany Bay, Captain Clonnard came round in a boat, on a visit of ceremony from Monsieur de la Peyrouse to the governor. He brought with him some dispatches, which he requested might be forwarded to the French ambassador at the court of London, by the first transports that sailed for England. The captain stayed all night, and returned the next morning. This day, for the first time, a Kangaroo was shot and brought into camp. Some of the natives passed pretty close to the Sirius, without seeming to express, by their countenance or actions, either fear, curiosity, or surprise. During the course of this week fourteen marriages were solemnized. The criminal court, consisting of six officers of his Majesty's forces by land or sea, with the judge advocate, sat for the first time; before whom several convicts were tried for petty larceny. Some of them were acquitted, others sentenced to receive corporal punishment, and one or two were, by the

the decision of the court, ordered to a barren rock, or little island, in the middle of the harbour, there to remain on bread and water for a stated time.

12th. The commissions were read a second time, at the desire of some of the officers, whose situation with the battalion prevented them from being present at the first reading; after which, the lieutenant governor and judge advocate were sworn in justices of the peace; and Lieutenant King (second of the Sirius) superintendant and commanding officer of New Norfolk Island; an appointment given him by the governor.

14th. The Supply sailed for Norfolk Island, with Lieutenant King and his detachment, consisting of Mr. Cunningham, master's mate, and Mr. Jameson, surgeon's first mate, of the Sirius, two marines, and twelve male and female convicts. The governor furnished him with provisions and stores of every kind for six months, and with tools for cutting down timber; which last employment was the purpose of his mission.

27th. Thomas Barrett, Henry Lovel, and Joseph Hall, were brought before the criminal court, and tried for feloniously and fraudulently taking away from the public

store

store beef and peafe, the property of the crown. They were convicted on the cleareft evidence; and fentence of death being paffed on them, they were, about fix o'clock the fame evening, taken to the fatal tree; where Barrett was launched into eternity, after having confeffed to the Rev. Mr. Johnfon, who attended him, that he was guilty of the crime, and had long merited the ignominious death which he was about to fuffer, and to which he faid he had been brought by bad company and evil example. Lovel and Hall were refpited until fix o'clock the next evening. When that awful hour arrived, they were led to the place of execution, and juft as they were on the point of afcending the ladder, the judge advocate arrived with the governor's pardon, on condition of their being banifhed to fome uninhabited place.

29th. Daniel Gordon and John Williams were tried and convicted of ftealing wine, the property of Mr. Zachariah Clarke. Williams being an ignorant black youth, the court recommended him to the governor as a proper object of mercy, and he was accordingly pardoned. Gordon, who was another black, had his fentence of death, while at the gallows, changed to banifhment with Lovel and Hall.

30th.

*Cassowary of New South Wales.*

London Published Dec: 29. 1789. by I. Debrett.

30th.   John Freeman was tried for ftealing from another convict feven pounds of flour. He was convicted, and fentenced to be hanged ; but while under the ladder, with the rope about his neck, he was offered his free pardon on condition of performing the duty of the common executioner as long as he remained in this country; which, after fome little paufe, he reluctantly accepted. William Sheerman, his accomplice, was fentenced to receive on his bare back, with a cat-o'nine-tails, three hundred lafhes, which were inflicted.

A *New Holland Caffowary* was brought into camp. This bird ftands feven feet high, meafuring from the ground to the upper part of the head, and, in every refpect, is much larger than the *common Caffowary* of all authors, and differs fo much therefrom, in its form, as to clearly prove it a new fpecies. The colour of the plumage is greatly fimilar, confifting of a mixture of dirty brown and grey; on the belly it was fomewhat whiter; and the remarkable ftructure of the feathers, in having two quills with their webs arifing out of one fhaft, is feen in this as well as the common fort. It differs materially in wanting the horny appendage on the top of the head. The head and beak

S                                                      are

are much more like thofe of the oftrich than the common Caffowary, both in fhape and fize. Upon the upper part of the head the feathers, with which it is but thinly covered, are very fmall, looking more like hair than feathers, and in having the neck pretty well clothed with them, except the chin and throat, which are fo thinly covered, that the fkin, which is there of a purplifh colour, may be feen clearly. The fmall wings are exceedingly fhort, which form a ridiculous contraft with the body, as they are even lefs than thofe of the Caffowary: they have no large quills in them, being only covered with the fmall feathers that grow all over the body. Another fingularity alfo prefents itfelf in this fpecies, which is in refpect to the legs. As to the back part of them, the whole length is indented, or fawed, in a remarkable manner. The toes are three in number, the middle one long, the other two fhort, with ftrong claws, not unlike the fame part of the common fpecies. On examining the vifcera, they differed from that of every other fpecies of the feathered kind which I had ever feen; particularly in having no gizzard, or fecond ftomach; and the liver was fo very fmall, that it did not exceed in fize that of a black-

3                                                                                  bird.

bird. To this liver was joined a large gall-bladder, well diftended with bile. The crop, or ftomach, was filled with at leaft fix or feven pounds of grafs, flowers, and a few berries and feeds. The inteftinal canal was at leaft fix yards long, very wide, and of a regular cylindrical fhape from the opening of the ftomach to the vent. The heart and lungs were feparated by a diaphragm or midriff, and bore a tolerable proportion to the fize of the bird. The flefh of this bird was very good, and tafted not unlike young tender beef.

This bird is fuppofed to be not uncommon in *New Holland*, as it has been frequently feen by our Settlers both at *Botany Bay* and *Port Jackfon*, but is exceedingly fhy, and runs fafter than a greyhound. One of them however has been fhot*.

March 9th. The governor, with two long boats manned and armed, returned from Broken Bay, fituated a little to the northward, which he had been exploring for feveral days. It affords good fhelter for fhipping, and the entrance is bold;

* A drawing was taken from this bird, of which an engraving is annexed. It has been lately fent to England by the governor, as a prefent to Lord Sydney, who, through the medium of Sir Jofeph Banks, has depofited it in the collections of Natural Hiftory of Mr. John Hunter in Leicefter Square.

it

it cannot, however, be compared to Port Jackſon. While he was there, he ſaw a great many of the natives, ſome of whom he thinks he had obſerved before, either at Botany Bay or in the neighbourhood of Port Jackſon. One of the females happened to fall in love with his great coat; and to obtain it, ſhe uſed a variety of means. Firſt, ſhe danced, and played a number of antic tricks; but finding this mode ineffectual, ſhe had recourſe to tears, which ſhe ſhed plentifully. This expedient not anſwering, ſhe ceaſed from weeping, and appeared as cheerful as any of the party around her. From this little incident it may be ſeen that they are not a people devoid of art. At Broken Bay many of the females, young and old, had the firſt joint of the little finger, on their left hand, cut off. As this was the caſe with thoſe who were married, or appeared to be ſo from their having young children, as well as with thoſe who were too young for a connection of that nature, it was not poſſible to account for the cauſe of ſuch an amputation. Thefts and depredations on one another have become ſo very frequent and glaring among the convicts, that ſcarcely a day paſſes without ſome of theſe miſerable delinquents being puniſhed. So hardened in wickedneſs and depravity are many of them, that they ſeem

I

infenfible

infenfible to the fear of corporal punifhment, or even death itfelf.

The principal bufinefs going forward at prefent is erecting cabbage-tree huts for the officers, foldiers, and convicts; fome ftore-houfes, &c.; and a very good hofpital; all which in the completion will coft a great deal of time and trouble, as the timber of this country is very unfit for the purpofe of building. Nor do I know any one purpofe for which it will anfwer, except for fire-wood; and for that it is excellent: but, in other refpects, it is the worft wood that any country or climate ever produced; although fome of the trees, when ftanding, appear fit for any ufe whatever, mafts for fhipping not excepted. Strange as it may be imagined, no wood in this country, though fawed ever fo thin, and dried ever fo well, will float. Repeated trials have only ferved to convince me that, immediately on immerfion, it finks to the bottom like a ftone.

The ftone of this country is excellent for building, could any kind of cement be found to keep it together. There is not any lime-ftone (I believe) in New South Wales. The governor, notwithftanding that he had collected together all the fhells which could be found, for the purpofe of

obtaining

obtaining from them the lime neceffary to the conftruction of a houfe for his own refidence, did not procure even a fourth part of the quantity which was wanted. The foundation ftone of a private houfe for him has been laid ; and a plate of copper, with the following infcription engraved on it, is to be placed in the wall :

## ARTHUR PHILLIP, Esq.

Captain General in and over his Majefty's Territory of New South Wales, and its Dependencies ;

Arrived in this Country on the 18th Day of January, 1788, with the firft Settlers ;

And on the 15th Day of May, in the fame Year, the firft of thefe Stones was laid.

The Supply tender returned from Norfolk Ifland ; where, with great difficulty and danger, the ftores fent with Lieutenant King were landed, on account of the rockynefs of its fhore, and the violence of the furf that almoft continually beats upon it. In her paffage there fhe fell in with an

ifland,

island, in lat. 31° 36′ S. long. 159° 4′ E. never before difcovered, to which Lieutenant Ball, who commanded the
Supply on this occafion, gave the name of Lord Howe's
Ifland. On her return to this port fhe ftopped at it, and
found the landing nearly, if not quite, as difficult as at
Norfolk Ifland. The fhore in many places was covered
with excellent turtle, eighteen of which were brought here,
and proved a feafonable fupply to the convicts afflicted with
the fcurvy, many of whom were in a deplorable fituation.

The fmalleft turtle brought from Lord Howe's Ifland did
not weigh lefs than 150 lb. They alfo found on it, in great
plenty, a kind of fowl, refembling much the Guinea fowl
in fhape and fize, but widely different in colour; they
being in general all white, with a red flefhy fubftance
rifing, like a cock's comb, from the head, and not unlike
a piece of fealing-wax. Thefe not being birds of flight,
nor in the leaft wild, the failors availing themfelves of their
gentlenefs and inability to take wing from their purfuits,
eafily ftruck them down with fticks. There were alfo many
birds of the dove kind, as tame as the former, and caught
with equal facility. Some of them were brought alive to
this place. Befides thefe, the fhore abounded with fea

birds

birds of several species. The island is very barren, and not more than twenty miles in circumference.

25th. The Scarborough, Lady Penrhyn, and Charlotte, transports, being cleared of government stores, were discharged from the service, and are shortly to depart for China, in order to load home with tea, they being chartered by the East India company for that purpose.

April 15th. His excellency, attended by Lieutenant Ball of the navy, Lieutenant George Johnston of the marines, the judge advocate, myself, three soldiers, and two seamen, landed in Manly Cove (so called from the manly conduct of the natives when the governor first visited it), on the north side of the entrance into Port Jackson harbour, in order to trace to its source a river, which had been discovered a few days before. We, however, found this impracticable, owing to a thicket and swamp which ran along the side of it. The governor, anxious to acquire all the knowledge of the country in his power, forded the river in two places, and more than up to our waists in water, in hopes of being able to avoid the thicket and swamp; but, notwithstanding all his perseverance, we were at length obliged to return, and to proceed along the sea shore, a mile or two to the northward.

At

*Great Brown Kings Fisher.*

London Published as the Act directs, Dec: 29, 1789 by I. Debrett.

At the end of this we fell in with a small salt-water lagoon, on which we found nine birds, that, whilst swimming, most perfectly resembled the *rara avis* of the ancients—a *black* swan. We discharged several shot at them, but the distance was too great for execution. Our frequent firing, however, caused them to take wing, and they flew towards the sea, which was very near, in the order that wild geese generally preserve; the one before the other. Had we not raised them, we should certainly have concluded that they were black swans; but their flight gave us an opportunity of seeing some white feathers, which terminated the tip of each wing; in every other part they were perfectly black. Their size appeared not equal to that of an European swan, but the shape exactly corresponded, except about the wings, which seemed rather small for the body. We not long after discovered the great brown King's Fisher, of which a plate is annexed. This bird has been described by Mr. *Latham* in his *General Synopsis of Birds*, vol. ii. p. 603, nearly to the following purport :—The length eighteen inches; the bill black above, and white beneath; the feathers of the head narrow, and pretty long, so as to form a kind of crest. They are of a brown colour, streaked with paler brown; the

T                                                    back

back and wings in general brown; the lower part of the back and rump pale blue-green; the outer edges of the quills blue; within and the tips black. On the wing covert is a patel of gloffy blue-green: the tail is barred with ferruginous, and fteel-black, gloffed with purple; the end, for one inch, white; the under part of the body is white, tranfverfely ftreaked with dufky lines; legs yellow, claws black.

This bird is not uncommon in many iflands of the *South Seas*, being pretty frequent at *New Guinea*, from whence the fpecimen came from which Mr. *Latham* took his defcription: it is alfo an inhabitant of *New Holland*, from whence feveral have been fent over to *England*.

We rounded this lagoon, and proceeded four or five miles weftward, along the banks of a fmall frefh-water river, which emptied itfelf into it, and had for its fource only a fwamp, or boggy ground. After we had paffed this fwamp, we got into an immenfe wood, the trees of which were very high and large, and a confiderable diftance apart, with little under or brufh wood. The ground was not very good, although it produced a luxuriant coat of a kind of four grafs growing in tufts or bufhes, which, at fome diftance, had the appearance of meadow land, and might be

miftaken

*Banksian* *Cockatoo*

S Stone Delin.

London Published as the Act directs, Dec: 29, 1789, by I. Debrett.

miftaken for it by fuperficial examiners. Here we pitched our tents (without which the governor never travelled) for the night, near a fwamp, out of which we were fupplied with water, not, indeed, either of the beft or cleareft kind. The night being cold, and a heavy dew falling, we kept up a large fire before the tents, which, though in one refpect an excellent precaution, far from chafing away, feemed to allure the mufquitos, which tormented us inexpreffibly during the whole night. We this day difcovered the Bankfian Cockatoo. This fpecies was firft defcribed by Mr. *Latham*, in his feventh volume or fupplement to the *General Synopfis of Birds*, and the one in the plate annexed differs from that in fome few particulars.—In Mr. *Latham*'s figure the general colour is dufky black, the feathers of the head longer than the reft, forming a creft; and each of thofe on the head, back of the neck, and major part of the wings, have a fpot of buff-colour at the tips; the under parts of the body barred with narrow bars of buff-colour; the tail is black at the bottom and ends of the feathers, but the middle of a fine red, barred irregularly with black.—In our fpecimen, the general colour of the bird is olive, or rufty black; the head feathers pretty

T 2 long,

long, and about the fides of the head and top of it is a mixture of fine yellow; but none of the feathers are marked with buff at the tips, nor is the under part of the body croffed with buff-colour. In the tail it differs fcarcely at all from Mr. *Latham*'s figure.

Thefe birds have been met with in feveral parts of *New Holland*.

We likewife faw feveral Blue-bellied Parrots. This is a very beautiful bird; and Mr. *Latham*, whofe leave we have to copy the account of it, from his *Syn.* vol. i. p. 213, N° 14. B. defcribes it thus: " The length is fifteen inches; " the bill is reddifh; orbits black; head and throat dark " blue, with a mixture of lighter blue feathers; back part " of the head green; towards the throat yellow green; " back and wings green; prime quills dufky, barred with " yellow; breaft red, mixed with yellow; belly of a fine " blue; thighs green and yellow; tail cuneiform; the two " middle feathers green; the others the fame, but bright " yellow on the outer edges; legs dufky."

This bird is a very common fpecies in various parts of *New Holland*, and in great plenty both at *Botany Bay* and *Port Jackfon*. It is found to differ much in plumage,

several

S. Stone Delin

*Blue Bellied Parrot.*

London Published as the Act directs Dec. 29. 1789. by I. Debrett.

several other varieties having been met with, which are natives of *Amboina* and others of the *Molucca Islands*.

16th. We pursued our route westward, proceeding many miles inland, without being able to trace, by a single vestige, that the natives had been recently in those parts. We saw, however, some proofs of their ingenuity, in various figures cut on the smooth surface of some large stones. They consisted chiefly of representations of themselves in different attitudes, of their canoes, of several sorts of fish and animals; and, considering the rudeness of the instruments with which the figures must have been executed, they seemed to exhibit tolerably strong likenesses. On the stones, where the natives had been thus exercising their abilities in sculpture, were several weather-beaten shells. The country all around this place was rather high and rocky; and the soil arid, parched, and inhospitable.

In the evening, after a long and fatiguing march, we fell in with the north-west branch of Port Jackson harbour. Here the two seamen, overcome with fatigue, and having their shoes torn from their feet through the ruggedness of the road along which we had travelled, could proceed no further. This circumstance induced the governor to consign them to

the

the care of Lieutenant Ball, and a marine, fupplying them with provifions fufficient to laft them till they reached the fhips. His excellency, with the reft of the party, pufhed on to the weftward, by the water fide, in hopes of finding better land, and a more open country. About four o'clock in the afternoon we came to a fteep valley, where the flowing of the tide ceafed, and a frefh-water ftream commenced. Here, in the moft defert, wild, and folitary feclufion that the imagination can form any idea of, we took up our abode for the night; dreffed our provifions, wafhed our fhirts and ftockings, and turned our inconvenient fituation to the beft advantage in our power. Saw this day the Anomalous Hornbill, of which a plate is annexed. This bird is fo very fingular in its feveral characteriftics, that it can fcarcely be faid to which of the prefent known genera to refer it. In the *bill* it feems moft allied to the *hornbill*, but the *legs* are thofe of a *toucan*, and the *tongue* is more like that of a *crow* than any other: it muft therefore be left to future ornithologifts to determine the point, refting here fatisfied with defcribing its external appearance.

The fize of the body is not much lefs than that of a crow: the bill is very large, and bent, particularly at the tip of the

upper

*Anamolous Hornbill.*

London Published Dec. 29. 1789 by I.Debrett

upper mandible ; the noſtrils and ſpace round the eyes are bare and red; the head, neck, and all beneath, are of a pale grey, croſſed over the thighs with duſky lines; the back and wings duſky lead-colour, with the end of each feather black; the tail is long and wedge-ſhaped, the feathers white at the ends; near which is a bar of black. The bill and legs are brown; the toes are placed two before and two behind, as in the *parrot* or *toucan* genus.

This ſingular bird was met with at *New Holland*, from whence three or four ſpecimens have found their way to England, but whether it is a numerous ſpecies has not been mentioned.

The next morning we hid our tents and the remains of our proviſions, and with only a little rum, and a ſmall quantity of bread, made a forced march into the country, to the weſtward, of about fourteen miles, without being able to ſucceed in the objeet of our ſearch, which was for good land well watered. Indeed, the land here, although covered with an endleſs wood, was better than the parts which we had already explored. Finding it, however, very unlikely that we ſhould be able to penetrate through this immenſe foreſt, and circumſtanced as we were, it was

thought

thought more prudent to return. We, accordingly, after an expeditious walk, reached the ſtream from whence we had ſet out in the morning, and taking up the tents and proviſions which we had left, proceeded a little farther down, to the flowing of the tide, and there pitched our tents for the night; during which it rained very heavily, with thunder and lightning. The Wattled Bee-eater, of which a plate is annexed, fell in our way during the courſe of the day. This bird is the ſize of a *miſſel thruſh*, but much larger in proportion; its total length being about fourteen inches. The feathers on the upper part of the head, longer than the reſt, give the appearance of a creſt; thoſe of the under part are ſmooth; the plumage for the moſt part is brown, the feathers long and pointed, and each feather has a ſtreak of white down the middle; under the eye, on each ſide, is a kind of *wattle*, of an orange colour; the middle of the belly is yellow; the tail is wedge-ſhaped, ſimilar to that of the *magpie*, and the feathers tipped with white; the bill and legs are brown.

This bird ſeems to be peculiar to *New Holland*, and is undoubtedly a ſpecies which has not hitherto been deſcribed.

18th. We began our progreſs early in the morning,

bending

*Wattled* *Bee Eater.*

S Stone Delin

London Published as the Act directs, Dec. 29, 1789 by I. Debrett.

bending our courfe down the river. Some places along the fhore, where the tide had flowed fo as to obftruct our paffage, we were obliged to ford; and, at times, we were under the neceffity of climbing heights nearly inacceffible. At length, after undergoing much fatigue, we were agreeably furprifed, and cheered, with the fight of two boats, fent by Captain Hunter to meet us, and juft then coming up with the tide. By them we learnt, that Lieutenant Ball, with his enfeebled party, had arrived fafe at the fhip the day after they had quitted us. We all went on board the boats, and fell down the river till we got to a pleafant little cove, where we dined, with great fatisfaction and comfort, upon the welcome provifions which were fent in the boats by the governor's fteward. After having refrefhed ourfelves, we again embarked, and about fix o'clock in the evening arrived in Sydney Cove.

We were likewife able, during this excurfion, to take one of the Gold-winged Pigeons, of which a plate is annexed. This bird is a curious and fingular fpecies, remarkable for having moft of the feathers of the wing marked with a brilliant fpot of golden yellow, changing, in various reflections of light, to green and copper-bronze; and, when the wing is clofed,

U                                                    forming

forming two bars of the fame acrofs it. The general colour of the bird otherwife is brown, changing to vinaceous red on the breaft, in the manner of our domeftic fpecies. The fore part of the head and chin are buff colour, with a ftreak of brownifh red paffing on each fide through the eye. The quills and tail are darker than the reft of the plumage, but all the feathers of the laft, except the two middle ones, incline to lead colour, with a bar of black near the tip. The bill and legs are of a dull red.

This fpecies is a native of *New South Wales*, feveral of them having been fent from *Port Jackfon*.

22d.   On the morning of this day the governor, accompanied by the fame party, with the addition of Lieutenant Creffwell of the marines and fix privates, landed at the head of the harbour, with an intention of penetrating into the country weftward, as far as feven days provifions would admit of; every individual carrying his own allowance of bread, beef, rum, and water. The foldiers, befide their own provifions, carried a camp kettle, and two tents, with their poles, &c. Thus equipped, with the additional weight of fpare fhoes, fhirts, trowfers, together with a great coat, or Scotch plaid, for the purpofe of fleeping in, as

the

*Golden Winged Pidgeon.*

London Published Dec: 29, 1789, by J.Debrett.

the nights were cold we proceeded on our deſtination. We likewiſe took with us a ſmall hand hatchet, in order to mark the trees as we went on; thoſe marks (called in America *blazing*) being the only guide to direct us in our return.  The country was ſo rugged as to render it almoſt impoſſible to explore our way by the aſſiſtance of the compaſs.

In this manner we proceeded for a mile or two, through a part well covered with enormous trees, free from under-wood.  We then reached a thicket of bruſh-wood, which we found ſo impervious, as to oblige us to return nearly to the place from whence we had ſet out in the morning. Here we encamped, near ſome ſtagnant water, for the night, during which it thundered, lightened, and rained. About eleven o'clock the governor was ſuddenly attacked with a moſt violent complaint in his ſide and loins, brought on by cold and fatigue, not having perfectly gotten the better of the laſt expedition.  The next morning being fine, his excellency, who was rather better, though ſtill in pain, would not relinquiſh the object of his purſuit; and therefore we proceeded, and ſoon got round the wood or thicket which had haraſſed us ſo much the day before.

U 2                                                After

After we had paſſed it, we fell in with an hitherto unperceived branch of Port Jackſon harbour, along the bank of
which the graſs was tolerably rich and ſucculent, and in
height nearly up to the middle, interſperſed with a plant
much reſembling the indigo. We followed this branch
weſtward for a few miles, until we came to a ſmall freſh
water ſtream that emptied itſelf into it. Here we took up
our quarters for the night, as our halts were always regulated
by freſh water, an eſſential point by no means to be
diſpenſed with, and not very abundant, or frequently to be
met with, in this country. We made a kettle of excellent
ſoup out of a white cockatoo and two crows which I had ſhot,
as we came along. The land all around us was ſimilar to
that which we had paſſed. At night we had thunder,
lightning, and rain. The governor, though not free from
pain, was rather recovering.

24th. As ſoon as the dew, which is remarkably heavy in
this country, was off the ground, we proceeded to trace
the river, or ſmall arm of the ſea. The banks of it were
now pleaſant, the trees immenſely large, and at a conſiderable
diſtance from each other; and the land around us flat, and
rather low, but well covered with the kind of graſs juſt
mentioned.

mentioned. Here the tide ceafed to flow; and all further progrefs for boats was ftopped by a flat fpace of large broad ftones, over which a frefh water ftream ran. Juft above this flat, clofe to the water-fide, we difcovered a quarry of flates; from which we expected to derive great advantage in refpect to covering our houfes, ftores, &c. it being a material beyond conception difficult to be procured in this country; but on trial it was found of no ufe, as it proved to be of a crumbling and rotten nature. On this frefh water ftream, as well as on the falt, we faw a great many ducks and teal; three of which we fhot in the courfe of the day, befides two crows, and fome loraquets. About four in the afternoon, being near the head of the ftream, and fomewhat apprehenfive of rain, we pitched our tents, before the grafs became wet; a circumftance which would have proved very uncomfortable during the night. Here we had our ducks picked, ftuffed with fome flices of falt beef, and roafted; and never did a repaft feem more delicious; the falt beef, ferving as a palatable fubftitute for the want of falt, gave it an agreeable relifh. The evening cleared up, and the night proved dry. During the latter, we heard a noife which not a little furprifed us, on account of its refemblance

3

to

to the human voice. What it proceeded from we could not discover; but I am of opinion that it was made by a bird, or some animal. The country round us was by no means so good, or the grass so abundant, as that which we had passed. The water, though neither clear, nor in any great quantity, was neither of a bad quality nor ill-tasted.

The next day, after having sowed some seeds, we pursued our route for three or four miles west, where we met with a mean hut, belonging to some of the natives, but could not perceive the smallest trace of their having been there lately. Close to this hut we saw a Kangaroo, which had come to drink at an adjacent pool of stagnated water, but we could not get within shot of it. A little farther on, we fell in with three huts, as deserted as the former, and a swamp, not unlike the American rice grounds. Near this we saw a tree in flames, without the least appearance of any natives; from which we suspected that it had been set on fire by lightning. This circumstance was first suggested by Lieutenant Ball; who had remarked, as well as myself, that every part of the country, though the most inaccessible and rocky, appeared as if, at certain times of the year, it had been all on fire. Indeed in

many

many parts we met with very large trees, the trunks of which and branches were evidently rent, and demolifhed by lightning. Clofe by the burning tree we faw three kangaroos. Though by this time very much fatigued, we proceeded about two miles farther on, in hopes of finding fome good water, but without effect; and about half paft four o'clock we took up our quarters near a ftagnant pool. The ground was fo very dry and parched, that it was with fome difficulty we could drive either our tent pegs or poles into it. The country about this fpot was much clearer of underwood than that which we had paffed during the day. The trees around us were immenfely large, and the tops of them filled with loraquets and paroquets of exquifite beauty, which chattered to fuch a degree, that we could fcarcely hear each other fpeak. We fired feveral times at them, but the trees were fo very high that we killed but few.

26th. We ftill directed our courfe weftward, and paffed another tree on fire; and others which were hollow, and perforated by a fmall hole at the bottom, in which the natives feemed to have fnared fome animal. It was certainly done by the natives, as the trees where thefe

holes

holes or perforations were, had in general many knotches cut, for the purpose of getting to the top of them. After this we croſſed a water-courſe; which ſhews, that at ſome ſeaſons the rain is very heavy here, notwithſtanding that there was, at preſent, but little water in it. Beyond the chaſm, we came to a pleaſant hill, the top of which was tolerably clear of trees, and perfectly free from underwood. His excellency gave it the name of *Belle Veüe*. From the top of this hill we ſaw a chain of hills or mountains, which appeared to be thirty or forty miles diſtant, running in a north and ſouth direction. The northernmoſt being conſpicuouſly higher than any of the reſt, the governor called it *Richmond Hill*; the next, or thoſe in the centre, *Lanſdown Hills*; and thoſe to the ſouthward, which are by much the loweſt, *Carmarthen Hills*.

In a valley below *Belle Veüe*, we ſaw a fire, and by it found ſome chewed root of a ſaline taſte, which ſhewed that the natives had recently been there. The country hereabout was pleaſant to the eye, well wooded, and covered with long four graſs, growing in tufts. At the bottom of this valley or flat, we croſſed another water-courſe, and

aſcended

afcended a hill, where the wood was fo very thick as to obftruct our view. Here, finding our provifions to run fhort, our return was concluded on, though with great reluctance; as it was our wifh, and had been our determination, to reach the hills before us if it had been poffible. In our way back, which we eafily difcovered by the marks made in the trees, we faw a hollow tree on fire, the fmoke iffuing out of the top part as through a chimney. On coming near, and minutely examining it, we found that it had been fet on fire by the natives; for there was fome dry grafs lighted and put into the hole wherein we had fuppofed they ufed to fnare or take the animal before alluded to. In the evening, where we pitched our tents, we fhot two crows and fome loraquets, for fupper. The night was fine and clear; during which we often heard, as before, a found like the human voice, and, from its continuance on one fpot, we concluded it to proceed from a bird perched on fome of the trees near us.

27th. We now found ourfelves obliged to make a forced march back, as our provifions were quite exhaufted; a circumftance rather alarming, in cafe of lofing our way; which, however, we met with no difficulty in difcovering,

X by

by the marked trees. By our calculation we had penetrated into the country, to the westward, not less than thirty-two, or thirty-three miles. This day we saw the dung of an animal as large as that of a horse, but it was more like the excrement of a hog, intermixed with grass. When we got as far back as the arm or branch of the sea which forms the upper part of Port Jackson harbour, we saw many ducks, but could not get within shot of any of them. It was now growing late; and the governor being apprehensive that the boats which he had ordered to attend daily, might be, for that day, returning before we could reach them, he sent Lieutenants Johnston and Cresswell, with a marine, a-head, in order to secure such provisions as might have been sent up; and to give directions for the boats to come for us the next morning, as it then appeared very unlikely that all the party, who were, without exception, much fatigued, could be there soon enough to save the tide down. Those gentlemen accordingly went forward, and were so fortunate as to be just in time; and they returned to us with a seasonable supply of bread, beef, rum, and wine. As soon as they had joined us, we encamped for the night, on a spot about the distance of a

mile

mile from the place where the boats were to take us up in the morning. His excellency was again indifposed, occafioned by a return of his complaint, which had been brought on by a fall into a hollow place in the ground, that being concealed by the long grafs, he was unable to difcern. We paffed the next day in examining different inlets in the upper part of the harbour. We faw there fome of the natives, who, in their canoes, came along-fide of the boat, to receive fome trifles which the governor held out to them. In the evening we returned to Sydney Cove.

May 1ft. James Bennet, a youth, was executed for robbing a tent belonging to the Charlotte tranfport, of fugar and fome other articles. Before he was turned off he confeffed his guilt, and acknowledged, that young as he was he had been an old offender. Some other trifling thefts were brought before the court at the fame time, and thofe concerned in them fentenced to receive corporeal punifhment.

The Supply tender failed for Lord Howe's Ifland to fetch turtle; as did the Lady Penrhyn tranfport for China. The Scarborough dropped down the harbour; fhe was followed the next day by the Charlotte, and they failed in company for

X 2

China.

China. Some of the natives came along-fide the Sirius, and made figns to have their beards taken off. One of them patiently, and without fear or diftruft, underwent the operation from the fhip's barber, and feemed much delighted with it.

21ft. William Ayres, a convict, who was in a ftate of convalefcence, and to whom I had given permiffion to go a little way into the country, for the purpofe of gathering a few herbs wherewith to make tea, was, after night, brought to the hofpital, with one of the fpears ufed by the natives fticking in his loins. It had been darted at him as he was ftooping, and while his back was turned to the affailant. The weapon was barbed; and ftuck fo very faft, that it would admit of no motion. After dilating the wound to a confiderable length and depth, with fome difficulty I extracted the fpear, which had penetrated the flefh nearly three inches. After the operation, he informed us that he received his wound from three of the natives, who came behind him at a time when he fufpected no perfon to be near him except Peter Burn, whom he had met a little before, employed on the fame bufinefs as himfelf. He added, that after they had wounded him, they beat him in a cruel manner, and ftripping the cloaths from his back,

3

carried

*Port Jackson Thrush.*

London Published Dec: 29. 1789. by J.Debrett

carried them off; making signs to him (as he interpreted them) to return to the camp. He further related, that after they had left him, he saw Burn in the possession of another party of the natives, who were dragging him along, with his head bleeding, and seemingly in great distress; while he himself was so exhausted with loss of blood, that, instead of being able to assist his companion, he was happy to escape with his life.

The *Port Jackson thrush*, of which a plate is annexed, inhabits the neighbourhood of Port Jackson. The top of the head in this species is blueish-grey; from thence down the hind part of the neck, and the back, the colour is a fine chocolate brown; the wings and tail are lead colour, the edges of the feathers pale; the tail itself pretty long, and even at the end; all the under parts from chin to vent are dusky-white, except the middle of the neck, just above the breast, which inclines to chocolate. The bill is of a dull yellow; legs brown.

25th. The Supply arrived from Lord Howe's Island without a single turtle, the object for which she was sent: a dreadful disappointment to those who were languishing under the scurvy; many of whom are since dead, and there

.is

is great reason to fear that several others will soon share the same fate. This disorder has now risen to a most alarming height, without any possibility of checking it until some vegetables can be raised; which, from the season of the year, cannot take place for many months. And even then I am apprehensive that there will not be a sufficiency produced, such are the labour and difficulty which attend the clearing of the ground. It will scarcely be credited, when I declare that I have known twelve men employed for five days, in grubbing up one tree; and when this has been effected, the timber (as already observed) has been only fit for firewood; so that in consequence of the great labour in clearing of the ground, and the weak state of the people; to which may be added the scarcity of tools, most of those we had being either worn out by the hardness of the timber, or lost in the woods among the grass, through the carelessness of the convicts; the prospect before us is not of the most pleasing kind. All the stock that was landed, both public and private, seems, instead of thriving, to fall off exceedingly. The number at first was but inconsiderable, and even that number is at present much diminished. The sheep, in particular, decreaser apidly, very few being now alive in the colony,

colony, although there were numbers, the property of Government or individuals, when first landed.

26th. Two men of the Sirius were brought before the criminal court, and tried for affaulting, and beating, in a cruel manner, another man belonging to the fame veffel, while employed on an ifland appropriated by the governor to the ufe of the fhip. They were fentenced to receive five hundred lafhes each, but could not undergo the whole of that punifhment, as, like moft of the perfons in the colony, they were much afflicted with the fcurvy.

28th. Captain Hunter, his firft lieutenant, and the furgeon of the Sirius, went to the point of land which forms the north head of Port Jackfon. In going there they difcovered an old man, with a little girl about five years of age, lying clofe to the ground watching their motions, and at the fame time endeavouring to conceal themfelves. The furgeon had his gun with him, the effects of which he let the old man fee, by fhooting a bird, which fell at his feet. The explofion at firft greatly alarmed him, but perceiving that they intended him no ill, he foon got over his fears. The bird was then given to him, which (having barely plucked, and not more than half broiled it) he devoured,

voured, entrails, bones, and all. The little girl was much frightened, and endeavoured to hide herself behind the old man, to escape the least observation.

30th. Captain Campbell of the marines, who had been up the harbour to procure some rushes for thatch, brought to the hospital the bodies of William Okey and Samuel Davis, two rush-cutters, whom he had found murdered by the natives in a shocking manner. Okey was transfixed through the breast with one of their spears, which with great difficulty and force was pulled out. He had two other spears sticking in him to a depth which must have proved mortal. His skull was divided and comminuted so much that his brains easily found a passage through. His eyes were out, but these might have been picked away by birds. Davis was a youth, and had only some trifling marks of violence about him. This lad could not have been many hours dead; for when Captain Campbell found him, which was among some mangrove-trees, and at a considerable distance from the place where the other man lay, he was not stiff, nor very cold; nor was he perfectly so when brought to the hospital. From these circumstances we have been led to think that while they were dispatching Okey, he had crept to the

trees

*Yellow Eared Fly Catcher.*

London Published Dec.r 29. 1789 by J.Debrett.

trees among which he was found; and that fear, united with the cold and wet, in a great degree contributed to his death. What was the motive or caufe of this melancholy cataftrophe we have not been able to difcover; but from the civility fhewn, on all occafions, to the officers, by the natives, whenever any of them were met, I am ftrongly inclined to think that they muft have been provoked and injured by the convicts. We this day caught a Yellow-eared Flycatcher (fee annexed plate). This bird is a native of *New Holland*, the fize of a martin, and nearly feven inches in length; the bill is broad at the bottom, and of a pale colour; the legs dufky; the plumage is moftly brown, mottled with paler brown; the edges of the wing feathers yellowifh; the under part of the body white, inclining to dufky about the chin and throat; the tail is pretty long, and, when fpread, feems hollowed out at the tip; beneath the eye, on each fide, is an irregular ftreak, growing wider, and finifhing on the ears, of a yellow or gold colour.

Early the next morning the governor, lieutenants G. Johnfton and Kellow, myfelf, fix foldiers, and two armed convicts, whom we took as guides, went to the place where

Y                                        the

the murder had been committed, in hopes, by some means
or other, to be able to find out, either the actual perpetrators, or those concerned. As most of their clothes, and
all their working tools were carried off, we expected that
these might furnish us with some clue; but in this we were
disappointed. We could not observe a single trace of the
natives ever having been there. We then crossed the
country to Botany Bay, still flattering ourselves that we
might be able to discover, among a tribe at that place,
some proof that they had been concerned; as the governor
was resolved, on whomsoever he found any of the tools
or clothing, to shew them his displeasure, and, by
every means in his power, endeavour to convince them
of his motives for such a procedure. In our route we
saw several kangaroos, and shot a very fine teal. A little
before sun-set, after a long and fatiguing march, we
arrived at Botany Bay. When we approached the bay,
we saw eleven canoes, with two persons in each, fishing;
most of them had a fire in their canoe, a convenience
which they seldom go without at any time or season, but
particularly at this, as the weather was very cold. Here
we pitched our tents, for (as I have before observed) we

never

never travel without them, and kindled large fires both in front and rear; still, however, the cold was so very intense that we could scarcely close our eyes during the night. In the morning the grass was quite white with a hoar frost, so as to crackle under our feet. After breakfast we visited the grave of the French abbé, who died whilst the Count de Peyrouse was here. It was truly humble indeed, being distinguished only by a common head-stone, stuck slightly into the loose earth which covered it. Against a tree, just above it, was nailed a board, with the following inscription on it:

HIC JACET

LE RECEVEUR

EX F. F. MINORIBUS GALLIA SACERDOS

PHYSICUS IN CIRCUMNAVIGATIONE MUNDI

DUCE D. DE LA PEYROUSE.

OBIIT DIE 17th FEBR. ANNO 1788.

As the painting on the board could not be permanent, Governor Phillip had the inscription engraved on a plate of copper, and nailed to the same tree; and at some future day he intends to have a handsome head-stone placed at

Y 2

the

the grave. We cut down some trees which stood between that on which the inscription is fixed and the
shore, as they prevented persons passing in boats from
seeing it.

Between this and the harbour's mouth, we found forty-
nine canoes hauled upon the beach, but not a native to
be seen. After we had passed them, we fell in with an
Indian path; and, as it took a turn towards the camp,
we followed it about two miles; when on a sudden, in a
valley or little bay, to the northward of Botany Bay, we
were surprised at hearing the sound of voices, which
we instantly found to proceed from a great number of
the natives, sitting behind a rock, who appeared to be
equally astonished with ourselves; as, from the silence we
observed, they had not perceived us till we were within
twenty yards of them. Every one of them, as they got
up, armed himself with a long spear, the short stick
before described, used in throwing it, a shield made of
bark, and either a large club, pointed at one end,
or a stone hatchet. At first they seemed rather hostilely
inclined, and made signs, with apparent tokens of anger,
for us to return; but when they saw the governor ad-

vance

vance towards them, unarmed, and with his hands opened wide (a fignal we had obferved among them of amity and peace), they, with great confidence, came up to him, and received from him fome trifles which he had in his pocket, fuch as fifh-hooks, beads, and a looking-glafs. As there appeared not to be lefs than three hundred of them in this bay, all armed, the foldiers were ordered to fix their bayonets, and to obferve a clofe, well connected, order of march, as they defcended the hill. Thefe people (as already mentioned) feem to diflike red coats, and thofe who carry arms; but, on the prefent occafion, they fhewed very little fear or diftruft; on the contrary they, in a few minutes, mixed with us, and conducted us to a very fine ftream of water, out of which fome of them drank, to fhew that it was good. The women and children kept at fome diftance, one or two more forward than the reft excepted, who came to the governor for fome prefents. While he was diftributing his gifts, the women danced (an exercife every defcription of people in this country feem fond of), and threw themfelves into fome not very decent attitudes.

The men in general had their fkins fmeared all over with

with greafe, or fome ftinking, oily fubftance; fome wore a fmall ftick, or fifh-bone, fixed crofs-ways, in the divifion of the nofe, which had a very ftrange appearance; others were painted in a variety of ways, and had their hair ornamented with the teeth of fifh, faftened on by gum, and the fkin of the kangaroo. As they conducted us to the water, a toadftool was picked up by one of our company, which fome of the natives perceiving, they made figns for us to throw it away, as not being good to eat. Soon after I gathered fome wood-forrel, which grew in our way, but none of them endeavoured to prevent me from eating it; on the contrary, if a conclufion may be drawn from the figns which they made relative to the toadftool, they fhewed, by their looks, that there was nothing hurtful in it.

We halted but a fhort time with them, as it was growing late, and we had a long way to walk. Before we parted from them, the governor gave them two fmall hand-axes, in exchange for fome of their ftone axes and two of their fpears. As we afcended a hill, after our departure from them, eight of them followed us until we had nearly reached the top, where one of thofe who had

been

been moſt familiar with us made ſigns for us to ſtop; which we readily complying with, he ran to the ſummit, and made a ſtrange kind of hallooing, holding at the ſame time his hands open above his head. As ſoon as we came up to him, we diſcovered another large body of them in a bay, about half a mile below us. Our new friend ſeemed anxious to carry us down to them; but it not being in our way, we declined his offer. Seeing us take another direction, he halted, and opened his hands, in order, as we ſuppoſed, to put us in mind that he had received nothing from us; upon which we preſented him with a bird, the only thing we had, with which he returned, to appearance, fully content and ſatisfied. We now proceeded towards the camp, where we arrived about ſun-ſet.

This was the greateſt number of the natives we had ever ſeen together ſince our coming among them. What could be the cauſe of their aſſembling in ſuch numbers gave riſe to a variety of conjectures. Some thought they were going to war among themſelves, as they had with them a temporary ſtore of half-ſtinking fiſh and fern-root, the latter of which they uſe for bread. This we remarked, as ſeveral of them were eating it at the time we were among them.

Others

Others conjectured that some of them had been concerned in the murder of our men, notwithstanding we did not meet with the smallest trace to countenance such an opinion, and that fearing we should revenge it, they had formed this convention, in order to defend themselves against us. Others imagined that the assemblage might be occasioned by a burial, a marriage, or some religious meeting.

The *Tabuan Parrot*, one of which was observed here, and of which a plate is annexed, is a bird about eighteen inches in length, and bigger than the Scarlet Lory. The head, neck, and under parts, are of a fine scarlet; the upper parts of the body and wings are of a beautiful green; across the upper part of the wing coverts is an oblique bar of yellowish green, more glossy than the rest; the lower part of the back and rump is blue; there is also a small patch of blue at the lower part of the neck behind, between a scarlet and green, dividing those colours; the tail is pretty long, and of an olive brown colour; the bill is reddish; the legs deep brown, nearly black.

The *Female* is mostly green; the head, neck, and under parts olive brown; belly red; rump blue; tail, on the upper surface, green; beneath, dusky.

The

*Tabuan Parrot*

London, Published Dec: 29, 1789 by I. Debrett

*The Tabuan Parrot, Female*

London Published as the Act directs Dec.29, 1789, by I.Debrett.

The above inhabits Botany Bay, and seems much allied to the *Tabuan Parrot* described by Mr. *Latham*, in his *Synopsis of Birds*; but in that the head, neck, and under parts, incline to purplish or chocolate colour; both quills and tail are blue, more or less edged with green, and a crescent of blue at the back part of the neck; it has also the under jaw surrounded with green feathers. It is probable, therefore, that our bird is only a variety of the Tabuan species.

June 4th. This being the anniversary of his Majesty's birth-day, and the first celebration of it in New South Wales, his excellency ordered the Sirius and Supply to fire twenty-one guns at sun-rise, at one o'clock, and at sun-set. Immediately after the King's ships had ceased firing, at one o'clock, the Borrowdale, Friendship, Fishburne, Golden Grove, and Prince of Wales, fired five guns each. The battalion was under arms at twelve, and fired three vollies, succeeded by three cheers. After this ceremony had taken place, the lieutenant-governor, with all the officers of the settlement, civil and military, paid their respects to his excellency, at his house. At two o'clock they all met there again to dinner, during which the band of musick

Z played

played "God fave the King," and feveral excellent marches. After the cloth was removed, his Majefty's health was drank with three cheers. The Prince of Wales, the Queen and royal family, the Cumberland family, and his Royal Highnefs Prince William Henry, fucceeded. His Majefty's minifters were next given; who, it was obferved, may be *Pitted* againft any that ever conducted the affairs of Great Britain.

When all the public toafts had gone round, the governor nominated the diftrict which he had taken poffeffion of, *Cumberland County*; and gave it fuch an extent of boundary as to make it the largeft county in the whole world. His excellency faid, that he had intended to have named the town, and laid the firft ftone, on this aufpicious day; but the unexpected difficulties which he had met with, in clearing the ground, and from a want of artificers, had rendered it impoffible; he therefore put it off till a future day. Its name, however, we underftand, is to be ALBION. The day was paffed in cheerfulnefs and good-humour; but it was a little damped by our perceiving that the governor was in great pain, from a return of his complaint. Though his countenance too plainly indicated

the

the torture which he fuffered, he took every method in his power to conceal it, left it fhould break in upon the feftivity and harmony of the day. His excellency ordered every foldier a pint of porter, befides his allowance of grog; and every convict half a pint of fpirits, made into grog, that they all may drink his Majefty's health; and, as it was a day of general rejoicing and feftivity, he likewife made it a day of forgivenefs; remitting the remainder of the punifhment to which the failors of the Sirius were fubject, and pardoning Lovel, Sideway, Hall, and Gordon, who had been confined on a little fterile ifland, or rather rock, fituated in the harbour, until a place of banifhment could be found. This act of lenity and mercy, added to many others which the governor had fhewn, it is to be hoped will work fome change on the minds of thefe men. Indeed fome good may be expected from Hall and Gordon, who, fince their fentence, have appeared penitent; but from Lovel and Sideway very little change for the better can be expected, becaufe they feem fo truly abandoned and incorrigible. At night every perfon attended an immenfe bonfire that was lighted for the occafion; after which the principal officers of the fettlement, and of

Z 2 the

the men of war, supped at the governor's, where they terminated the day in pleasantry, good humour and cheerfulness.

The next morning we were astonished at the number of
thefts which had been committed, during the general festi-
vity, by the villanous part of the convicts, on one another,
and on some of the officers, whose servants did not keep a
strict look-out after their marquées. Availing themselves thus
of the particular circumstances of the day, is a strong instance
of their unabated depravity and want of principle. Scarcely
a day passes without an example being made of some one
or other of these wretches; but it seems to have no manner
of effect upon them.

10th. John Ascott and Patrick Burn, two convicts,
were brought before the criminal court, and prosecuted by
Lieutenant G. William Maxwell of the Sirius, and Mr.
Kelter the Master of the same ship, for having, a few nights
before, in a riotous manner, with many more of the convicts, attacked some seamen belonging to the men of war,
and behaving in an insolent and contemptuous manner to
them. After a long and judicious hearing, the prisoners
were acquitted, as the charge brought against them was by
no means substantiated.

26th.

26th. About four in the afternoon a flight shock of
an earthquake was felt at Sidney Cove, and its environs. This incident had so wonderful an effect on Edward Corbett, a convict, who had eloped about three weeks before, on a discovery being made of his having stolen a frock, that he returned and gave himself up to justice. A few days antecedent to his return, he had been outlawed; and was supposed to have driven off with him four cows, the only animals of this kind in the colony. This, however, he declared himself innocent of; but confessed his having committed the theft laid to his charge. The strictest search was made, but in vain, after the cows. It is probable that they have strayed so far off in this endless wild, as to be irrecoverably lost. Previously to the return of Corbett he must have suffered very severely from hunger; his eyes were sunk into his head, and his whole appearance shewed that he had been half starved. While he was absent, he says, he frequently fell in with the natives, who, though they never treated him ill, did not seem to like his company. He informed us, that in a bay adjacent to that where the governor and his party had met with so many of the natives, he saw the head of one of the convicts lying near

the

the place where the body had been burnt in a large fire. This, in all likelihood, was Burn, who was carried off at the time Ayres was wounded, as he has not been heard of since.

The natives of this country, though their mode of sub-fisting seems to be so very scanty and precarious, are, I am convinced, not cannibals. One of their graves, which I saw opened, the only one I have met with, contained a body which had evidently been burned, as small pieces of the bones lay in the bottom of it. The grave was neatly made, and well covered with earth and boughs of trees.

The *Pennantian Parrot* (of which see plate annexed) was about this time first noticed. The general colour of the body, in the *male*, is crimson; the feathers of the back black in their middle; the chin and throat blue; the wings blue, with a bar of a paler colour down the middle of them; the tail is long, and blue also, and all but the two middle feathers have the ends very pale.

The *female* differs, in having the upper parts of the neck and body of a greenish colour; the top of the head red, and a patch of the same under each eye; the chin and

throat

*Pennantian Parrot*

London Published Dec: 29, 1789, by I. Debrett.

*Pennantian Parrot, Female.*

London Published Dec. 29, 1789, by I. Debrett.

throat blue; lower part of the neck and breaſt red; as are the rump and vent; the middle of the belly duſky green; tail dark blue, fringed with cheſnut; ſhoulders blue; the reſt of the wing the ſame, but darker; bill and legs as in the male.

24th. The governor revoked the decree by which Corbett was outlawed, and he was tried by the criminal court, ſimply for the theft he had committed, and ſentenced to be hanged. Samuel Payton, a convict, likewiſe received the ſame ſentence, for feloniouſly entering the marquée of Lieutenant Fuzer, on the night of the fourth of June, and ſtealing from thence ſome ſhirts, ſtockings, and combs. His trial had been put off to the preſent time, on account of a wound in his head, which he had received from Captain Lieutenant Meredith, who, on his return from the bonfire, found Payton in his marquée. When brought to the hoſpital, in conſequence of the wound which he had received, he was perfectly ſenſeleſs. During the time he remained under my care, I frequently admoniſhed him to think of the perilous ſituation he then ſtood in, and to make known the accomplices whom he was ſuppoſed to have; but he firmly and uniformly denied his guilt; and diſclaimed his having any knowledge

knowledge of, or concern in, robbing Lieutenant Fuzer. He further faid, that he did not recollect how he came to Captain Lieutenant Meredith's tent, or any circumftance relative to it. However, fince he received his fentence, he has confeffed that he robbed Lieutenant Fuzer; and gave him information where to find the articles he had been robbed of: he at the fame time acknowledged that he entered Mr. Meredith's marquée with an intention to rob him, doubting not but he fhould be able to make his efcape undifcovered, as every one feemed fo fully engaged on the pleafures of the day.

When he and Corbett were brought to the fatal tree, they (particularly Payton) addreffed the convicts in a pathetic, eloquent, and well-directed fpeech. He acknowledged the juftice of his fentence; a fentence, which (he faid) he had long deferved. He added, that he hoped and trufted that the ignominious death he was about to fuffer, would ferve as a caution and warning to thofe who faw and heard him. They both prayed moft fervently, begging forgivenefs of an offended GOD. They likewife hoped, that thofe whom they had injured, would not only forgive them, as they themfelves did all mankind, but offer up their prayers to

a merciful

a merciful Redeemer that, though so great sinners, they might be received into that bliss, which the good and virtuous only can either deserve or expect. They were now turned off; and in the agonizing moments of the separation of the soul from the body seemed to embrace each other. The execution of these unhappy youths, the eldest of whom was not twenty-four years of age, which seemed to make a greater impression on the convicts than any circumstance had done since their landing, will induce them, it is to be hoped, to change their conduct, and to adopt a better mode of life than, I am sorry to say, they have hitherto pursued.

The principal business now going forward, is the erecting huts for the marines and convicts, with the cabbage-tree. We have been here nearly six months, and four officers only as yet got huts: when the rest will be provided with them seems uncertain; but this I well know, that living in tents, as the rainy season has commenced, is truly uncomfortable, and likely to give a severe trial to the strongest and most robust constitution.

The trees of this country are immensely large, and clear of branches to an amazing height. While standing, many

A a                                                of

of them look fair and good to the eye, and appear fufficient to make a maft for the largeft fhip; but, when cut down, they are fcarcely convertible to any ufe whatever. At the heart they are full of veins, through which an amazing quantity of an aftringent red gum iffues. This gum I have found very ferviceable in an obftinate dyfentery that raged at our firft landing, and ftill continues to do fo, though with lefs obftinacy and violence. When thefe trees are fawed, and any way expofed to the fun, the gum melts, or gets fo very brittle, that the wood falls to pieces, and appears as if the pieces had been joined together with this fubftance. How any kind of houfes, except thofe built of the cabbage tree, can be raifed up, the timber being fo exceedingly bad, it is impoffible to determine.

I have already faid that the ftone of this country is well calculated for building, could any kind of cement be found to keep them together. As for lime-ftone, we have not yet difcovered any in the country; and the fhells collected for that purpofe have been but inconfiderable. From Captain Cook's account, one would be led to fuppofe that oyfter and cockle fhells might be procured in fuch quantities, as to make a fufficiency of lime, for the

purpofe

purpofe of conftructing at leaft a few public buildings; but this is by no means the cafe. That great navigator, notwithftanding his ufual accuracy and candour, was certainly too lavifh of his praifes on Botany Bay.

The peculiarity I have mentioned relative to the wood of this place is ftrange. There are only three kinds of it, and neither of them will float on the water. We have found another refin here, not unlike the balfam Tolu in fmell and effect, but differing widely in colour, being of a clear yellow, which exudes from the tree. This, however, is not to be met with in fuch quantities as the red gum before mentioned, nor do I think that its medicinal virtues are by any means fo powerful. A kind of earth has been difcovered which makes good bricks, but we ftill are in want of a cement for them as well as for the ftone.

What animals we have yet met with have been moftly of the Opoffum kind. The Kangaroo, fo very accurately delineated by Captain Cook, is certainly of that clafs, and the largeft animal feen in the country. One has been brought into camp which weighed a hundred and forty-nine pounds. See plate annexed. The conformation of this animal is peculiarly fingular. Its hinder parts have great mufcular

A a 2                    power,

power, and are, perhaps, beyond all parallel, out of proportion, when compared with the fore parts. As it goes, it jumps on its two hind legs, from twenty to twenty-eight feet, and keeps the two fore ones clofe to the breaſt; thefe are fmall and ſhort, and it feems to ufe them much like a fquirrel. The tail of thefe animals is thick and long; they keep it extended, and it ferves as a kind of counterpoife to the head, which they carry erect, when bounding at full fpeed. The velocity of a Kangaroo as far outſtrips that of a greyhound, as that animal exceeds in fwiftnefs a common dog. It is a very timid, ſhy, and inoffenſive creature, evidently of the granivorous kind. Upon our firſt difcovering one of them, as it does not ufe its fore feet to aſſiſt it in running, or rather jumping, many were of opinion that the tail, which is immenfely large and long, was made ufe of by them in the act of progreſſion; but this is by no means the cafe. Had it been ufed in fuch a manner, the hair would probably have been worn away from the part which, of courfe, muſt be applied to the ground. The tail, from its fize and weight, feems to ferve it for a weapon both of defence and offence; for it does not appear that nature has provided it with any other. Its mouth and head,

even

even when full grown, are too small for it to do much execution with the teeth ; nor is the conformation of either at all calculated for the purpose. Indeed, its fore feet, which it uses, as a squirrel or monkey, to handle any thing with, and which assist it in lying down, are too small, and out of proportion, as are all the superior parts, to admit of its either possessing or exerting much strength. It has been reported by some convicts who were out one day, accompanied by a large Newfoundland dog, that the latter seized a very large Kangaroo, but could not preserve its hold. They observed that the animal effected its escape by the defensive use it made of its tail, with which it struck its assailant in a most tremendous manner. The blows were applied with such force and efficacy, that the dog was bruised, in many places, till the blood flowed. They observed that the Kangaroo did not seem to make any use of either its teeth or fore feet, but fairly beat off the dog with its tail, and escaped before the convicts, though at no great distance, could get up to secure it.

The female has a pouch or pocket, like the Opossum, in which she carries her young. Some have been shot with a young one, not larger than a walnut, sticking to a teat

in

in this pocket. Others, with young ones not bigger than a rat : one of which, moſt perfectly formed, with every mark and diſtinguiſhing characteriſtic of the Kangaroo, I have ſent to Mr. Wilſon, of Gower Street, Bedford Square.

There is a peculiar formation in the generative parts of this animal. Of its natural hiſtory we at preſent know little; and therefore as we are ſo unacquainted with its habits, haunts, and cuſtoms, to attempt particular and accurate deſcriptions of it might beget error, which time, or a fuller knowledge of its properties, would directly contradict. As to mere conjectures (and ſuch too often are impoſed upon the public for inconteſtible facts), it cannot be improper to ſuppreſs them.

Every animal in this country partakes, in a great meaſure, of the nature of the Kangaroo. We have the Kangaroo Opoſſum, the Kangaroo Rat, &c. In fact every quadruped that we have ſeen, except the flying ſquirrel, and a ſpotted creature, nearly the ſize of a Martin, reſembles the Kangaroo in the formation of the fore legs and feet, which bear no proportion to the length of the hind legs.

The ſcarcity of boats will prevent our being ſo well ſupplied with fiſh, as otherwiſe might be expected. Fiſh

is

is far from abounding at the cold feafon of the year; but, in the fummer, judging from the latter end of the laft, we have every reafon to conclude that the little bays and coves in the harbour are well ftored with them. The fifh caught here are, in general, excellent; but feveral of them, like the animals in fome degree refembling the Kangaroo, partake of the properties of the fhark. The land, the grafs, the trees, the animals, the birds, and the fifh, in their different fpecies, approach by ftrong fhades of fimilitude to each other. A certain likenefs runs through the whole.

July 8th. A party of the natives came to the place where the Sirius's boat had been to haul the feine, and having beaten the crew, took from them by force a part of the fifh which they had caught. It is a great misfortune to us that we cannot find proper wood in this place wherewith to build a boat; particularly as fifh is not only fo very plentiful in the fummer, but the only change from falt provifions which we can procure, there being neither wild nor domeftic animals fit for food. Here, where no other animal nourifhment is to be procured, the Kangaroo is confidered as a dainty; but in any other country I am fure that fuch food would be thrown to

the

the dogs; for it has very little or no fat about it, and, when skinned, the flesh bears some likeness to that of a fox or lean dog.

A few days since a civil court of jurisdiction (which consisted of the judge advocate, the Reverend Mr. Johnson, and myself), was convened, by his excellency, to hear a complaint made against Duncan Sinclair, master of the Alexander transport, by Henry Coble and Susannah his wife (the Norwich convicts who so much excited the public attention), for the non-delivery of a parcel sent on board the Alexander, by Mrs. Jackson of Somerset Street, containing wearing apparel, books, and other things, for the use of the said Henry Coble, his wife, and child, value twenty pounds. The parcel was proved (and this even by the acknowledgment of the master) to have been received on board; and it likewise appeared in evidence that, on moving it from one part of the ship to another, the package had broken, and the books had fallen out, which books the convict said had been delivered to him. The court, after deducting five pounds (the value of the books received), gave a verdict in favour of the couple, in whose cause the world had seemed so much to interest

themselves,

and in confequence of the authority unto them granted by Act of Parliament, in fuch cafes made and provided, they adjudged the mafter of the tranfport fully to compenfate the lofs of the convicts, amounting to fifteen pounds. Sinclair confidered it as oppreffive to be obliged to pay for that on account of which he had not received any freightage ; but this objection had no weight with the court, as the fhip was in the fervice of government, and paid for the fole purpofe of conveying thefe people, and the little property which they poffeffed, to this country.

July 13th. The Alexander, Friendfhip, and Prince of Wales tranfports, with the Borrowdale victualler, failed for England. His Majefty's brig the Supply failed at the fame time for Norfolk Ifland, with provifions, &c. for the people there.

21ft. I went down the harbour, with the mafter of the Golden Grove victualler, to look for a cabbage tree, as a covering for my hut. On our return, we fell in with three canoes that had been out fifhing. We rowed towards them, when the natives in them fuddenly appeared intimidated, and paddled away with all poffible difpatch. Willing to

B b                                                     convince

convince them that they had nothing to dread from us, we rowed after them, in order to prefent them with fome trifles which we had about us.     When we approached the canoes, an old woman in one of them began to caft her fifh overboard, in great hafte; whether it was for fear that we fhould take them from her, or whether fhe threw them to us, we could not afcertain.     However, when we came along-fide, our conduct foon convinced her that her alarms, with refpect to us, were groundlefs.     She had in the canoe with her a young girl, whom, as fhe wore a complete apron, we could not help confidering as fuch an inftance of female decency, as we had not at any other time obferved among the natives.     The girl did not betray the leaft fign of apprehenfion, but rather feemed pleafed at the interview. She laughed immoderately, either at us, or at the petulance fhown by the old woman, who, I believe, was more terrified on the girl's account than on her own.     After this we left them fully fatisfied that we did not mean to offer them any injury.

We difcovered the *New Holland Creeper*; (See plate annexed).     The general colour of the bird is black, fpotted in various parts with white: the bill is dufky, growing paler

towards

*New Holland Creeper.*

London Published Dec. 29, 1789, by I.Debrett.

towards the tip. The neck, breaft, belly, and fides are more or lefs ftreaked with white; over the eye is alfo a white ftreak, and the fides of the neck and beginning of the back have likewife fome ftreaks of the fame. The quills and tail feathers are marked with yellow on the outer margins; the laft are rounded in fhape, and two or three of the outer feathers fpotted within, at the tip, with white; legs dufky; is about the fize of a *nightingale*, and meafures feven inches in length. It is probably a non-defcript fpecies.

A party of convicts, who had croffed the country to Botany Bay to gather a kind of plant refembling balm, which we found to be a good and pleafant vegetable, were met by a fuperior number of the natives, armed with fpears and clubs, who chafed them for two miles without being able to overtake them; but if they had fucceeded in the purfuit, it is probable that they would have put them to death; for wherever perfons unarmed, or inferior in num-bers, have fallen in with them, they have never failed to maltreat them. The natives had with them fome middling fized dogs, fomewhat refembling the fpecies called, in England, fox-dogs. A fervant of Captain Shea being

one

one day out fhooting, he found a very young puppy, belonging to the natives, eating part of a dead Kangaroo. He brought it to the camp, and it thrives much. The dog, in fhape, is rather fhort and well made; has very fine hair of the nature of fur, and a fagacious look. When found, though not more than a month old, he fhowed fome fymptoms of ferocity. It was a confiderable time before he could be induced to eat any flefh that was boiled, but he would gorge it raw with great avidity. (See plate annexed).

23d. The blackfmith's fhop, which was built of common brufh wood, was burnt down. Very fortunately for us, the bellows and the other tools were, through the exertion of the people, faved. To effect this was no eafy point, as, in the courfe of three or four minutes, the wood being very dry, every part of the fhop was in flames.

29th. One of the convicts was met by fome of the natives, who wounded him very feverely in the breaft and head with their fpears. They would undoubtedly have deftroyed him had he not plunged into the fea, near which he happened to be, and by that means faved himfelf. When he was brought to the hofpital he was

very

very faint from the loſs of blood, which had flowed plentifully from his wounds. A piece of a broken ſpear had entered through the ſcalp and under his ear, ſo that the extraction gave him great pain. Their ſpears are made of a kind of cane which grows out of the tree that produces the yellow gum; they are ten or twelve feet long; pointed, and ſometimes barbed, with a piece of the ſame cane or the teeth of fiſh. Theſe they throw, with the aſſiſtance of the ſhort ſtick already mentioned, which has a ſhell made faſt to the end of it with the yellow gum. With this gum they likewiſe faſten their barbs to their ſpears and fiſh-gigs. The latter of theſe differ from the former by having four prongs, and being always barbed; which is not generally the caſe with the ſpears. Their ſpears, the only weapon they are ever ſeen to have that may be conſidered in any degree as dangerous, they throw thirty or forty yards with an unerring preciſion. When equipped for any exploit, they are alſo armed with a ſhield made of the bark of a tree, with which they very dexterouſly ward off any thing thrown at them. An humble kind of ſcymitar; a bludgeon, or club, about twenty inches long, with a large and pointed end;

and

and fometimes a ftone hatchet; make up the catalogue of their military implements.

We this day fhot a *Knob-fronted Bee-eater*; (See plate annexed). This is about the fize of a blackbird; the plumage moftly brown above and white beneath; the head and upper part of the neck are fparingly covered with narrow feathers, almoft like hairs; but the fore part of the neck and breaft are furnifhed with long ones, of a white colour and pointed at the ends; the tail is pretty long, and the feathers tipped with white; the bill is about one inch in length, and pale; but what is moft remarkable, on the forehead, juft at the bafe of the bill, is a fhort blunt knob, about a quarter of an inch in length, and of a brownifh colour; the tongue is nearly of the length of the bill, and briftly at the end; the legs are brown. This inhabits *New South Wales*, and is fuppofed to be a non-defcript fpecies.

This day three canoes, with a man and woman in each, came behind the point on which the hofpital is built, to fifh. I went over to them, as did two other gentlemen, my affiftants, without their fhewing any fear at our coming; on the contrary, they manifefted a friendly confidence.

We

*Knob-fronted*                    *Bee Eater*

London Published Dec: 29, 1789 by J.Debrett.

We gave them some bread, which they received with apparent pleasure, but did not eat any of it while in our presence. We likewise presented them with a looking-glass, but this they received with indifference, and seemed to hold in no kind of estimation. I gave one of the women a pocket handkerchief, which she immediately tied round her head, and shewed great satisfaction. She had a young child between her knees in the canoe, (the way in which they always carry their infants), for whom she solicited something, in the most suppliant tone of voice I ever heard. The only thing I had about me was a narrow slip of linen, which I gave her; and trifling as it was, she appeared to be perfectly satisfied with it, and bound it round the child's head. She would not come out of the canoe, though along-side the rocks; but the man quitted it, and shewed us some wild figs that grew near at hand. Such as were green and unripe he did not pull; but, after some search, having found one that was tolerably ripe, he made me pluck it and put it into his mouth. He eat it with an apparent relish, and smacked his lips, after he had swallowed it, to convince us how good it was.

At

At some little distance from the place where we were a sheep lay dead. As soon as he had discovered it, he took it by the horns, and, as well as we could understand him, he was extremely inquisitive and anxious to know what it was. When his curiosity was satisfied, he went into the canoe, where the woman had been waiting for him. About ten or twenty yards from the shore, among the long grass, in the shallow water, he struck and took with his fish-gig several good fish; an acquisition to which, at this season of the year, it being cold and wet, we were unequal. While he was engaged in watching for them, both he and the woman chewed something, which they frequently spit into the water; and which appeared to us, from his immediately striking a fish, to be a lure. While they were thus employed, one of the gentlemen with me sung some songs; and when he had done, the females in the canoes either sung one of their own songs, or imitated him, in which they succeeded beyond conception. Any thing spoken by us they most accurately recited, and this in a manner of which we fell greatly short in our attempts to repeat their language after them.

While we were thus amicably engaged, all on a sudden they

*Sacred Kings Fisher*

London Published Dec: 29. 1789 by I.Debrett.

they paddled away from us. On looking about to difcover the caufe, we perceived the gunner of the Supply
at fome little diftance, with a gun in his hand; an
inftrument of death, againft which they entertain an
infuperable averfion. As foon as I difcovered him, I
called to him to ftay where he was, and not make a nearer
approach; or, if he did, to lay down his gun. The
latter requeft he immediately complied with; and when
the natives faw him unarmed, they fhewed no further
fear, but returning to their employment, continued
alternately to fing fongs, and to mimic the gentlemen
who accompanied me.

We this day fhot the *Sacred Kings-Fifher* (See Plate
annexed). This bird is about the fize of a thrufh, and
meafures nearly ten inches in length: the top of the
head is blue, and crefted; fides of the head, and back
part of it, black; over the eye, from the noftrils, a rufty
coloured ftreak; the chin, the middle of the neck, all
round, and all the under part of the body, buff-colour,
more or lefs inclining to ruft; the upper part of the
plumage chiefly blue; but the beginning of the back is
black, as are alfo the quills and tail feathers within,

C c                                   being

being blue only on the outer edges; the bill is large and black, but the baſe of the under jaw is whitiſh; the legs are brown. This bird is ſubject to great variety, ſeveral of them being mentioned by Mr. Latham in his *Synopſis*. The preſent ſeems to come neareſt his Var. **C.** See vol. ii. page 622, of that work.

Auguſt 12th. Celebrated the Prince of Wales's birth-day. The men of war fired a royal ſalute, and all the officers in the colony, civil and military, dined with the governor. The evening was ſpent in making bonfires, and teſtifying ſuch other demonſtrations of joy as could be ſhewn in this country. The weather is now very wet and cold, and has been ſo for the laſt ſix weeks. Several mornings we have had a hoar froſt, and a few diſtinct pelicles of ice were formed on ſhallow ſpots of water; the thermometer frequently as low as the freezing point.

16th. A convict who had been out gathering what they called ſweet tea, about a mile from the camp, met a party of the natives, conſiſting of fourteen, by whom he was beaten, and alſo ſlightly wounded with the ſhell-ſtick uſed in throwing their ſpears; they then made him

ſtrip,

ſtrip, and would have taken from him his clothes, and probably his life, had it not been for the report of two muſquets; which they no ſooner heard, than they ran away. This party were returning from the wood with cork, which they had been cutting, either for their canoes or huts; and had with them no other inſtruments than thoſe that were neceſſary for the buſineſs on which they were engaged; ſuch as a ſtone hatchet, and the ſhell ſtick before mentioned. Had they been armed with any other weapons, the convict would probably have loſt his life.

That which we call the ſweet tea, is a creeping kind of vine, running to a great extent along the ground; the ſtalk is not ſo thick as the ſmalleſt honey-ſuckle; nor is the leaf ſo large as the common bay leaf, though ſomething ſimilar to it; and the taſte is ſweet, exactly like the liquorice root of the ſhops. Of this the convicts and ſoldiers make an infuſion which is tolerably pleaſant, and ſerves as no bad ſuccedaneum for tea. Indeed were it to be met with in greater abundance, it would be found very beneficial to thoſe poor creatures, whoſe conſtant diet is ſalt proviſions. In uſing it for medical purpoſes,

I have

I have found it to be a good pectoral, and, as I before obſerved, not at all unpleaſant. *(See Plate annexed).* We have alſo a kind of ſhrub in this country reſembling the common broom; which produces a ſmall berry like a white currant, but, in taſte, more ſimilar to a very ſour green gooſeberry. This has proved a good antiſcorbutic; but I am ſorry to add, that the quantity to be met with is far from ſufficient to remove the ſcurvy. That diſorder ſtill prevails with great violence, nor can we at preſent find any remedy againſt it, notwithſtanding that the country produces ſeveral ſorts of plants and ſhrubs, which, in this place, are conſidered as tolerable vegetables, and uſed in common. The moſt plentiful, is a plant growing on the ſea ſhore, greatly reſembling ſage. Among it are often to be found ſamphire, and a kind of wild ſpinage, beſides a ſmall ſhrub which we diſtinguiſh by the name of the vegetable tree, and the leaves of which prove rather a pleaſant ſubſtitute for vegetables.

22d. His Excellency Governor Phillip, Lieutenant George Johnſton, his Adjutant of Orders, Lieutenant Creſſwell of the Marines, myſelf, and ſix ſoldiers, landed in Manly Cove, in order to examine the coaſt to Broken Bay. At a
ſhort

fhort diftance from the fhore, we faw fixteen canoes, with two perfons in each, and in fome three, employed in fifhing. They feemed to take very little notice as we paffed them, fo very intent were they on the bufinefs in which they were engaged.  On our landing, we faw fixty more of the natives, about two hundred yards diftant from us.  Some of them immediately came up to us, and were very friendly.  A black man, who carried our tents, gave two of them a ftocking each, with which they feemed much pleafed; and pointing to the naked leg, expreffed a great defire to have that alfo clothed.  The morning was fo cold, that thefe poor wretches ftood fhivering on the beach, and appeared to be very fenfible of the comfort and advantage of being clothed.

We fent back our boats, and proceeded northward along the coaft about fix miles, where we were forced to halt for near two hours, until the tide had run out of a lagoon, or piece of water, fo as to admit of its being forded. While we were detained here, an old native came to us, and, in the moft friendly manner, pointed out the fhalloweft part of the water we had to crofs; but the tide ran with too much rapidity at that time for us to attempt it.  After we

had

had waded through, one of our company shot a very fine duck, which we had dressed for supper, on a little eminence by the side of a cabbage tree swamp, about half a mile from the runof the tide. Here the whole party got as much cabbage, to eat with their salt provisions, as they chose. While we had been detained by the tide, several natives were on the opposite side, who also pointed out to us the shoalest water, and appeared, by their signs and gestures, to wish us very much to come over; but before the tide was sufficiently low, they went away. One of them wore a skin of a reddish colour round his shoulders. Near the place where we pitched our tent, we saw several quails exactly like those in England. I fired four or five times at them, but without success, as my shot was too large.

23d. As soon as the dew was off the grass, we began our march, and about twelve o'clock fell in with the south branch of *Broken Bay*: but finding the country round this part very rugged, and the distance too great for our stock of provisions, we returned to the sea shore, in order to examine the south part of the entrance into the bay. This, like every other part of the country we have seen, had a very indifferent aspect. From the entrance

of

of *Port Jackſon* to *Broken Bay*, in ſome places from fifty to a hundred, in others to two hundred yards diſtant from the ſea, the coaſt indeed is very pleaſant, and tolerably clear of wood; the earth a kind of adheſive clay, covered with a thick and ſhort four graſs.

All along the ſhore we met the natives, who ſeem to have no fixed reſidence or abode; but, indiſcriminately, whenever they meet with a hut, or, what is more common, a convenient excavation or hole in the rocks, take poſſeſſion of it for the time. In one of their huts, at *Broken Bay*, which was conſtructed of bark, and was one of the beſt I had ever met with, we ſaw two very well made nets, ſome fiſhing lines not inferior to the nets, ſome ſpears, a ſtone hatchet of a very ſuperior make to what they uſually have, together with two vehicles for carrying water, one of cork, the other made out of the knot of a large tree hollowed. In this hut there were two pieces of coarſe linen, which they muſt have obtained from ſome of our people, and every thing about it beſpoke more comfort and convenience than I had obſerved in any other. A little way from it we fell in with a large party of natives, whom we ſuppoſed to be the proprietors;

they

they were armed with ſpears and ſtone hatchets. One of the latter they very earneſtly wiſhed to exchange for one of ours. Though we would readily have obliged them, it was not in our power to comply with their wiſhes, as we had only a ſufficient number wherewith to cut wood for our own fires. However, notwithſtanding our refuſal, they parted from us without appearing at all diſſatisfied.

As we proceeded along the ſandy beach, we gathered ſome beans, which grew on a ſmall creeping ſubſtance not unlike a vine. They were well taſted, and very ſimilar to the Engliſh long-pod bean. At the place where we halted, we had them boiled, and we all eat very heartily of them. Half an hour after, the governor and I were ſeized with a violent vomiting. We drank warm water, which, carrying the load freely from our ſtomachs, gave us immediate relief. Two other gentlemen of the party ate as freely of them as we had done, without feeling the ſmalleſt inconvenience or bad effect. About this place we got ſome raſberries; but they had not that pleaſant tartneſs peculiar to thoſe in Europe.

24th. We returned by the ſame paſſage, along the coaſt,

with

without ſeeing any objects worth notice, until we came to a convenient ſpot to encamp for the night, where there was great plenty of cabbage trees, and tolerable water; a circumſtance, as I have already obſerved, not generally to be met with in this country, except on the ſea coaſt; and even there by no means in abundance.

While ſoup was making of ſome birds we had lately killed (which proved very good), and every thing was getting ready for the night, the governor, the two other gentlemen, and myſelf, took our guns, and aſcended a hill juſt above us. From this eminence we ſaw the ſouthern branch of Broken Bay, which ran far into the country. During our return, we picked up, in the diſtance of about half a mile, twenty-five flowers of plants and ſhrubs of different genera and ſpecies, ſpecimens of which I have tranſmitted to Mr. *Wilſon,* particularly the Red Gum Tree. (See Plate annexed). On the ſpot where we encamped, the graſs was long, dry, and ſour; and in ſuch abundance, that we ſet it on fire all around, for fear the natives ſhould ſurpriſe us in the night by doing the ſame; a cuſtom in which they ſeem always happy to indulge themſelves.

25th. We ſet off early in the morning to look at the

D d

branch

branch of Broken Bay which we had ſeen the evening
before; and were led to it by a path not very much
frequented.   At the head of this branch we found a freſh
water river, which took its riſe a little above, out of a
ſwamp.   Such is the origin and ſource of every river
we have yet diſcovered in this country; though few, when
compared to thoſe in any other part of the world.   It is
very extraordinary that in all this extenſive tract, a living
ſpring has not yet been explored.   On this river we ſaw
many ducks and teal.   Mr. Creſſwell ſhot one of the latter,
and I ſhot one of the former.   They were both well taſted,
and good of their kind.   At the head of this branch we
found the country rough and impaſſable.   Having followed
the courſe of the river to its origin,  we that day returned
to Manly Cove, where we ſurpriſed two old men, an old
woman, a grown-up girl, and thirteen children, in a hut.
When the children ſaw us approach, they all gathered
themſelves cloſely together around the girl; they cried,
and ſeemed much terrified.   The old men ſhowed ſuch
diſlike to our looking at them, that the governor and the
reſt of the party withdrew to ſome little diſtance to dine.
Some of the children, on ſeeing all the party gone but

myſelf

myſelf and another gentleman, began to laugh, and thus proved that their fears had vaniſhed. When we joined the reſt of the party, the old man followed us in a very friendly manner, and took part of every kind of proviſion we had, but he ate none of it in our ſight. The women and children ſtood at ſome diſtance, and beckoned to us when the men, of whom they ſeemed to ſtand in very great dread, had turned their backs.

As ſoon as we had dined, and refreſhed ourſelves, the governor, by himſelf, went down to them, and diſtributed ſome preſents among them, which ſoon gained their friendſhip and confidence. By this time ſixteen canoes, that were out fiſhing, came cloſe to the ſpot where we were, and there lay on their paddles, which they managed with wonderful dexterity and addreſs; mimicking us, and indulging in their own merriment. After many ſigns and entreaties, one of the women ventured to the governor, who was by himſelf, and with ſeemingly great timidity, took from him ſome ſmall fiſhing lines and hooks; articles which they hold in great eſtimation. This made her leſs fearful; and in a little time ſhe became perfectly free and unreſtrained. Her conduct influenced many others,

Dd 2                                    who

who came on ſhore for what they could procure. Many of them were painted about the head, breaſt, and ſhoulders, with ſome white ſubſtance. None of thoſe who were thus ornamented came on ſhore, till by ſigns we made them underſtand that we intended to offer them ſome preſents; and even then, only one of them ventured. To this perſon Lieutenant Creſſwell gave a white pocket handkerchief, with which ſhe ſeemed much pleaſed. Every gentleman now ſingled out a female, and preſented her with ſome trinkets, not forgetting, at the ſame time, to beſtow gifts upon ſome of her family, whom ſhe took conſiderable pains to make known, left they ſhould fall into the hands of ſuch as did not belong to her. It was remarked that all the women and children, (an old woman excepted) had the little finger of the left hand taken off at the ſecond joint; the ſtump of which was as well covered as if the operation had been performed by a ſurgeon.

While we were thus employed among the women, a body of men came out of the woods with a new canoe, made of cork. It was one of the beſt we had obſerved in this country; though it fell very ſhort of thoſe

which

which I have ſeen among the American or Muſquito-ſhore Indians; who, in improvements of every kind, the Indians of this country are many centuries behind. The men had alſo with them ſome new paddles, ſpears, and fiſh-gigs, which they had juſt been making. They readily ſhowed us the uſe of every thing they had with them. Indeed they always behave with an apparent civility when they fall in with men that are armed; but when they meet perſons unarmed, they ſeldom fail to take every advantage of them.

Thoſe females who were arrived at the age of puberty did not wear a covering; but all the female children and likewiſe the girls wore a ſlight kind of covering before them, made of the fur of the kangaroo, twiſted into threads. While we went towards the party of men that came out of the woods with the new canoe, all the women landed, and began to broil their fiſh, of which they had a large quantity. There ſeemed to be no harmony or hoſpitality among them. However, the female to whom I paid the moſt attention gave me, but not un-till I aſked her for it, ſome of the fiſh which ſhe was eating.

eating.   She had thrown it on the fire, but it was ſcarcely
warm.

Many of the women were ſtrait, well formed, and lively.
My companion continued to exhibit a number of coquettiſh
airs while I was decorating her head, neck, and arms,
with my pocket and neck handkerchiefs, which I tore into
ribbons, as if deſirous of multiplying two preſents into
ſeveral.   Having nothing left, except the buttons of my
coat, on her admiring them, I cut them away, and with a
piece of ſtring tied them round her waiſt.   Thus ornamented, and thus delighted with her new acquirements,
ſhe turned from me with a look of inexpreſſible arch-
neſs.

Before the arrival of the boats, which was late, the
natives pointed to a hawk, and made ſigns to us to ſhoot
it.    It had alighted upon an adjoining tree, and the
governor deſired that I would bring it down.   The report
of the gun frightened them very much.   Some ran away;
but on perceiving that no harm was intended againſt them,
they returned, and were highly pleaſed to ſee the hawk
preſented by the governor to a young girl, who appeared

to

to be the daughter of the moſt diſtinguiſhed amongſt them.

While the boats were preparing for our reception, an old woman, perfectly grey with age, ſolicited us very much for ſome preſent; and in order to make us comply, threw herſelf, before all her companions, into the moſt indecent attitudes.

The cockſwain of the boat informed us, that while he was waiting for our return, the day before, two parties of the natives met, and commenced hoſtilities againſt each other. The man thus deſcribed the manner in which this encounter was carried on. A champion from each party, armed with a ſpear and a ſhield, preſſed forwards before the reſt; and, as ſoon as a favourable opportunity offered (till which he advanced and retreated by turns), threw his ſpear, and then retired; when another immediately took his place, going through the ſame manœuvres; and in this manner was the conflict carried on for more than two hours. The boats crew and two midſhipmen, who ſaw the whole of the proceeding, perceived that one of the natives walked off with a ſpear in his ſide. During the engagement, the women belonging to them, who ſtood

at

at ſome diſtance, diſcovered ſtrong marks of concern, and ſcreamed loudly when any of the combatants appeared to be wounded.    As the boat was returning cloſe along ſhore, a ſpear was thrown at the people by ſome of the natives, who were lurking behind the trees and rocks.   It was hurled with ſuch force, that it flew a conſiderable way over the boat, although we were between thirty and forty yards from the ſhore.

It was late in the evening before we arrived in Sydney Cove; and as ſoon as the governor landed, he was informed that a gold mine had been diſcovered, near the entrance of the harbour, by a convict.   During his excellency's abſence, the convict had made this diſcovery known to the lieutenant governor and the judge advocate; for which, he ſaid, that he hoped and expected to have his freedom, and a pecuniary reward.   The gentlemen to whom he applied anſwered, that they could not promiſe to grant his requeſt until he ſhould have put them in poſſeſſion of the mine; but, that they were well aſſured that the governor would beſtow on him a proper recompence, after ſufficient proof of the diſcovery.   A boat was, in conſequence, ordered from the Sirius, to carry him and Captain Campbell down to the

place

place where he declared that the mine was ſituated. At their landing, he begged leave to withdraw a little, on ſome neceſſary occaſion; when, inſtead of returning to Captain Campbell, he went back to the camp, and waiting on the lieutenant governor and judge advocate, aſſerted that he had put Captain Campbell in poſſeſſion of the mine, who had diſpatched him over land for another officer and a proper guard. His account not being doubted, he was well fed and treated; and Lieutenant Paulden, with a guard and all neceſſary articles, was ordered to attend him to the place. But, before they could ſet out, to the great aſtoniſhment of all, Captain Campbell arrived, and unravelled the whole of this extraordinary deception. This produced an unexpected revolution. Inſtead of receiving a reward for his golden diſcoveries, the impoſtor was immediately taken into cuſtody, with two others, ſuppoſed to be concerned in carrying on the artifice. The next day he was examined, with great privacy and ſtrictneſs; but no ſatisfactory elucidation being obtained from him, he was ordered to be ſeverely whipped. Subſequently to this puniſhment, of which he was prepared to expect a weekly repetition, between the intervals of hard labour, and to be

E e                                                 loaded

loaded inceſſantly with heavy irons, during the time of his remaining in the colony, he moſt audaciouſly perſiſted in endeavouring to maintain the deluſion, and declared that if an officer was ſent with him, he would ſhow him the mine; adding, that he was heartily ſorry for what had happened. Accordingly, he was ſuffered to accompany Lieutenant G. Johnſton, the Governor's Adjutant of Orders, to the place in queſtion. Before the boat had reached its deſtination Mr. Johnſton argued with him, yet not without proteſting, that if he either attempted to deceive *him* as he had impoſed upon Captain Campbell, or preſumed to move five yards from him and his party, he would inſtantly order him to be ſhot. Finding that this officer was not to be trifled with, but ſeemed determined, he acknowledged that it was unneceſſary to proceed any farther; that he was ignorant of the exiſtence of any ſuch mine, and that the ſpecimens ſhown by him were only a compoſition of braſs and gold, which he had filed down and melted. Mr. Johnſton brought him back; when he was again examined, and ordered to be puniſhed. It is needleſs to add that no further diſcovery was made. He is now at liberty. He is, however, obliged to wear a large *R* on

his

his back. The man, whoſe name is Daily, appears inſane; yet others cannot be perſuaded that he is a lunatic, but are rather of opinion that he is a deſigning miſcreant, and that time will diſcloſe a deep-laid ſcheme, which he had planned for ſome purpoſe hitherto undiſcovered. For my own part, I freely confeſs, that I cannot coincide with their ſentiments. He was ſo artful as to circulate a report that he had ſold ſeveral pounds weight of the ore to the maſter of the Golden Grove, and ſome of his ſeamen. This rumour was received with ſuch credulity, that, in conſequence of the impreſſion which it made, none of the ſailors were ſuffered to leave the ſhip after a certain hour in the evening. In a word, ſo many ridiculous circumſtances attended this affair, that to attempt a complete enumeration of them would prove not leſs difficult than unintereſting.

26th. The Supply arrived from Norfolk Iſland, after a long and rough paſſage. She had landed, but neither in apparent ſafety nor with facility, the ſtores which ſhe carried to that place: and, upon the preſent occaſion, I am ſorry to add, that the hazard of landing and embarking from this little iſland is ſo very great, that Mr. Cunningham, a midſhipman of the Sirius (who reſided on it with

Lieutenant

Lieutenant King, the ſuperintendant), was loſt, with three ſeamen, in a boat that was ſwamped by the ſurf, which on every part of the coaſt runs high, and beats againſt the ſhore with great violence; ſo that I much fear, from the difficulty of acceſs, and its ſituation, it never will prove of any great conſequence, although it promiſed ſome advantages; particularly in furniſhing us with pine trees, which grow here to a ſize nearly equal to thoſe of Norway. In the whole iſland there is not a harbour capable of admitting even ſo ſmall a veſſel as the Supply, and the anchorage on every part of the coaſt is equally bad.

The iſland produces a kind of gladiolus luteus, or iris paluſtris, of which, as may be ſeen by the ſpecimens ſent Mr. Wilſon, exceeding good hemp is to be made; and which is to be procured in any quantity, the plants growing in great abundance throughout the whole iſland. The foregoing articles, were the iſland larger and more eaſy of acceſs, with even a tolerable harbour, might, in any other country, be of the firſt conſequence to a maritime nation. But from every information which I have gained from the officers and crew of the Supply, the procuring of this beneficial acquiſition is at preſent ſomewhat doubtful. The

people

people settled upon it, when they can venture out, get great plenty of fish; and, at certain seasons, turtle. In the island also are pigeons, as tame as domestic fowls; and the soil seems well adapted for the growth of all kinds of grain and vegetables. It produces a wild banana, or plantain tree, which, by cultivation, may assist the settlers, as a succedaneum for bread: and I am not without hopes that we shall be able to make some additions from thence to such necessaries of life as may in time be produced here.

A few days since the natives landed near the hospital, where some goats belonging to the Supply were browsing; when they killed, with their spear, a kid, and carried it away. Within this fortnight, they have also killed a he-goat of the governor's. Whenever an opportunity offered, they have seldom failed to destroy whatever stock they could seize upon unobserved. They have been equally ready to attack the convicts, on every occasion which presented itself; and some of them have become victims to these savages. I have already observed that they stand much in fear of a musquet, and therefore they very seldom approach any person by whom it is carried; and their apprehensions are almost equally great when they perceive a red garment.

September

September 5th. About half after fix in the evening, we faw an aurora auftralis, a phænomenon uncommon in the fouthern hemifphere.

October 2d. His Majefty's fhip the Sirius failed for the Cape of Good Hope, for a fupply of flour, it being difcovered that our ftock of this article bore no proportion to the falt beef and pork.

The fame day the Golden Grove failed for Norfolk Ifland, with a reinforcement of male and female convicts; two free men, as gardeners; a midfhipman from the Sirius, to fill up the vacancy occafioned by the death of Mr. Cunningham; a fergeant, corporal, and fix privates; and a fupply of neceffaries for eighteen months.

4th. A convict, named Cooper Handley, who went out with an armed party of marines to collect wild vegetables and fweet tea, ftrayed from them, and was afterwards met by the natives, who murdered and mutilated him in a fhocking manner. The natives were fo near our men, that they heard them very diftinctly fhouting and making a great noife, yet were unable to overtake them in the purfuit. In the evening, a party of foldiers and convicts were fent out to bury the deceafed.

10th.

10th.   A general court martial was convened by warrant from the governor.   When the members, with the deputy judge advocate, were affembled, they gave it as their opinion, that notwithftanding the governor has full power and authority to grant and hold court martials among regular troops; yet, as a corps of marines, under the influence of a particular code of laws, and inftructions from the Admiralty, and only amenable to that board, they could not proceed to trial; the board of Admiralty not having delegated any part of their authority over the marine corps, particularly that of holding court martials, to the governor; neither did any part of the act of Parliament for forming a colony in New South Wales contain directions relative to that fubject.   The marine inftructions, with refpect to court martials, ftate, that no general court martial can be ordered but by the Lord High Admiral, or three commiffioners for executing the office; nor any fentence be carried into execution until approved of by him or them, unlefs the marines, as in America, fhould be, by act of Parliament, confidered as a part of the army; which is not the cafe here.   They are truly and literally governed and regulated by the fame rules and inftructions as the marine divifions at

Chatham,

Chatham, Portfmouth, or Plymouth; and, confequently, their proceeding to trial would not only be illegal, but a direct infult to the governance and power of the Board under which they act, and to whom every appeal from them muft come; unlefs an act of Parliament, in that cafe made and provided, otherwife directs.

28th. A marine went to gather fome greens and herbs, but has not returned; as he was unarmed, it is feared that he has been met and murdered by the natives.

31ft. A fergeant and four privates, who had been miffing three days, returned. They were fent by the commanding officer to look for the marine, and loft themfelves in the woods. In the evening of this day we had very loud thunder, and a fhower of hail; many of the hail-ftones were meafured, and found to be five-eights of an inch in diameter.

November 2d. This day more hail; the weather dark and gloomy, with dreadful lightning. The mercury during the whole of the day ftood between 66 and 68.

7th. A criminal court fentenced a convict to five hundred lafhes for ftealing foap, the property of another convict, value eight pence.

10th.

10th. The Golden Grove returned from Norfolk Island with a few spars, and some timber for the governor. While she lay there, she was obliged to cut her cable and stand to sea, there being (as before observed) no harbour in the whole island, where a ship can ride in safety. The master of the ship was swamped in the surf and nearly lost, with his boat and crew.

11th. Thomas Bulmore, a private marine, died in consequence of the blows which he received during a battle with one of his companions; who is to be tried for his life, on the 17th instant, by a criminal court. So small is our number, and so necessary is every individual who composes it, for one purpose or another, that the loss of even a single man may truly be considered as an irreparable disadvantage!

The preceding is all the account I am able at present to send you of the territories of New South Wales, and its productions. The unsettled state in which you must naturally suppose every thing, as yet, to remain, will not permit me to be as copious as I could wish; but, by the next dispatch,

F f

I hope

I hope to be able to fend you no inconfiderable additions to the Natural Hiftory, and at the fame time fuch further information concerning our affairs here as during the interim fhall have occurred.

# APPENDIX.

F.P. Nodder delin.

*The Banksia Serrata in Bud.*

London. Publish'd as the Act directs Dec. 29. 1789. by I. Debrett.

# NATURAL HISTORY.

## THE DIFFERENT SPECIES OF BANKSIA.

THE fineſt new genus hitherto found in *New Holland* has been deſtined by *Linnæus*, with great propriety, to tranſmit to poſterity the name of Sir *Joſeph Banks*, who firſt diſcovered it in his celebrated voyage round the world. It is indeed one of the moſt magnificent genera with which we are acquainted, being nearly allied to *Protea* and *Embothrium* in habit and botanical characters, but ſufficiently diſtinguiſhed from both by its fruit. Four ſpecies of *Bankſia* are deſcribed in the *Supplementum Plantarum* of *Linnæus*; ſpecimens of which we have ſeen in his *Herbarium* now in the poſſeſſion of Dr. *Smith* of *Marlborough Street*; and we have depoſited with the ſame gentleman

ſpecimens

fpecimens of all the plants we are about to defcribe in this work. Dr. *Gaertner*, in his admirable book on fruits and feeds, has figured the fruit of feveral *Bankfias*, fome of them defcribed by *Linnæus*. Having had his plates, with the names, engraved before he faw the *Supplementum* of *Linnæus*, his nomenclature differs from that of the laft mentioned author; but he quotes his fynonyms in the letter prefs. We mention this, that he may not be accufed of *wantonly* changing *Linnæan* names, and that for the worfe, as it would appear to any one uninformed of this circumftance.

The character of the genus is very badly made out in *Linnæus*. *Gaertner* has greatly corrected it, but it is ftill a doubt whether the flowers are conftantly *monopetalous* or *tetrapetalous*, nor have we materials fufficient to remove this difficulty. All we can fay is, that *Bankfia* is next in natural arrangement to *Protea*, from which it is effentially diftinguifhed by having an hard woody bivalve capfule, containing two winged feeds, with a moveable membranous partition between them. It is ftrangely mifplaced in *Murray*'s 14th edition of *Syftema Vegetabilium*, being put between *Ludwigia* and *Oldenlandia!*

Mr. White has fent imperfect fpecimens and feeds of

four

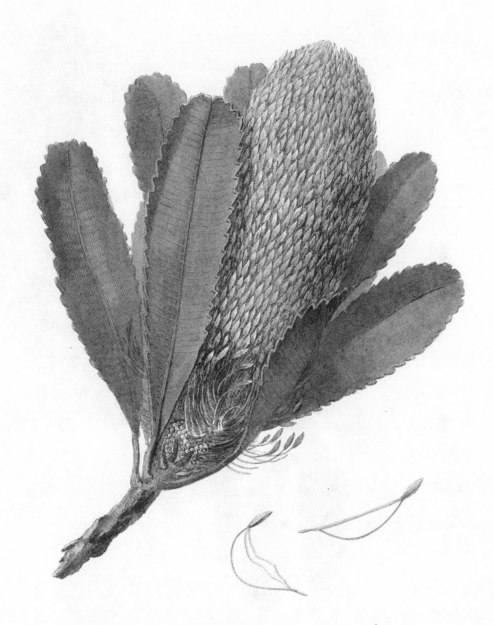

F. P. Nodder, delin.

*The Banksia serrata in Flower*

London Published as the Act directs Dec.r 29. 1789. by I. Debrett.

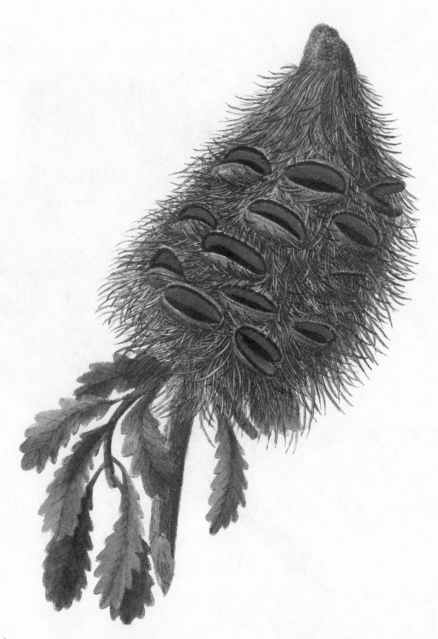

F. P. Nodder, delin.

*The Banksia serrata in Fruit.*

London Published as the Act directs Dec:29.1789. by I.Debrett.

four fpecies of Bankfia, which we have endeavoured to fettle as follows:

1. B. ferrata. *Linn. Supp.* 126.
   B. conchifera. *Gaertn.* 221. *t.* 48.

This is the moft ftately of the genus. Its trunk is thick and rugged. Leaves alternate, ftanding thick about the ends of the branches on fhort footftalks, narrow, obtufe, ftrongly ferrated, fmooth and of a bright green colour above, beneath opaque and whitifh, with a ftrong rib running through their middle. A very large cylindrical fpike of flowers terminates each branch. Moft of the flowers are abortive, a few only in each fpike producing ripe feed. The form of the capfules may be underftood from the figure, which reprefents a whole fpike in fruit, about half the natural fize. The capfules are covered with thick down. Another plate of the plant in flower fhews the curved pofition in which the ftyle is held by the corolla; the increafe of the former in length being greater and more rapid than that of the latter.

2. B.

2.  B. pyriformis.   *Gaertn.* 220. *t.* 47.*f.* **1.**

This fpecies was unknown to Linnæus; and as Gaertner has
given no fpecific character of it, we beg leave to offer the
following:

*B. floribus folitariis, capfulis ovatis pubefcentibus, foliis*
*lanceolatis integerrimis glabris.*

Bankfia with folitary flowers, ovate downy capfules, and
lance-fhaped entire fmooth leaves.

The capfules are larger than in any other known fpecies.
In the figure they are reprefented fomewhat fmaller than
the life; but the feed is given as large as life.

3.  B. gibbofa.   B. dactyloides *Gaertn.* 221. *t.* 47. *f.* 2. ?

*B. floribus folitariis, capfulis ovatis gibbofis rugofis, foliis*
*teretibus.*

Bankfia with folitary flowers; ovate, tumid, rugged capfules; and cylindrical leaves.

We fufpect this to be the Bankfia dactyloides of *Gaertner*;
but if fo, his figure is by no means a good one; as he is
generally very accurate, we are rather inclined to believe

ours

*The Banksia pyriformis*

Published as the Act directs Dec: 29. 1789 by I.Debrett.

*Fig:1.*

*Fig:2.*

*1 The Banksia. 2 The Banksia gibbosa.*

London Published as the Act directs Dec: 29, 1789, by I.Debrett.

ours a different plant, and have therefore given it a new
name. The leaves are very peculiar, being perfectly cylindrical, about two inches long and one line in diameter,
pale, green and smooth. The flowers we have not seen.

Fig. 1. of the same Plate reprefents the capfule of another
Bankfia, belonging to thofe which bear the flowers in fpikes,
but we cannot with certainty determine the fpecies. The
capfules are fmooth, at leaft when ripe, and a little fhining.
We think this is neither the B. ferrata, integrifolia, nor dentata
of Linnæus, nor probably his ericifolia; fo that it feems to
be a fpecies hitherto undefcribed. The leaves and flowers
we have not feen.

G g                              THE

# THE PEPPERMINT TREE.

## EUCALYPTUS PIPERITA.

*An Eucalyptus obliqua, L'Heritier Sert. Angl. p.* 18 ?

(See Plate annexed.)

This tree grows to the height of more than an hundred feet, and is above thirty feet in circumference. The bark is very fmooth, like that of the poplar. The younger branches are long and flender, angulated near the top, but as they grow older the angles difappear. Their bark is fmooth, and of a reddifh brown. The leaves are alternate, lanceolate, pointed, very entire, fmooth on both fides, and remarkably unequal, or oblique, at their bafe ; the veins alternate and not very confpicuous. The whole furface of both fides of the leaves is marked with numerous minute refinous fpots, in which the effential oil refides. The foot-ftalks are about half an inch in length, round on the under fide, angular above, quite fmooth. The flowers we have not feen. What Mr. WHITE has fent as the ripe capfules of this tree (although not attached to the fpecimens of the leaves) grow in clufters, from fix to eight in each, feffile

and

*The Peppermint Tree.*

London, Published Dec 29, 1789, by J.Debrett.

F.P.Nodder, Delin

and conglomerated. Thefe clufters are fupported on angular alternate footftalks, which form a kind of panicle. Each capfule is about the fize of an hawthorn berry, globular, but as it were cut off at the top, rugged on the outfide, hard and woody, and of a dark brown colour. At the top is a large orifice, which fhews the internal part of the capfule divided into four cells, and having a fquare column in the center, from which the partitions of the cell arife. Thefe partitions extend to the rim of the capfule, and terminate in four fmall projections, which look like the teeth of a calyx. The feeds are numerous, fmall, and angular.

The name of Peppermint Tree has been given to this plant by Mr. WHITE on account of the very great refemblance between the effential oil drawn from its leaves and that obtained from the Peppermint (*Mentha piperita*) which grows in England. This oil was found by Mr. WHITE to be much more efficacious in removing all cholicky complaints than that of the Englifh Peppermint, which he attributes to its being lefs pungent and more aromatic. A quart of the oil has been fent by him to Mr. *Wilfon*.

The tree above defcribed appears to be undoubtedly of the fame genus with that cultivated in fome greenhoufes

in

in England, which *Mr. L'Heritier* has deſcribed in his *Sertum Anglicum* by the name of *Eucalyptus obliqua*, though it is commonly called in the gardens *Metroſideros obliqua*; but we dare not aſſert it to be the ſame ſpecies, nor can this point be determined till the flowers and every part of both be ſeen and compared; we have compared the beſt ſpecimens we could procure of each, and find no ſpecific difference. The *Eucalyptus obliqua* has, when dried, an aromatic flavour ſomewhat ſimilar to our plant. We have remarked indeed innumerable minute white ſpots, beſides the reſinous ones, on both ſurfaces of the leaves in ſome ſpecimens of the garden plant, which are not to be ſeen in ours, and the branches of the former are rough, with ſmall ſcaly tubercles. But how far theſe are conſtant we cannot tell. The obliquity in the leaves, one ſide being ſhorter at the baſe than the other, as well as ſomewhat narrower all the way up, as in the *Begonia nitida* of the *Hortus Kewenſis*, is remarkable in both plants.

The figure repreſents a branch of the Peppermint Tree in leaf: on one ſide of it part of a leaf ſeparate, bearing the gall of ſome inſect; on the other the fruit above deſcribed.

TEA

## TEA TREE OF NEW SOUTH WALES.

### MELALEUCA ? TRINERVIA.

This is a fmall fhrub, very much branched. The bark full of longitudinal fiffures, and eafily feparated from the branches. Leaves on fhort footftalks, alternate, lanceolate, pointed, entire, about three quarters of an inch in length, fmooth on both fides, marked with three longitudinal ribs, and reticulated with tranf-verfe veins; they are alfo full of refinous fpots, the feat of an aromatic effential oil. The flowers we have not feen, nor can we determine with certainty the genus of this plant. It moft nearly approaches the Leptofpermum virgatum of Forfter, re-ferred by the younger Linnæus, perhaps improperly, to Mela-leuca. At leaft it may fafely be determined to belong to the fame genus with the Melaleuca virgata Linn. Supp. though a diftinct fpecies. The fpecific difference between them is, that the leaves of our plant have three ribs, whereas M. virgata has leaves perfectly deftitute of ribs or veins. Hence we judge the figure and defcription of Rumphius, Herb. Amboin. V. 2. t. 18. to belong rather to our Tea Tree, than to M. virgata; and if this conjecture be right, the plants are ftill further diftin-guifhed by the inflorefcence, which in M. virgata is an umbel, whereas in the figure above mentioned the flowers are folitary.

*a.* Reprefents a leaf flightly magnified.

SWEET

## SWEET TEA PLANT.

### Smilax? glyciphylla.

This is a tree or fhrub whofe leaves only we have feen, but from them we judge it to belong to the genus of Smilax. For want of the ftem we cannot fettle its fpecific character. Thefe leaves are about two inches long, ovato-lanceolate, pointed, entire, marked with three longitudinal ribs, and many tranfverfe elevated veins, fmooth and fhining above, glaucous beneath, with a thick cartilaginous edge of the fubftance of the ribs. The leaves have the tafte of liquorice root accompanied with bitter. They are faid to make a kind of tea, not unpleafant to the tafte, and good for the fcurvy. The plant promifes much in the laft refpect, from its bitter as a tonic, as well as the quantity of faccharine matter it contains.

Leaves of this plant are reprefented on the fame plate with the Tea Tree. A. is the front, B. the back of a leaf.

THE

B

a

A

F.P.Nodder Delin

The Tea-Tree of New South Wales.

London Published as the Act directs Dec: 29. 1789. by J.Debrett.

*Bark of the Red Gum Tree.*

*London Published Dec: 29, 1789 by J. Debrett.*

*J. P. Nodder, delin:*

# THE RED GUM TREE.

## EUCALYPTUS RESINIFERA.

*Floribus pedunculatis, calyptrá conicá acutá.*

(See Plate annexed.)

This is a very large and lofty tree, much exceeding the Englifh Oak in fize. The wood is extremely brittle, and, from the large quantity of refinous gum which it contains, is of little ufe but for firewood. Of the leaves Mr. WHITE has given no account, nor fent any fpecimens. The flowers grow in little clufters, or rather umbels, about ten in each, and every flower has a proper partial footftalk, about a quarter of an inch in length, befides the general one. The general footftalk is remarkably compreffed (*anceps*), and the partial ones are fo in fome degree. We have perceived nothing like *bractéæ*, or floral leaves. The flowers appear to be yellowifh, and are of a very fingular ftructure. The calyx is hemifpherical, perfectly entire in the margin, and afterwards becomes the capfule. On the top of the calyx, rather within the margin, ftands a conical pointed calyptra,

which

of the fame colour with the calyx, and about as long as that and the footftalk taken together. This calyptra, which is the effential mark of the genus, and differs from that of the *Eucalyptus obliqua* of *L'Heritier* only in being conical and acute, inftead of hemifpherical, is perfectly entire, and never fplits or divides, though it is analogous to the corolla of other plants. When it is removed, we perceive a great number of red ftamina, ftanding in a conical mafs, which before the calyptra was taken off, were completely covered by it, and filled its infide. The *Antheræ* are fmall and red. In the center of thefe ftamina is a fingle ftyle or pointal, rifing a little above them, and terminated by a blunt ftigma. The ftamina are very refinous and aromatic. They are inferted into the margin of the calyx, fo that the genus is properly placed by Mr. *L'Heritier* in the clafs *Icofandria*. Thefe ftamina and ftyle being removed, and the germen cut acrofs about the middle of the calyx, it appears to be divided into three cells, and no more, as far as we have examined, each containing the rudiments of one or more feeds, for the number cannot with certainty be determined. Whether the calyptra in this fpecies falls off, as in that defcribed by Mr. *L'Heritier*, or be permanent,

we

we cannot tell. From one specimen sent by Mr. WHITE, the latter should seem to be the case; and that the calyx swells and rises around it nearly to the top, making a pear-shaped fruit, with the point of the calyptra sticking out at its apex; but as this appears only in a single flower, and none of the others are at all advanced towards ripening seed, the flower in question may possibly be in a morbid state, owing to the attacks of some insect. *(See Fig. g.)* Future observations will determine this point. We have been the more diffuse in our description on account of the singularity of the genus, and the value of the plant.

On making incisions in the trunk of this tree, large quantities of red resinous juice are obtained, sometimes even more than sixty gallons from a single tree. When this juice is dried, it becomes a very powerfully astringent gum-resin, of a red colour, much resembling that known in the shops by the name of Kino, and, for all medical purposes, fully as efficacious. Mr. WHITE administered it to a great number of patients in the dysentery, which prevailed much soon after the landing of the convicts, and in no one instance found it to fail. This gum-resin dissolves almost entirely in spirit of wine, to which it gives a blood red tincture. Water

H h

dissolves

diſſolves about one ſixth part only, and the watery ſolution is of a bright red. Both theſe ſolutions are powerfully aſtringent.

The Plate repreſents a portion of the bark of the *Eucalyptus reſinifera*, with the fructification annexed.

   *a.* Is a bunch of the flowers the ſize of nature.

   *b.* The flower, its calyptra, or hood, being removed.

   *c.* Calyx.

   *d.* Stamina.

   *e.* Piſtillum.

   *f.* Calyptra ſeparate.

   *g.* The enlarged flower, which we ſuſpect to be in a diſeaſed ſtate.

THE

## THE YELLOW RESIN TREE.

This is about the fize of an Englifh walnut tree. Its trunk grows pretty ftraight for about fourteen or fixteen feet, after which it branches out into long fpiral leaves, which hang down on all fides, and refemble thofe of the larger kinds of grafs or fedge. From the center of the head of leaves arifes a fingle footftalk, eighteen or twenty feet in height, perfectly ftraight and erect, very much refembling the fugar cane, and terminating in a fpike of a fpiral form, not unlike an ear of wheat. This large ftem or footftalk is ufed by the natives for making fpears and fifh gigs, being pointed with the teeth of fifh or other animals, fome of which are reprefented, in the plate of Implements, from originals now in Mr. Wilfon's poffeffion.

But the moft valuable produce of this plant feems to be its refin, the properties of which vie with thofe of the moft fragrant balfams. This refin exudes fpontaneoufly from the trunk; the more readily, if incifions are made in its bark. It is of a yellow colour; fluid at firft, but being infpiffated in the fun, it acquires a folid form. Burnt on hot coals, it

H h 2

emits

emits a fmell very much refembling that of a mixture of balfam of Tolu and benzoin, fomewhat approaching to ftorax. It is perfectly foluble in fpirit of wine, but not in water, nor even in effential oil of turpentine, unlefs it be digefted in a ftrong heat. The varnifh which it makes with either is very weak, and of little ufe. With refpect to its medicinal qualities, Mr. White has found it, in many cafes, a good pectoral medicine, and very balfamic. It is not obtainable in fo great abundance as the red gum produced by the Eucalyptus refinifera.

The plant which produces the yellow gum feems to be perfectly unknown to botanifts, but Mr. White has communicated no fpecimens by which its genus or even clafs could be determined.

THE

*The Crested Cockatoo,*

London Published as the Act directs Dec. 29. 1789 by I. Debrett.

# THE CRESTED COCKATOO.

## PSITTACUS CRISTATUS. Lin.

I cannot regard this bird in any other view than as a variety of the Pſittacus Criſtatus of Linnæus, or large white Cockatoo, which has been deſcribed by almoſt all ornithologiſts, and figured in ſeveral works of Natural Hiſtory. The bird ſeems liable to great variation both as to ſize and colour; the white in ſome being of a much purer appearance than in others, and the yellow on the creſt and tail more predominant. All the varieties yet known agree in having the beak and legs blackiſh. The individual ſpecimen here figured ſeemed of a ſomewhat ſlenderer form than uſual. The colour not a pure white, but ſlightly tinged on the upper parts, and particularly on the neck and ſhoulders, with duſky. The feathers on the front white, but the long lanceolate feathers below them, which form the creſt, of a pale jonquil-yellow. The tail white above, and pale yellow beneath; as are alſo the wings.

THE

# THE WHITE FULICA.

## Fulica alba.

*Fulica alba, roſtro fronteque rubris, humeris ſpinoſis, pedibus flavis ?*

*Corpus magnitudine fere gallinæ domeſticæ.   Humeri ſpina parva incurvata.
In ſpecimine exſiccato pedes flavi ; ſed fortaſſe in viva ave roſtro concolores.*

White Fulica, with the bill and front red, ſhoulders ſpined, legs and feet
yellow ?

The body is about the ſize of a domeſtic fowl.   The ſhoulders
are furniſhed with a ſmall crooked ſpine.   In the dried ſpecimen the
legs and feet are yellow ; but, perhaps, in the living bird might have
been of the ſame colour with the beak.

THIS bird is the only ſpecies of its genus yet known of a
white colour.   The birds of this genus rank in the order
called by Linnæus Grallæ, and moſt of the ſpecies frequent
watery places.   To this genus belongs the well-known bird
called the Moor-hen, or Fulica chloropus ; as alſo a very
beautiful exotic ſpecies called the Purple Water-hen, which
is the Fulica porphyrio of Linnæus, and which in ſhape
much reſembles the White Fulica now deſcribed.

THE

*The White Fulica.*

London Published as the Act directs Dec.29.1789. by I.Debrett.

S. Stone Delin.

The Southern Motacilla

London Published as the Act directs Dec.29.1789. by I.Debrett.

## THE SOUTHERN MOTACILLA.

### MOTACILLA AUSTRALIS.

*M. cinera, subtus flava.*
N. B. *Gula fere albida.*

Ash-coloured Motacilla, yellow beneath.
*N. B.* The throat inclines a little to whitish.

IT is not perhaps absolutely clear whether this bird should be referred to the genus Motacilla, or Muscicapa : the probability, however, is in favour of Motacilla.

The bird is about the size of the Motacilla flava of Linnæus, or yellow wagtail, but seems of a stouter make. The beak is of a pale colour, and the legs brown. The two middle tail-feathers have the very extremities slightly marked with white.

The genus Motacilla is extremely numerous, and it is not easy to fix upon a proper or expressive trivial name. Such names should, if possible, convey some idea either of the colour, or some other circumstance relative to the manners or habits of the animal; but in new species, whose history is unknown, this is impracticable. The trivial name, therefore, of Australis may be allowable, though it cannot be regarded as sufficiently distinctive.

WATTLED

## WATTLED BEE-EATER, or MEROPS, Female.

The female Bea-eater is ftouter in the body and in the legs, more brilliant in the plumage, the bill more curved: and the tail cuneated and tipped with white; but fhorter than in the male. The feathers on the head are fmall, each tipped with white, and fomewhat erected: it has no wattles, but on the chin the feathers are dark, long, and hang dif-fufely.

The general colour of the bird is a blackifh chocolate, lighter on the breaft, and towards the vent; darker on the abdomen and towards the tip of the tail. The feathers on the neck and breaft have each a ftreak of white through the middle. On the wing the outer long feathers are flightly edged with whitifh, thofe of the middle region round-ended and tipped only; and on the upper part of the wing each feather bears a ftreakd own the middle, fuddenly dilating at the tip.

The legs yellower than thofe of the male; claws blackifh.

THE

*The Wattled Bee Eater, Female*

London Published as the Act directs Dec: 29, 1789, by I.Debrett.

*The Crested Goatsucker.*

London Published as the Act directs, Dec 29, 1789, by I Debrett.

# THE CRESTED GOAT-SUCKER.

## Caprimulgus cristatus.

*C. cinereo-fuscus, subtus pallidus, remigibus caudaque fasciis pallidis numerosis, vibrissis utrinque erecto-cristatis.*

*Corpus supra punctis minutissimis subalbidis irroratum.*

Cinereous-brown Goat-sucker, pale beneath; with the long feathers of the wings and tail sprinkled with numerous pale fasciæ, and the vibrissæ (or bristles on the upper mandible) standing up on each side, in the manner of a crest.

The body on the upper part is sprinkled with very small whitish specks.

The birds of this genus are remarkable for the excessive widenefs of the mouth, though the beak is very small; in their manner of life, as well as general structure, they are very nearly allied to the genus Hirundo, or swallow; and indeed may be regarded as a kind of nocturnal swallows. They feed on infects, particularly on beetles. The name Caprimulgus, or Goat-sucker, was given to this genus from an idea that prevailed amongst the more ancient naturalists of their sometimes sucking the teats of goats and sheep; a circumstance in itself so wildly improbable, that it would scarce deferve to be seriously mentioned, were it not that so accurate a naturalist as the late celebrated Scopoli seems in some degree to have given credit to it.

I i

THE

## THE SCINCOID, or SKINC-FORMED LIZARD.

### Lacerta Scincoides.

This Lizard comes nearer to the Scincus than any I am acquainted with, but is still a distinct species.

In the two specimens sent over by Mr. White, one had a process on the upper part of the tail, near the top, almost like a supernumerary or forked tail, but which I rather conceive to be natural; and as this one was a male, I am inclined to think that this is peculiar to that sex, which would in some degree have been more clearly made out, if the other, which had not this process, had proved a female; but as its being gutted and stuffed before I saw it, prevented my examination, this remains still to be proved: but what makes the conjecture very probable, is, that it is mentioned by Mr. White that some are without, and some with this process. Now if it was a monster, arising either from accident, or originally so formed, it would hardly be so common as to be taken notice of. The tail is longer than that of the Scincuses, and not so taper; the animal is of a dark iron-grey colour, which is of different shades in different parts, forming a kind of stripes across the back and tail.

The

Fig: 1

3

4

2

1 The Skink-formed Lizard, 2 Eggs, 3 The Egg as broken, 4 The Young.

Published as the Act directs Dec. 29 1789 by E Debrett.

The scales of the cuticle are strong, but not so much so as those of the Scincus. Its legs are short and strong, covered with the same kind of scales as the body, but the scales of the feet are not. On the cuticle are small knobs, as if it were studded.

The toes on each foot are pretty regular; the difference in length not great, and the same on both the fore and hind foot; which is not the case with the Sincus, it having a long middle toe.

There are small short nails on each toe; on their upper surface they are covered with a series of scales, which go half round, like a coat of mail.

Just within the verge of the external opening of the ear, on the anterior edge, is a membrane, covering about one third of it, which is scolloped on its loose or unattached edge; this can hardly be called an external ear, nor can it be called the reserve, viz. a valve; but if it is an assistant to hearing, which it most probably is, it should be considered as the external ear.

The teeth are in a row on each side of each jaw, becoming gradually larger backwards. They are short above the gum, and rounded off, fitted for breaking or bruising of substances, more than cutting or tearing.

THE

# THE MURICATED LIZARD.

## Lacerta Muricata.

*L. cauda tereti longa, corpore griseo, squamis carinatis mucronatis.*

*Corpus supra fasciis tranversis fuscis; subtus pallidum.   Valde affinis Agamæ et Calotæ.*

L. with long rounded tail, body greyish, scales carinated and sharp pointed.

The animal on its upper part is fasciated with transverse dusky bars, and is pale beneath.   This species is very nearly allied to the L. Agama and Calotes.

This species measures somewhat more than a foot in length.   The general colour is a brownish grey, and the whole upper part of the animal is marked with transverse dusky bars, which are most conspicuous on the legs and tail. The tail is very long; the scales on every part of the animal are of a sharp form, and furnished with a prominent line on the upper surface; toward the back part of the head the scales almost run into a sort of weak spines; the feet are furnished with moderately strong, sharp claws.

THE

London Published as the Act directs Dec. 29.1789 by I.Debrett.

1 Snake, 2 Muricated Lizard.

Fig. 2.

Fig. 1.

*1 Ribbon Lizard.    2 Broad-tailed Lizard.*

Published as the Act directs Dec. 29. 1789. by J. Debrett.

# THE RIBBONED LIZARD.

## LACERTA TÆNIOLATA.

*L. lævis, cauda tereti longa, corpore supra tæniolis albis nigrisque, subtus albo.*

*Affinis L. lemniscatæ. Crura supra albo nigroque striata: digiti unguiculati: aures conspicuæ: squamæ totius corporis lævissimæ, nitidissimæ, cauda vix distincte striata, subferruginea.*

This is a very elegant species. The length of the animal is about six inches and a half; and is distinguished by a number of parallel stripes, or bands of black and white, disposed longitudinally throughout the whole upper part of the body, except that on the tail the bands are not carried much above the base; the remainder being of a pale ferruginous colour. In some specimens a tinge of this colour is also visible on the back; the lower part of the body is of a yellowish white; the tail is perfectly round, of a great length, and gradually tapers to the extremity.

THE

# THE BROAD-TAILED LIZARD.

## LACERTA PLATURA.

*L. cauda depreſſo-plana lanceolata, margine ſubaculeato, corpore griſeo-fuſco ſcabro.*

*Ungues quaſi duplicati. Lingua brevis, lata, integra, ſeu non forficata; apice autem leniter emarginato.*

L. with a depreſſed lanceolate tail, almoſt ſpiny on the margin; the body of a duſky grey colour, and rough.

The claws appear as if double; the tongue is ſhort and broad, not forked, but ſlightly emarginated at the tip.

This Lizard is ſtrikingly diſtinguiſhed by the uncommon form of its tail, which is of a depreſſed or flattened ſhape, with very thin edges, and gradually tapers to a ſharp extremity. This depreſſed form of the tail is extremely rare in Lizards; there being ſcarcely more than two other ſpecies yet known in which a ſimilar ſtructure takes place. One of theſe is the L. Caudiverbera of Linnæus, in which the tail

appears

appears to be not only depreffed, but pinnated on the fides. Another fpecies with a depreffed tail has been figured by the Count De Cepede, in his Hiftory of Oviparous Quadrupeds.

The prefent fpecies is about four inches and a half in length. The head is large in proportion; and the whole upper furface of the animal is befet with fmall tubercles, which in fome parts, efpecially towards the back of the head, and about the tail, are lengthened into a fharpened point. The lower furface is of a pale colour, or nearly white.

THE

# THE BLUE FROG.

## Rana Cærulea.

*R. cærulea, subtus griseo-punctata, pedibus tetradactylis, posterioribus pal-*
*matis.*

*Magnitudo Ranæ temporariæ.*

Blue Frog, speckled beneath with greyish; the feet divided into four toes; the hind-feet webbed.

Size of the common Frog.

Plate

Blue Frogs.

London, Published as the Act directs Dec. 2 & 1789, by I. Debrett.

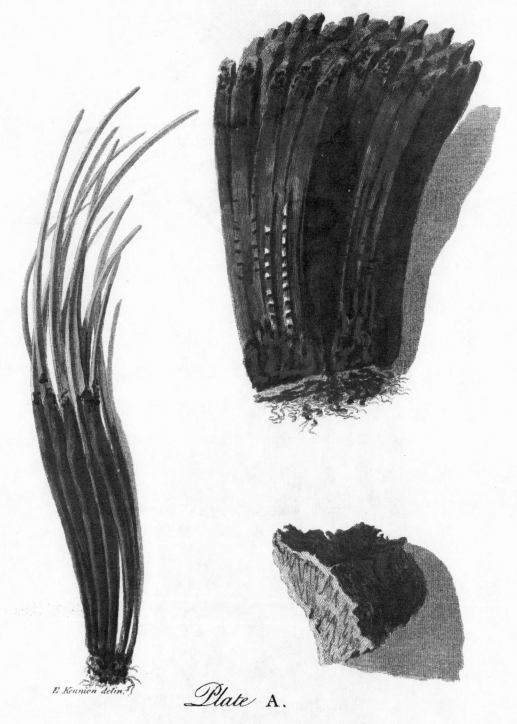

E. Kennion delin.

*Plate* A.

London, Published as the Act directs, Dec.ʳ 29,1789, by I.Debrett.

Plate A. annexed, reprefents a production of which Mr. WHITE has fent no defcription, nor can we give any fatisfactory account of it. This is faid to come from the root of the Yellow Gum Tree, and is a congeries of fcales, cemented, as it were, together by the gum. Whether they are the bafes of the leaves of that tree, or part of a parafitical plant growing upon it, future obfervations muft determine. The latter fuppofition feems to be countenanced by the appearance of fibrous roots at the bafe of this fingular production.

K k                    THE

# THE WHITE HAWK.

## FALCO ALBUS.

*Falco-albus, rostro nigro, cera pedibusque flavis.*

White Hawk, with black beak, cere and legs yellow.

This species, in shape and general appearance, seems very nearly allied to the bird called, in England, the Hen-Harrier, which is the Falco cyaneus of Linnæus. It is very nearly of the same size, and the legs and thighs are of a slender form, as in that species.

The whole plumage is white, without any variegation.

THE

The White Hawke.

S. Stone Delin.

London. Publish'd as the Act directs Dec. 29, 1789, by J Debrett

S. Stone Delin.

The White Vented Crow.

London, Published as the Act directs, Dec. 29, 1789, by I. Debrett.

# THE WHITE-VENTED CROW.

## Corvus Graculinus.

*Corvus niger, remigum rectricumque basi apiceque caudæ albis.*

Black Crow, with the bases of the wing and tail feathers, and the tip of the tail, white.

This bird is about the size of a Magpye; and in shape is not much unlike one, except that the tail is not cuneated, but has all the feathers of equal length. The bird is entirely black, except the vent, the base of the tail feathers, the base of the wing feathers, and the extremity of the tail, which are white. The small part of the white base of the wing feathers gives the appearance of a white spot when the wings are closed. The beak is very strong; the upper mandible slightly emarginated near the tip, and the lower mandible is of a pale colour towards the tip. The *capistrum reversum*, or set of bristles, which are situated forward on the base of the upper mandible in most of the birds of this genus, is not very conspicuous in this species; but the whole habit and general appearance of the bird sufficiently justify its being regarded as a species of Corvus.

K k 2                    THE

# FULIGINOUS PETERIL.

## Procellaria Fuliginosa.

*Procellaria fuliginosa, rostro albido.*

Fuliginous Peteril, with whitish beak.

This is probably nothing more than a variety of the Procellaria Æquinoctialis of Linnæus. Its size is nearly that of a raven. The whole bird is of a deep sooty brown, or blackish; except that on the chin is a small patch of white, running down a little on each side from the lower mandible. The beak is of a yellowish white.

VARIE-

Sterna Stolida

Fuliginous Peteril.

Published as the Act directs Dec: 29, 1789 by F. Debrett.

The Variegated Lizard

Published as the Act directs—Dec. 29.1799 by J. Dobner.

# VARIEGATED LIZARD.

## LACERTA VARIA.

*Lacerta cauda longa carinata, corpore maculis transverfis variis.*

Lizard with long carinated tail, the body tranfverfely variegated.

This Lizard approaches fo extremely near to the Lacerta Monitor of Linnæus, or Monitory Lizard, as to make it doubtful whether it be not in reality a variety of that fpecies. The body is about 15 inches in length, and the tail is confiderably longer. The animal is of a black colour, variegated with yellow marks and ftreaks of different fhapes, and running in a tranfverfe direction. On the legs are rows of tranfverfe round fpots; and on the tail broad alternate bars of black and yellow. In fome fpecimens the yellow was much paler than in others, and nearly whitifh.

THE

# THE LONG-SPINED CHÆTODON.

## CHÆTODON ARMATUS.

*Chætodon albescens, corpore fasciis septem nigris, spinis pinnæ dorsalis sex, tertia longissima.*

Whitish Chætodon, with seven black stripes on the body, six spines on the dorsal fin, the third very long.

This appears to be a new and very elegant species of the genus Chætodon. The total length of the specimen was not more than four inches. The colour a silvery white, darker, and of a bluish tinge, on the back; the transverse fasciæ, or bands, of a deep black; the fins and tail of a pale brown. The third ray or spine of the first dorsal fin is much longer than the rest.

MURICATED

Fig.1.

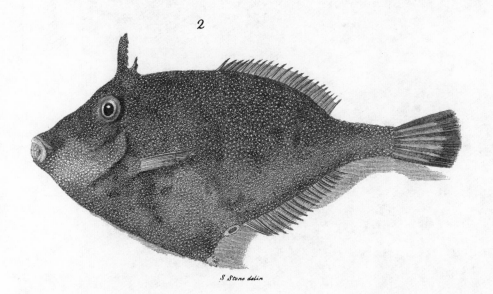

2

S Stone delin

1 The Pungent Chœtedon.    2 Granulated Balistes.

London Published as the Act directs Dec: 29, 1789, by I. Debrett.

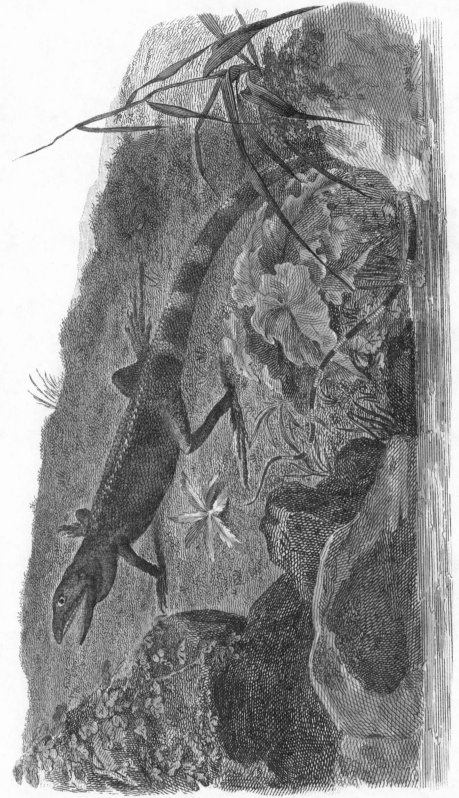

Muricated Lizard, variety.

London Published as the Act directs Dec.8.9.1789 by ID.

# MURICATED LIZARD.

### Lacerta Muricata. Var.

This variety chiefly differs from that reprefented in a preceding Plate, p. 244, in having the head lefs diftinctly acculeated, and the fcales on the body not fo ftrongly carinated.

Figure 1. in the above mentioned Plate is a fmall Snake, about a foot in length, of a white colour, tinged with ferruginous; the body marked by diftant black bands, and each fcale on the back marked with a fmall black fpeck.

SUPERB

# APPENDIX.

## SUPERB WARBLERS.

### MOTACILLA SUPERBA.

*Motacilla nigra, remigibus fuscis, abdomine albo, fronte genisque cæruleis.*

Black Warbler, with the long feathers of the wings brown; the belly white; the forehead and cheeks blue.

This beautiful species is generally found in the state described in the specific character; but it appears to be subject to great variety, two of which are exhibited; the lower and largest specimen having not only more blue on the head than usual, but also a patch of brilliant blue on each side the back, and a mark of reddish brown or orange near the shoulders.

The upper specimen is considerably less than that beneath, and has still more blue upon the head; the beak and legs smaller in proportion, darker in colour, and the latter almost black. The head is crowned with a small crest of bright azure; the cheek, and upper part of the back and wings, are of the same colour; the lower parts of each brown. The outer feathers of the wing whitish, near the shoulder marked with brown. The head, neck, and breast deep black; abdomen white, faintly tinged with dusky. Tail black, highly cuneated. In this bird the blue is most lucid, composed of short, stiff feathers, resembling fish-scales, with shining surfaces; but it has not the beautiful scapulary of prismatic violet-colour, found in the other. Legs, feet, and claws black, and extremely slender.

SMALL

S Stone Delt

*Superb Warblers*

Published as the Act directs Dec.29.1789. by J. Debrett.

*S Stone delin*

*Motacilla♀.*

*London Publish'd as the Act directs Dec 29, 1789, by J. Debrett.*

# MOTACILLA, or WARBLER.

## Motacilla Pusilla.

*M. fusca, subtus pallida, cauda prope apicem fascia fusca.*

Brown Warbler, pale beneath, with a band of brown towards the tip of the tail.

This little bird is about the same size with the Superb Warbler, and has evidently some affinity with that species, but (exclusive of the difference in colour) the tail is not in the least cuneated, but even at the end.

L l SERPENTS.

# S E R P E N T S.

The species of Serpents are much less easily ascertained than those of most other animals; not only on account of the great number of species, but from the innumerable variations to which many of them are subject in point of colour. Amongst those lately received from New Holland, the following are the most remarkable.

SNAKE, No. 1, about three feet and a half in length, of a bluish ash-colour, coated with scales rather large than small, and having nearly the same general proportion with the common English snake, or Coluber Natrix of Linnæus.

SNAKE, No. 2, nearly three feet in length, slender, and of a tawny yellowish colour, with numerous indistinct bars of dark brown, and somewhat irregular, or flexuous, in their disposition.

SNAKE,

*Snake, Nº 1*

London, Published as the Act directs, Dec. 29 1789 by I. Debrett.

J.Stone Delin

Snake, N.º 2

London.Published as the Act directs Dec.29,1789, by I.D.Sowerby.

S.r Stone Delin

Snake, N.º 5

London, Published as the Act directs Dec 29 1789 by T. Debrett.

2

Snakes.

London Publish'd as the Act directs. Dec. 29, 1789. by I. Debrett.

Snake, No. 5, upwards of eight feet in length, of a darkifh colour, varied with fpots and marks of a dull yellow: the belly alfo is of a yellowifh colour. The fcales are fmall in proportion to the fize of the animal; the tail gradually tapers to a point.

S N A K E S. See Plate containing Two Figures.

No. 1. Small, about fourteen inches in length, coated with very fmall fcales, and varied with irregular markings of yellow on a dark brown or blackifh ground. It is probably a young fnake.

No. 2. Small, about fifteen inches in length, and fafciated with alternate bars of black and white.

None of the above Serpents appear to be of a poifonous nature: they belong to the Linnæan genus Coluber; yet No. 5. has fome characters of the genus Anguis.

INSECTS.

## I N S E C T S.

The Infects received from New Holland are:

No. 1. The large Scolopendra, or Centipede (Scolopendra Morfitans Lin.) The fpecimens feemed of a fomewhat darker colour than ufual. See Plate of large Scolopendra, &c. annexed.

No. 2. A fmaller Spider, of a dark colour; with a fmall thorax and large round abdomen, and with the joints of the legs marked with whitifh.

No. 3. A fmall fpecies of Crab, or Cancer, of a pale colour, and which fhould be ranked amongft the Cancri brachyuri in the Linnæan divifion of the genus.

No. 4. A Caterpillar, befet with branchy prickles, and confequently belonging to fome fpecies of Papilio or butterfly.

**LIZARD**

*Fig: 1*

2          3

4

*1 Large Scolopendra,   2 Spider,  3 Crab, 4 Caterpillar.*

*Published as the Act directs Dec: 29, 1789. by I.Debrett.*

# L I Z A R D   E G G S.

With the specimens of Lacertæ, several Eggs were received. They were of an oval shape, and of a livid brown colour, whitish within and not much larger than pease. On opening them the young Lizards were extracted, perfectly formed, and in all respects resembling the Scincoid Lizard, except that the tail was longer in proportion. See Plate of the Skinc-formed Lizard, Fig. 2, 3, and 4, which are given of the natural size. Fig. 1. represents the Eggs in the proportion they bear to the adult specimen.

SMALL

# SMALL PAROQUET.

## Psittacus Pusillus.

*Pſittacus ſubmacrourus viridis, capiſtro rectricumque baſi rubris.*

*Cauda ſubtus flaveſcens, baſi rubra.　Remiges latere interiore fuſcæ.　Magnitudo Pſittaci Porphyrionis.　Roſtrum ſubflaveſcens, ſeu fuſco-flaveſcens　Pedes ſubfuſci.*

Green Paroquet, with ſomewhat lengthened tail; the feathers round the beak, and the baſe of the tail feathers, red.

About the ſize of the violet-coloured Otaheite Paroquet.　The beak is yellowiſh, or browniſh yellow.　The feet duſky.　The tail feathers yellowiſh beneath, and red at the baſe.　The wing feathers duſky on the interior margin.

RED

*The Small Paroquet.*

London Published as the Act directs Dec. 29 1789 by I. Debrett.

*The Red Shoulder'd Paroquet.*

London Published as the Act directs Dec. 29, 1789 by J. Debrett.

# RED SHOULDERED PAROQUET.

## PSITTACUS DISCOLOR.

*Pſittacus macrourus viridis, rectricibus baſi ferrugineis, humeris ſubtus ſanguineis.*

Long tailed Green Parrot, with the tail feathers ferruginous towards the baſe, the ſhoulders blood-red beneath.

This ſpecies, which appears to be new, is of that ſort generally termed Paroquets. It is about ten inches in length: the general colour of the bird a fine green: the outer edge of the wing, near the ſhoulders, blue: the edge of the ſhoulders deep red; the under part the ſame. On the ſides of the body a patch of red: round the beak a few red feathers: long feathers of the wings of a deep blackiſh blue, edged ſlightly with yellow: tail deep ferruginous toward the baſe, each feather becoming blue at the tip: bill and feet pale brown.

CYPRI-

# CYPRINACEOUS LABRUS.

## LABRUS CYPRINACEUS.

*Labrus corpore albefcente.*

Labrus with whitifh body.

The length of this fifh was about fix inches: the colour whitifh: fcales large.

From the bad condition of the fpecimen it was not poffible to make fo accurate an examination of its characters as might have been wifhed.

DOUBT-

*Fig. 1*

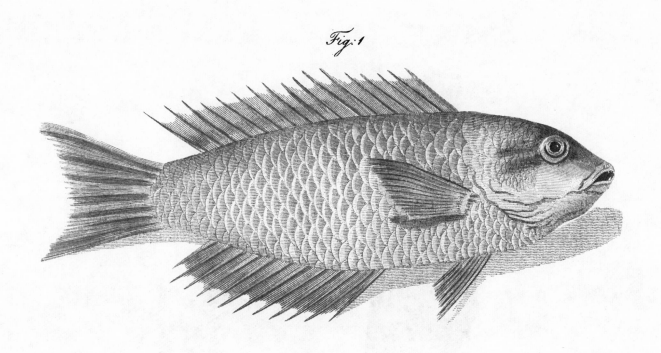

2

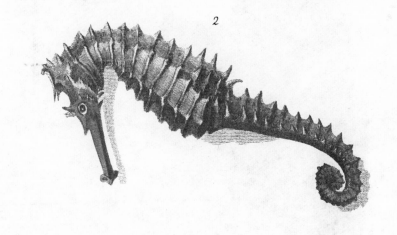

1. *Cyprinaceous Labrus.*          2. *The Hippocampus or Sea-Horse.*

*Published as the Act directs, Dec: 29. 1789. by I. Debrett.*

The Doubtfull Lophius.

Published as the Act directs Dec: 23 1789 by I. Debrett

# DOUBTFUL LOPHIUS.

## LOPHIUS DUBIUS.

*Lophius nigricans, subtus pallidus.*

Blackish Lophius, pale beneath.

This fish was about six inches in length; its general colour a very deep brown, almost black; the mouth extremely wide, and furnished with several rows of slender sharp teeth. On opening it many ova were found, which were very large in proportion to the fish.

M m SOUTHERN

## SOUTHERN COTTUS.

### Cottus Australis.

*Cottus albidus, capite aculeato, corpore fasciis transversis lividis.*

Whitish Cottus, with aculeated head, body marked with transverse livid bands.

This fish did not exceed four inches in length, and is sufficiently described in its specific character.

**DOUBTFUL**

*Fig. 1.*

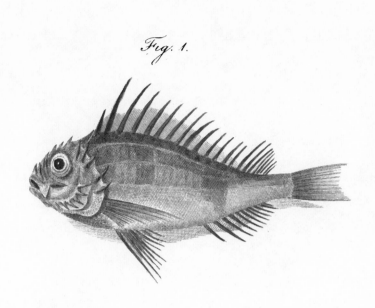

2

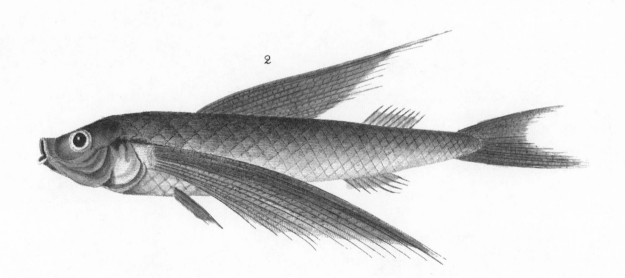

*1 The Southern Cottus.    2 The Flying-Fish.*

London, Published as the Act directs Dec.29,1789. by I. Debrett.

## DOUBTFUL, or COMPRESSED SPARUS.

### SPARUS? COMPRESSUS.

*Sparus? Argenteus, compreſſus.*

Sparus? Of a ſilvery colour, the body much compreſſed.

The ſpecimen figured was nearly ſix inches in length; the colour a ſilvery white; ſcales of a moderate ſize, and the body much compreſſed. It ſeemed to poſſeſs the characters of a Sparus, though they could ſcarce be determined with ſufficient certainty, from the bad condition of the ſpecimen.

# FASCIATED MULLET.

## MULLUS FASCIATUS.

*Mullus subflavescens, fasciis longitudinalis fuscis.*

Pale yellowish Mullet, with longitudinal brown bands.

**Length about five inches : scales large.**

The

*London Published as the Act directs Dec 29 1789, by P Debrett.*

*Fig.1*

2

*1 Fasciated Mullet.    2 Doubtful Sparus.*

The Non-defcript Animals of New South Wales occupied a great deal of Mr. WHITE's attention, and he preferved feveral fpecimens of them in fpirits, which arrived in England in a very perfect ftate. There was no perfon to whom thefe could be given with fo much propriety as Mr. Hunter, he, perhaps, being moft capable of examining accurately their ftructure, and making out their place in the fcale of animals; and it is to him that we are indebted for the following obfervations upon them; in which the anatomical ftructure is purpofely avoided, as being little calculated for the generality of readers of a work of this kind.

It is much to be wifhed that thofe gentlemen who are defirous of obliging their friends, and promoting the ftudy of Natural Hiftory, by fending home fpecimens, would endeavour to procure all the information they can relating to fuch fpecimens as they may collect, more efpecially animals. The fubjects themfelves may be valuable, and may partly explain their connection with thofe related to them, fo as, in fome meafure, to eftablifh their place in nature, but they cannot do it entirely; they

only

only give us the form and conftruction, but leave us in other refpects to conjecture, many of them requiring further obfervations relative to their œconomy. A neglect in procuring this information has left us, almoft to this day, very ignorant of that part of the Natural Hiftory of animals which is the moft interefting. The Opoffum is a remarkable inftance of this. There is fomething in the mode of propagation in this animal that deviates from all others; and although known in fome degree to be extraordinary, yet it has never been attempted, where opportunity offered, to complete the inveftigation. I have often endeavoured to breed them in England; I have bought a great many, and my friends have affifted me by bringing them or fending them alive, yet never could get them to breed; and although poffeffed of a great many facts refpecting them, I do not believe my information is fufficient to complete the fyftem of propagation in this clafs. In collecting animals, even the name given by the natives, if poffible, fhould be known; for a name, to a Naturalift, fhould mean nothing but that to which it is annexed, having no allufion to any thing elfe; for when it has, it divides the idea. This obfervation applies particularly to the animals

which

which have come from New Holland; they are, upon the whole, like no other that we yet know of; but as they have parts in some respect similar to others, names will naturally be given to them expressive of those similarities; which has already taken place: for instance, one is called the Kangaroo Rat, but which should not be called either Kangaroo or Rat; I have therefore adopted such names as can only be appropriated to each particular animal, conveying no other idea.

Animals admit of being divided into great classes; but will not so distinctly admit of subdivision, without interfering with each other. Thus the class called Quadruped is so well marked, that even the whole is justly placed in the same class. Birds the same; Amphibia (as they are called) the same; and so of fish, &c.; but when we are subdividing these great classes into their different tribes, genera, and species, then we find a mixture of properties; some species of one tribe partaking of similar properties with a species of another tribe.

*Of*

## Of the KANGAROO.

This animal (probably from its fize) was the principal one taken notice of in this ifland; the only parts at firft brought home were fome fkins and fculls; and I was favoured with one of the fculls from Sir Jofeph Banks. As the teeth of fuch animals as are already known, in fome degree point out their digeftive organs, I was in hopes that I might have been able to form an opinion of the particular tribe of the animals already known, to which the Kangaroo fhould belong; but the teeth did not accord with thofe of any one clafs of animals I was acquainted with, therefore I was obliged to wait with patience till I could get the whole: and in many of its other organs the deviation from other animals is not lefs than in its teeth. In its mode of propagation it very probably comes nearer to the Opoffum than any other animal; although it is not at all fimilar to it in other refpects. Its hair is of a greyifh brown colour, fimilar to that of the wild rabbit of Great Britain, is thick and long when the animal is old; but it is

late

*A Kangaroo.*

London Published as the Act directs Dec: 29. 1789 by J.Debrett.

late in growing, and when only begun to grow, it is like a ſtrong down ; however, in ſome parts it begins earlier than others, as about the mouth, &c. In all of the young Kangaroos yet brought home (although ſome as large as a full grown cat), they have all the marks of a fœtus ; no hair ; ears lapped cloſe over the head ; no marks on the feet of having been uſed in progreſſive motion. The large nail on the great toe ſharp at the point ; and the ſides of the mouth united ſomething like the eye-lids of a puppy juſt whelped, having only a paſſage at the anterior part. This union of the two lips on the ſides is of a particular ſtructure, it wears off as it grows up, and by the time it is of the ſize of a ſmall rabbit, diſappears.

## Of the Teeth of the Kangaroo.

The teeth of this animal are ſo ſingular, that it is impoſſible, from them, to ſay what tribe it is of. There is a faint mixture in them, correſponding to thoſe of different tribes of animals.

Take the mouth at large, reſpecting the ſituation of the teeth, it would claſs in ſome degree with the *Scalpris*

N n *dentata* ;

*dentata**; in a fainter degree with the Horfe, and Ruminants; and with regard to the line of direction of all the teeth, they are very like thofe of the *Scalpris dentata*. The fore teeth in the upper jaw agree with the Hog; and thofe in the lower, in number, with the *Scalpris dentata*; but with regard to pofition, and probably ufe, with the Hog. The grinders would feem to be a mixture of Hog and Ruminants; the enamel on their external and grinding furfaces, rather formed into feveral cutting edges, than points. There are fix incifors in the upper jaw, and only two in the lower; but thefe two are fo placed as to oppofe thofe of the upper; five grinders in each fide of each jaw, the moft anterior of which is fmall. The proportions of fome of the parts of this animal bear no analogy to what is common in moft others. The difproportions in the length between the fore legs and the hind are very confiderable; alfo in their ftrength; yet perhaps not more than in the Jerboa. This difproportion between the fore legs and the hind is principally in the more adult; for in the very young, about the fize of a half grown rat, they are pretty

* This tribe includes the Rat, &c.

well

well proportioned; which fhews that at the early period of life they do not ufe progreffive motion. The proportions of the different parts of which the hind legs are compofed, are very different. The thigh of the Kangaroo is extremely fhort, and the leg is very long. The hind foot is uncommonly long; on which, to appearance, are placed three toes, the middle toe by much the largeft and the ftrongeft, and looks fomething like the long toe of an Oftrich. The outer toe is next in fize; and what appears to be the inner toe, is two, inclofed in one fkin or covering.

The great toe nail much refembles that of an Oftrich, as alfo the nail of the outer toe; and the inner, which appears to be but one toe, has two fmall nails, which are bent and fharp.

From the heel, along the under fide of the foot and toe, the fkin is adapted for walking upon.

The fore legs, in the full grown Kangaroo, are fmall in proportion to the hind, or the fize of the animal; the feet, or hands, are alfo fmall; the fkin on the palm is different from that on the back of the hand and fingers. There are five toes or fingers on this foot; the middle rather the largeft; the others become very gradually fhorter, and are all nearly of

N n 2

the

the fame fhape. The nails are fharp, fit for holding. The tail is long in the old; but not fo long, in proportion to the fize of the animal, in the young. It would feem to keep pace with the growth of the hind legs, which are the inftruments of progreffive motion in this animal; and which would alfo fhew that the tail is a kind of fecond inftrument in this action.

The under lip is divided in the middle, each fide rounded off at the divifion.

It has two clavicles; but they are fhort, fo that the fhoulders are not thrown out.

WHITE-

*White-Jointed Spider*

London, Published as the Act directs Dec 29. 1789. by I. Debrett.

## WHITE JOINTED SPIDER.

The species of Spiders, unless seen recent, and in the utmost state of perfection, are not easily distinguished. The present species is most remarkable for the lucid surface of its thorax and legs, which latter are furnished with several long moveable spines, that may be either elevated or depressed at the will of the animal: this however is not peculiar to the present species, but is seen in some others. The eyes are eight in number, and are arranged in the same manner as those of the great American Spider, or Aranea Avicularia of Linnæus. The colour of this Spider is a clear chesnut brown, except the body, which is a pale brown, with a very deep or blackish fascia on its upper part, reaching about half way down. The orifice at the tip of each fang is very visible by so slight a magnifying power as that of a glass of two inches focus: this Spider is therefore of the number of those which poison their prey before they destroy it.

The Plate exhibits the back and front view, of the natural size. A. the order in which the Spines are placed. The lesser a. two Spines enlarged, shewing the Bracket on which they turn, and the Groove or Niche they shut into when closed. C. the Fangs magnified.

WHA

## WHA TAPOAU ROO.

This animal is about the fize of a Racoon, is of a dark grey colour on the back, becoming rather lighter on the fides, which terminates in a rich brown on the belly. The hair is of two kinds, a long hair, and a kind of fur, and even the long hair, at the roots, is of the fur kind.

The head is fhort; the eyes rather prominent; the ears broad, not peaked.

The teeth refemble thofe of all the animals from that country I have hitherto feen.

The incifors are not continued into the grinders by intermediate teeth, although there are two teeth in the intermediate fpace in the upper jaw, and one in the lower. The incifors are fimilar to thofe of the Kangaroo, and fix in number in the upper jaw, oppofed by two in the lower, which have an oblique furface extending fome diftance from their edge, fo as to increafe the furface of contact.

There are two cufpidati on each fide in the upper jaw, and only one in the lower; five grinders on each fide of each jaw,

White Tapoa Roo.

Published as the Act directs Dec. 19, 1789 by J. White.

Mortimer delin.

jaw, the firſt rather pointed, the others appear nearly of the ſame ſize, and quadrangular in their ſhape, with a hollow running acroſs their baſe from the outſide to the inner, which is of ſome depth; and another which croſſes it, but not ſo deep, dividing the grinding ſurface into four points.

On the fore foot there are five toes, the inner the ſhorteſt, reſembling, in a ſlight degree, a thumb. The hind foot reſembles a hand, or that of the Monkey and Opoſſum, the great toe having no nail, and oppoſing the whole ſole of the foot, which is bare. The nails on the other toes, both of the fore and hind foot, reſemble, in a ſmall degree, thoſe of the cat, being broad and covered; and the laſt bone of the toe has a projection on the under ſide, at the articulation. Each nail has, in ſome degree, a ſmall ſheath, covering its baſe when drawn up.

The tail is long, covered with long hair, except the under ſurface of that half towards the termination, of the breadth of half an inch, becoming broader near the tip or termination: this ſurface is covered with a ſtrong cuticle, and is adapted for laying hold.

A DINGO,

## A DINGO, or DOG, of NEW SOUTH WALES.

This animal is a variety of the Dog, and, like the shep-herd's dog in most countries, approaches near to the original of the species, which is the wolf, but is not so large, and does not stand so high on its legs.

The ears are short, and erect, the tail rather bushy; the hair, which is of a reddish dun colour, is long and thick, but strait. It is capable of barking, although not so rea-dily as the European dogs; is very ill-natured and vicious, and snarls, howls, and moans, like dogs in common.

Whether this is the only Dog in New South Wales, and whether they have it in a wild state, is not mentioned; but I should be inclined to believe they had no other; in which case it will constitute the wolf of that country; and that which is domesticated is only the wild dog tamed, without having yet produced a variety, as in some parts of America.

TAPOA

*Dog of New South Wales.*

London, Published as the Act directs Dec. 29, 1789, by J. Debrett.

A Tapoa Tafa.

Published as the Act directs Dec 29 1789 by I. Debrett.

# THE TAPOA TAFA, or TAPHA.

This animal is the fize of a rat, and, has very much the appearance of the martin cat, but hardly fo long in the body in proportion to its fize.

The head is flat forwards, and broad from fide to fide, efpecially between the eyes and ears; the nofe is peaked, and projecting beyond the teeth, which makes the upper jaw appear to be confiderably longer than the lower; the eyes are pretty large; the ears broad, efpecially at their bafe, not becoming regularly narrower to a point, nor with a very fmooth edge, and having a fmall procefs on the concave, or inner furface, near to the bafe. It has long whifkers from the fides of the cheeks, which begin forwards, near the nofe, by fmall and fhort hairs, and become longer and ftronger as they approach the eyes. It has very much the hair of a rat, to which it is fimilar in colour; but near to the fetting on of the tail, it is of a lighter brown, forming a broad ring round it. The fore feet are fhorter than the hind, but much in the fame proportion as thofe of the rat; the hind feet are

O o                                         more

more flexible. There are five toes on the fore feet, the middle the largeſt, falling off on each ſide nearly equally; but the fore, or inner toe, is rather ſhorteſt: they are thin from ſide to ſide, the nails are pretty broad, laterally, and thin at their baſe; not very long but ſharp; the animal walks on its whole palm, on which there is no hair. The hind feet are pretty long, and have five toes; that which anſwers to our great toe is very ſhort, and has no nail; the next is the longeſt in the whole, falling gradually off to the outer toe; the ſhape of the hind toes is the ſame as in the fore feet, as are likewiſe the nails; it walks nearly on the whole foot. The tail is long and covered with long hair, but not all of the ſame colour.

The teeth of this creature are different from any other animal yet known. The mouth is full of teeth. The lower jaw narrow in compariſon to the upper, more eſpecially backwards, which allows of much broader grinders in this jaw than in the lower, and which occaſions the grinders in the upper jaw to project conſiderably over thoſe in the lower. In the middle the cuſpidati oppoſe one another, the upper piercers, or holders, go behind thoſe of the lower; the ſecond claſs of inciſors in the lower jaw overtop thoſe of

the

the upper while the two firſt in the lower go within, or behind thoſe of the upper. In the upper jaw, before the holders, there are four teeth on each ſide, three of which are pointed, the point ſtanding on the inner ſurface; and the two in front are longer, ſtand more obliquely forwards, and appear to be appropriated for a particular uſe. The holders are a little way behind the laſt fore teeth, to allow thoſe of the lower jaw to come between. They are pretty long, the cuſpidati on each ſide become longer and larger towards the grinders; they are points or cones placed on a broad baſe.

There are four grinders on each ſide, the middle two the largeſt, the laſt the leaſt; their baſe is a triangle of the ſcalenus kind, or having one angle obtuſe and two acute. Their baſe is compoſed of two ſurfaces, an inner and an outer, divided by proceſſes or points: it is the inner that the grinders of the lower jaw oppoſe, when the mouth is regularly ſhut. The lower jaw has three fore teeth, or inciſors, on each ſide; the firſt conſiderably the largeſt, projecting obliquely forwards; the other two of the ſame kind, but ſmaller, the laſt the ſmalleſt.

The holder in this jaw is not ſo large as in the upper jaw,

and

and clofe to the incifors. There are three cufpidati, the middle one the largeft, the laft the leaft; thefe are cones ftanding on their bafe, but not on the middle, rather on the anterior fide. There are four grinders, the two middle the largeft, and rather quadrangular, each of which has a high point or cone on the outer edge, with a fmaller, and three more diminutive on the inner edge. It is impoffible to fay critically, what the various forms of thefe teeth are adapted for from the general principles of teeth. In the front we have what may divide and tear off; behind thofe, there are holders or deftroyers; behind the latter, fuch as will affift in mafhing, as the grinders of the lion, and other carniverous animals; and laft of all, grinders, to divide parts into fmaller portions, as in the graminiverous tribe: the articulation of the jaw in fome degree admits of all thofe motions.

THE

# THE TAPOA TAFA.

Another animal of the fame fpecies; only differing from the Tapoa Tafa in its external colour, and in being fpotted.

THE

## THE POTO ROO, or KANGAROO RAT.

The head is flat fideways, but not fo much fo as the true Scalpris Dentata. The ears are neither long nor fhort, but much like thofe of a moufe in proportion to the fize of the animal.

The fore legs are fhort in comparifon to the hind. There are four toes on the fore feet, the two middle are long, and nearly of equal lengths, with long narrow nails, flightly bent; the two fide toes are fhort, and nearly equal in fize, but the outer rather the largeft. From the nails on the two middle toes, one would fuppofe that the animal burrowed. Their hind legs are long, and it is in their power to ftand either on the whole foot, or on the toes only.

On the hind legs are three toes, the middle one large, and the two fide ones fhort. The tail is long. The hair on the body is rather thin; it is of two kinds, a fur, and a long hair, which laft becomes exterior from its length. The fur is the fineft, and is compofed of ferpentine hairs; the long hair is ftronger, and is alfo ferpentine, for more than two

thirds

*A Poto Roo*

Published as the Act directs Dec. 29.1789. by J. Debrett.

thirds of its length near to the ſkin, and terminates in a pretty ſtrong pointed end, like the quill of a hedge hog. It is of a browniſh grey colour, ſomething like the brown, or grey rabbit, with a tinge of a greeniſh yellow.

It has a pouch on the lower part of the belly, the mouth opens forwards, and the cavity extends backwards to the pubis, where it terminates ; on the abdominal ſurface of this pouch are four nipples or two pair, each pair placed very near the other.

THE

## THE HEPOONA ROO.

This animal is of the fize of a fmall rabbit : it has a broad
flat body, the head a good deal refembles that of the fquirrel : the eyes are full, prominent, and large : the ears broad
and thin : its legs fhort, and its tail very long. Between
the fore and hind legs, on each fide, is placed a doubling of
the fkin of the fide, which, when the legs are extended
laterally, is as it were pulled out, forming a broad lateral wing
or fin, and when the legs are made ufe of in walking, this
fkin, by its elafticity, is drawn clofe to the fide of the animal,
and forms a kind of ridge, on which the hair has a peculiar
appearance. In this refpect it is very fimilar to the flying
fquirrel of America.

It has five toes on each fore foot, with fharp nails. The
hind foot has alfo five toes, but differs confiderably
from the fore foot ; one of the toes may be called a thumb,
having a broad nail, fomething like that of the Monkey or
Opoffum : what anfwers to the fore and middle toes are
united in one common covering, and appear like one toe

with

Hapoona Roo

Published as the Act directs Dec. 29 1789, by J. Debrett.

C. Catton Jun. Delin.

with two nails; this is somewhat similar to the Kangaroo, the two other toes are in the common form, these four nails are sharp like those on the fore foot. This formation of the foot is well calculated for holding any thing while it is moving its body, or its fore foot, to other parts, a property belonging (probably) to all animals who move from the hind parts; such as the Monkey, Mocock, Mongoose, Opossum, Parrot, Leech, &c.

Its hair is very thick and long, making a very fine fur, especially on the back. It is of a dark brown grey on the upper part, a light white grey on the lower side of what may be termed the wing, and white on the under surface, from the neck to the parts adjacent to the anus.

P p                    FEATHER

## FEATHER OF THE CASSOWARY.

The feathers of the New Holland Caſſowary are of a remarkable conſtruction ; and may, perhaps, be more eaſily delineated than deſcribed. The ſpecimen is figured of the exact ſize, and conſiſts of two long ſlender ſhafts, extremely flaccid, iſſuing from one ſmall quill. The feather at the baſe of each ſhaft is cloſely ſet, ſoft, and floſſy, widening and growing harder gradually to the tip, reſembling the texture of a dried plant.

The colour browniſh aſh, whitening towards the quill.

It ſeems incapable of reſiſting water, or of holding air. This circumſtance in the feather, added to the great pliability of the ſhaft, is a moſt admirable proviſion for a bird whoſe ſafety is entruſted ſolely to its feet.

FISH

*Fish Hooks of* *New S.º Wales.*

A

*A Feather of the Cassowary*

B

E. Kennion delin.

London, Published as the Act directs, Dec.ʳ 29. 1789, by J. Debrett.

## FISH HOOKS of NEW SOUTH WALES.

Fig. A. reprefents a hook of the fame fize, formed of a hard black wood-like fubftance, neatly executed, and finifhed with a fmall knob to affift in faftening it to the line; it is well mounted: the line confifts of two ftrands very evenly laid, and twifted hard; made with a graffy fubftance dark in colour, and nearly as fine as raw filk: the length of it is fhewn by the top of the rod being broken off.

Fig. B. is a hook of mother of pearl, formed by an internal volute of fome fpiral fhell, affifted by grinding it a little on one fide only: the point of this hook, as well as of the former, feems, to an European, to turn fo much as to render them almoft ufelefs.

Pp 2                                        IMPLEMENTS

## IMPLEMENTS of NEW SOUTH WALES.

AA. is a War Spear, formed of a light reed-like substance produced by the Yellow Gum Tree, vide p. 235, which if the ends marked with the letters were joined together, would shew its full length: the long pointed head is of hard wood, of a reddish colour, and is fastened into the shaft in the firmest manner by a cement of the yellow gum only.

B. is a Stick, at one end of which is a small peg fastened with the same cement, and forming a hook: the other end is ornamented with the shell of the Limpet or Patella, stuck on with the gum; and, thus constructed, it is used to throw the spear—in this manner: The shell end of the stick being held in the right hand, and the spear poised in the left, the end of the hook at B. is inserted into a hollow at the foot of the spear at D. and thus thrown with a force similar to that of a stone from a sling: this is shewn more particularly in a reduced figure at the upper part of the Plate, *a. b.*

CC. is a Spear or Gig, of a substance similar to the former, for striking fish in the water: the true length of which will be

known

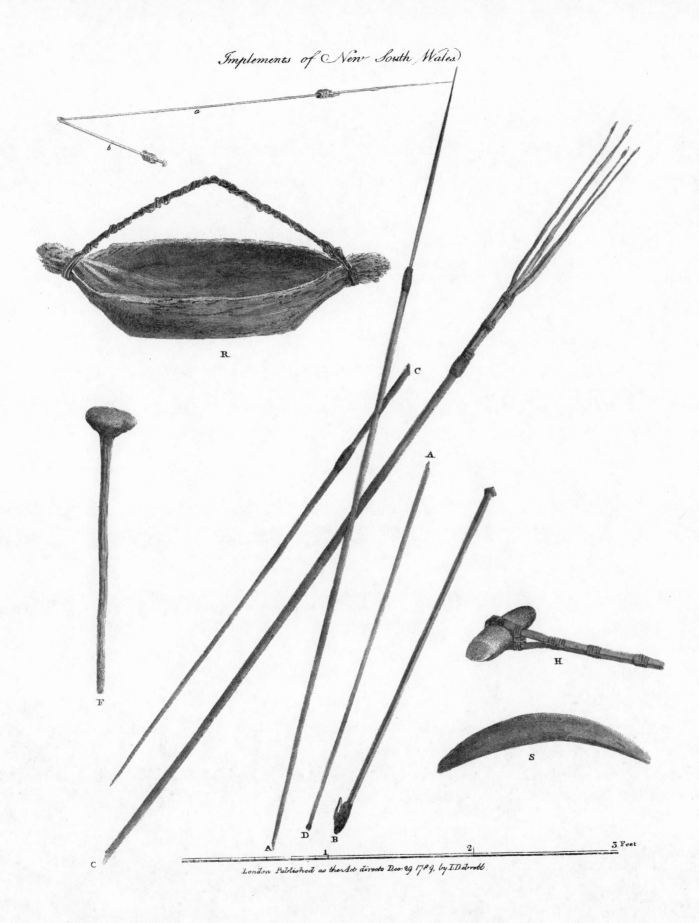

Implements of New South Wales.

London Published as the Act directs Dec. 29. 1789. by I. Debrett

known by fuppofing the parts joined together at the lettered ends : the fhaft confifts of two pieces, a large and a fmall one, joined by the gum: and the head is compofed of four fticks inferted into the fhaft with gum, and tied together above with flips of bark, which are afterwards tightened by little wedges, driven within the bandage: each of thefe fticks is terminated by the tooth of a fifh, very fharp, and ftuck on by a lump of the gum cement: the fhaft of this inftrument is punctured in many places with very fmall holes, to the pith in the centre, but for what purpofe is not known.

H. is a Hatchet, of which the head is a very hard black pebble ftone, rubbed down at one end to an edge; the handle is a ftick of elaftic wood, fplit, which being bent round the middle of the ftone, and the extremities brought together, is ftrongly bound with flips of bark, and holds the head very firmly, as fmiths chiffels are held by hazel fticks in Europe.

S. is a kind of blunt Sword, of hard wood, like the head of the fpear A.

F. feems to be an inftrument of offence; it is a ftick of the natural growth, with the bark on; the root of which is cut round into a large knob; the end F. is made rough with notches, that it may be held more firmly in the hand.

R. is

R. is a Basket, formed by a single piece of a brown fibrous bark. This separated whole from the tree is gathered up at each end in folds, and bound in that form by withes, which also make the handle. The Basket is patched in several places with yellow gum, from which it appears to have been sometimes used for carrying water.

These Implements are drawn from exact measurements, and fitted to a scale of three feet, inserted at the foot of the Plate.

FLYING-

# APPENDIX.

## FLYING-FISH.

### EXOCÆTUS VOLITANS.

This fish is so well known to Naturalists, and is so frequently seen in every voyage, that it is unnecessary to give a particular description of it.  See Plate page 266.

## SEA-HORSE, OR HIPPOCAMPUS.

This animal, like the Flying-fish, being commonly known, a description is not necessary.  It is the Syngnathus Hippocampus of Linnæus.  See Plate page 264.

## GRANULATED BALISTES.

### BALISTES GRANULATA.

*Balistes pinna dorsali anteriore biradiata, corpore granoso.*
*Valde affinis B. Papilloso Linnæi.  Corpus albido-cinerascens, papillis parvulis aspersum.*
*Thorax velut in sacculum productus.*

Balistes with the anterior dorsal fin two-spined, and the body covered with granules.
This fish is extremely nearly allied to the Balistes Papillosus of Linnæus.
    The body is of a whitish ash-colour, and covered with small papillæ.
The thorax as it were produced into a Sacculus beneath.  See Plate page 254.

SOUTHERN

## SOUTHERN ATHERINE.

### ATHERINA AUSTRALIS.

*Au vere diſtincta ab A. Hepſeto Lin.?*
*A. pinna ani radiis ſedecim.*
*Corpus ſubferrugineum.*    *Cauda forficata.*    *Faſcia lateralis nitidiſſima.*

Doubtful whether really diſtinct from the A. Hepſetus of Linnæus.
Atherine with the anal fin furniſhed with ſixteen rays.
The body is of a ſubferruginous caſt.   The tail forked.   The lateral line
     extremely bright.

## THE TOBACCO-PIPE FISH.

This fiſh is ſo well known, that a particular deſcription
need not be given.   It is the Fiſtularia Tabacaria of Linnæus.

## REMORA, or SUCKING-FISH.

### The Echeneis Remora of Linnæus.

This fiſh, like the preceding, does not require a particular deſcription; is met with in moſt ſeas, and poſſeſſes powerfully the faculty of adheſion, by the top of the head: frequently to ſhips bottoms, whence it is named Remora.

NEW

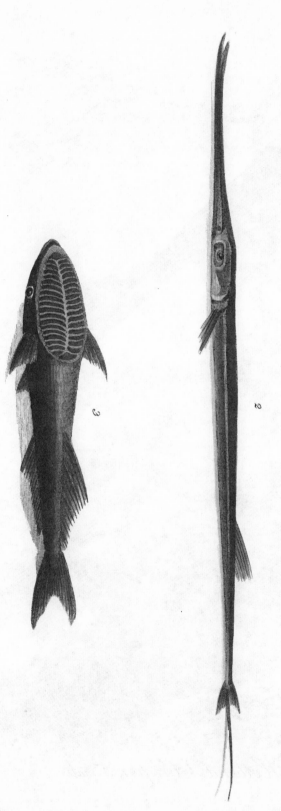

1 The Atherine. 2 The Tobacco Pipe Fish. 3 The Remora.

London. Published as the Act directs Dec. 29, 1789 by I. Debrett.

Fig. 1

2

3

*New Holland Creeper, Female.*

London Publish'd as the Act directs Dec 29. 1789 by F.Debrett.

## NEW HOLLAND CREEPER, Female.

The general colours of the female are the fame as in the male, but lefs vivid ; nor has it the white markings on the front of the head and over the eye, but on the cheeks only. The back and breaft are black without white interfperfions. The abdomen black, ftreaked with dufky white ; the yellow on the wings and tail inclining to an olivaceous green, the feathers in the latter obtufely pointed. A fcapulary of brown adorns the fhoulders, terminating in a lanceolate fhape, half way down the back.

In this bird the bill is longer, and the legs and general form ftouter than the male.

Q q                                    DEATHS

## DEATHS between December 1786 and July 1788.

*On the Passage.*

| | |
|---|---:|
| Marines - - - - - - - - - - - - - - - - | 1 |
| Marines Wives - - - - - - - - - - - - - | 1 |
| Marines Children - - - - - - - - - - - - | 1 |

*After the Landing.*

| | |
|---|---:|
| Marines - - - - - - - - - - - - - - - | 3 |
| Marines Children - - - - - - - - - - - - | 2 |
| Total | 8 |

*On the Passage.*

| | |
|---|---:|
| Male Convicts - - - - - - - - - - - - - | 36 |
| Female Convicts - - - - - - - - - - - - | 4 |
| Convicts Children - - - - - - - - - - - | 5 |

*After the Landing.*

| | |
|---|---:|
| Male Convicts, including two murdered - - - - - - | 22 |
| Female Ditto - - - - - - - - - - - - - | 8 |
| Convicts Children - - - - - - - - - - - | 9 |
| Total | 84 |

| | |
|---|---:|
| Executed, by a sentence of the Criminal Court - - - - - | 4 |
| Condemned to death by the Court, but pardoned by the Governor - - - - - - - - - - - - - | 6 |
| Missing, including one Female - - - - - - - - - | 9 |

# ESTABLISHMENT OF NEW SOUTH WALES.

## CIVIL DEPARTMENT.

ARTHUR PHILLIP, Efq.——Governor in Chief, Captain General &c. &c.

ROBERT ROSS, Efq.——Lieut. Governor, and Commander of the Troops.

Rev. RICHARD JOHNSON—Chaplain.

ANDREW MILLER——Commiffary, and Secretary to his Excellency.

DAVID COLLINS————Judge Advocate.

JOHN WHITE————Surgeon.

D. CONSIDOR————Firft Affiftant Ditto.

THOMAS ARNDELL————Second Ditto Ditto.

WILLIAM BALMAIN————Third Ditto Ditto.

WILLIAM BREWER————Provoft Marſhal.

H. T. AUGUSTUS ALT, Efq. Surveyor of Lands.

## MILITARY DEPARTMENT.

Captains————JAMES CAMPBELL.

———— JOHN SHEA.

Capt. Lieutenants ———— MEREDITH.

———— WATKIN TENCH.

Firft Lieutenants——G. JOHNSTON.

———— JOHN CRESSWELL.

———— ROBERT KELLOW.

———— JOHN POULDEN.

———— JOHN JOHNSTON.

———— JAMES MAITLAND SHAIRP.

———— THOMAS TIMMINS.

———— THOMAS DAVY.

Second Lieutenants ———— CLARKE.

———— WILLIAM FEDDY.

———— JOHN LONG, Adjutant.

Firft Lieutenant————JAMES FURZAR, Quartermaſter.

Firft Lieutenant————JAMES MAXWELL, } Returning to Europe for the recovery of their health.

Second Lieutenant—— COLLINS, }

# A
# DIARY

OF THE

## Winds, Weather, Temperature of the Air, &c.

WITH THE DIFFERENT

## LATITUDES AND LONGITUDES,

IN A

# VOYAGE

TO

## PORT JACKSON, NEW SOUTH WALES.

DIARY of the Winds, Weather, Temperature of the Air, &c. with the different Latitudes and Longitudes.

## MAY 1787.

| Days. | Winds. | Weather. | Latitude in | Long. in | Longitude per Time-keeper, and Lunar Ob. | Therm. | Barom. | Variation per Az. and Am. | REMARKS. |
|---|---|---|---|---|---|---|---|---|---|
| 13 | S. E. | Clear | — | — | — | 52 0 | — | — | { Squally in the evening, and a high swell. |
| 14 | S. E. | Clear | — | — | — | 52 0 | — | — | Some small rain. |
| 15 | Variable | Clear | 49 49 N. | 4 49 W. | — | 52 0 | 30 8 | — | Strong breezes, at times rain. |
| 16 | E. S. E. | Cloudy | 48 47 | 6 26 | 4 33 | 54 0 | 29 9 | — | Strong breezes. |
| 17 | S. S. W. | Rain | 49 0 | 7 30 | 6 12 | 59 0 | 30 0 | — | |
| 18 | S. W. | Clear | 49 2 | 8 56 | 7 51 | 60 0 | 30 8 | — | Little wind. |
| 19 | South | Cloudy | 48 33 | 10 43 | 9 21 | 58 0 | 29 44 | — | Much rain. |
| 20 | W. N. W. | Foggy | 47 37 | 11 36 | — | 60 0 | 30 20 | — | Light airs of wind. |

| | Wind | Weather | | | | | | | Remarks |
|---|---|---|---|---|---|---|---|---|---|
| 21 | W. S. W. | Clear | 47  2 N. | 11 38 W. | 11 45 W. / 11 40 | 60  0 | 30 12 | — | |
| 22 | W. by N. | Clear | 47  2 | 11 11 | 11 35 | 63  0 | 30 21 | — | Fresh gales in the evening. |
| 23 | N. N. W. | Clear | 45 42 | 11 23 | 11 2 | 57  0 | 30 14 | — | Some rain in the evening. |
| 24 | N. N. W. | Clear | 44 15 | 12 12 | 10 38 | 59  0 | 29 93 | — | Strong gales, and high sea. |
| 25 | North | Clear | 42 24 | 13 9 | 11 30 | 60  0 | 30 25 | | |
| 26 | N. E. | Cloudy | 40 42 | 13 59 | 12 20 | 61  0 | 30 12 | 20 17 / 20 36 | |
| 27 | N. E. | Clear | 38 44 | 14 59 | 12 46 | 64  0 | 30 26 | — | Saw some Gulf weed. |
| 28 | N. E. | Cloudy | 36  9 | 16 24 | 13 52 | 61  0 | 30 15 | — | { Fresh gales, with a following sea. |
| 29 | N. E. | Cloudy | 33 56 | 16 24 | — | 63  0 | 30 10 | — | { Ditto weather: no observation. |
| 30 | N. E. | Clear | 32 18 | 15 50 | 16 30 | 65  0 | 30 3 | — | { Saw the Deserter Isles, also some turtle. |
| 31 | North | Clear | 30 47 | 15 16 | — | 70  0 | 30 0 | — | Mercury in the Sun 98. |

## JUNE 1787.

| Days. | Winds. | Weather. | Latitude in | Long. in | Longitude per Time-keeper, and Lunar Ob. | Therm. | Barom. | Variation per Az. and Am. | REMARKS. |
|---|---|---|---|---|---|---|---|---|---|
| 1 | S. W. | Clear | 29 52 N. | 15 18 W. | 15 17 W. | 71 0 | 30 3 / 30 2 | — | Little wind: faw many small fish. |
| 2 | Calm | Clear | 29 40 | 15 24 | — | 74 0 | — | 18 27 0 / 18 0 | Anchored in Santa Cruz Road, in the Island of Teneriffe. |
| 3 | S. W. | Clear | — | — | — | 73 0 | — | — | |
| 4 | S. W. | Clear | — | — | — | 74 0 | — | — | |
| 5 | S. W. | Cloudy | — | — | — | 72 0 | — | — | Still at anchor. |
| 6 | South | Clear | — | — | — | 75 0 | — | — | |
| 7 | S. by E. | Clear | — | — | — | 75 0 | — | — | |

| Day | Wind | Weather | | | | | | | Remarks |
|---|---|---|---|---|---|---|---|---|---|
| 8 | S. W. | Cloudy | — | — | — | 73 0 | — | — | } Still at anchor. |
| 9 | S. E. | Cloudy | — | — | — | 75 0 | — | — | } |
| 10 | Variable | Cloudy | — | — | — | 75 0 | — | — | { We failed ; very little wind, an Iris round the Sun at equal distance. |
| 11 | Calm | Clear | — | — | — | 76 0 | — | — | |
| 12 | Calm | Clear | — | — | — | 78 0 | — | — | { Current setting us to the westward. |
| 13 | South | Cloudy | 26 33 N. | 17 11 W. | — | 73 0 | 29 98 | — | Sea luminous. |
| 14 | N. E. | Cloudy | 25 8 | 18 29 | — | 72 0 | 30 0 | — | |
| 15 | N. E. | Cloudy | 23 24 | 19 40 | 19 40 | 73 0 | 30 1 | 15 40 / 15 45 | Saw a flying-fish. |
| 16 | N. E. | Cloudy | 21 23 | 21 2 | 21 10 | 73 30 | 30 2 | — | { A great number of flying-fish. |

## JUNE 1787.

| Days. | Winds. | Weather. | Latitude in | Long. in | Longitude per Time-keeper, and Lunar Ob. | Therm. | Barom. | Variation per Az. and Am. | REMARKS. |
|---|---|---|---|---|---|---|---|---|---|
| 17 | N. E. | Cloudy | 18 53 N. | 22 8 W. | 22 22 W. | 74 0 | 30 11 | — | Saw a strange sail. |
| 18 | N. E. | Hazy | 16 27 | 23 11 | — | 76 0 | 30 0 | — | { Horizon line about two miles. |
| 19 | N. E. | Hazy | 14 53 | 23 11 | — | 76 0 | 30 0 | — | { Passed the Islands of Sal, Bonavista, and Mayo: looked into Port Praya. |
| 20 | E by N. | Hazy | 13 29 | 22 56 | — | 81 0 | 29 96 | | |
| 21 | East | Clear | 11 52 | 22 45 | 23 10 | 82 0 | 30 6 | 10 23 | |
| 22 | East | Clear | 10 43 | 22 57 | 22 57 | 82 0 | 30 14 | — | Lightning. |
| 23 | N. E. | Cloudy | 9 49 | 22 51 | — | 82 0 | 30 8 | — | { Heavy rain, lightning, and distant thunder. |

| | | | | | | | | | Remarks |
|---|---|---|---|---|---|---|---|---|---|
| 24 | Eaſt. | Cloudy | 9 2 | 22 46 | — | 81 0 | 30 3 | — | Ditto weather. |
| 25 | Variable | Showery | 8 32 | 22 56 | — | 82 0 | 30 2 | — | { Strong current ſetting to the N. W. |
| 26 | Variable | Clear | 8 45 | 22 50 | 22 34 | 85 0 | 30 3 | — | Light airs. |
| 27 | Variable | Calms | 8 12 | 22 31 | 21 45 | 82 0 | 30 4 | — | { Heavy rain, with thunder in the evening. |
| 28 | S. W. | Clear | 7 29 | 22 19 | 21 41 | 80 0 | 30 3 | — | { In the evening moderate breezes. |
| 29 | S. S. W. | Clear | 7 28 | 21 33 | — | 81 0 | 30 4 | — | |
| 30 | W. S. W. | Clear | 7 19 | 21 7 | 19 43 | 82 0 | 30 5 | — | { Ditto weather in the evening. |

## JULY 1787.

| Days. | Winds. | Weather. | Latitude in | Long. in | Longitude per Time-keeper, and Lunar Ob. | Therm. | Barom. | Variation per Az. and Am. | REMARKS. |
|---|---|---|---|---|---|---|---|---|---|
| 1 | S. S. W. | Cloudy | 6 48 N. | 20 37 W. | 18 51 W. | 79 0 | 30 7 | — | Heavy rain: saw a gull, and many flying-fish. |
| 2 | South | Clear | 6 36 | 20 33 | — | 80 0 | 30 6 | — | Tacked Ship, and stood to the westward. |
| 3 | S. S. E. | Cloudy | 6 36 | 21 29 | — | 80 0 | 30 5 | | |
| 4 | S. S. E. | Cloudy | 6 18 | 22 5 | — | 80 20 | 30 8 | | |
| 5 | S.W.by S. | Cloudy | 5 53 | 22 25 | — | 81 0 | 30 6 | — | A great variety of fish in chace of one another. |
| 6 | S. S. W. | Cloudy | 5 38 | 21 39 | — | 80 40 | 30 1 | — | Fresh breezes: a swell from the S. E. |
| 7 | S. by E. | Cloudy | 5 15 | 22 19 | — | 80 0 | 30 4 | — | Caught a Boneta. |
| 8 | S. by E. | Cloudy | 4 36 | 23 0 | — | 79 0 | 30 7 | — | Fish round us in great numbers. |

| No. | Wind | Weather | Lat. | Long. | | | | | | Remarks |
|---|---|---|---|---|---|---|---|---|---|---|
| 9 | S.E. by S. | Clear | 3 57 N. | 23 28 W. | — | 78 | 0 | 30 | 7 | — | Moderate weather, the sea very luminous. |
| 10 | S.E. by S. | Cloudy | 3 29 | 24 18 | — | 78 | 0 | 30 | 5 | — | Caught an Albacore, and several Bonetoes. |
| 11 | S. by E. | Hazy | 2 59 | 24 54 | — | 77 | 0 | 30 | 6 | | |
| 12 | S.E. by S. | Hazy | 2 24 | 25 6 | — | 77 | 0 | 30 | 6 | | |
| 13 | S E. by E. | Cloudy | 1 22 | 26 6 | — | 78 | 0 | 30 | 6 | — | Sea luminous, with Dolphins; caught two. |
| 14 | E. S. E. | Cloudy | 0 18 N. | 26 37 | — | 77 | 0 | 30 | 3 | — | Pleasant weather; sea quite luminous with ditto. |
| 15 | E. S. E. | Clear | 0 25 S. | 26 24 | — | 77 | 40 | 30 | 5 | — | Saw a Noddy, and two Pintado birds. |
| 16 | East | Clear | 1 24 | 26 22 | — | 78 | 0 | 30 | 3 | — | Sea perfectly luminous with fish; struck 14 with a gig. |
| 17 | East | Clear | 2 54 | 26 19 | — | 79 | 0 | 30 | 7 / 5 9 W. 4 40 | | |

b

## J U L Y   1787.

| Days. | Winds. | Weather. | Latitude in | Long. in | Longitude per Time-keeper, and Lunar Ob. | Therm. | Barom. | Variation per Az. and Am. | REMARKS. |
|---|---|---|---|---|---|---|---|---|---|
| 18 | E. by N. | Clear | ° ' 4 18 S. | ° ' 26 5 W. | — | 80 0 | 30 6 | 5 0 / 6 0 W. | |
| 19 | E. by S. | Clear | 6 3 | 25 53 | — | 80 40 | 30 7 | 6 0 / 6 0 W. | |
| 20 | East | Clear | 6 57 | 25 49 | — | 79 0 | 30 7 | 6 35 W. / 6 52 | |
| 21 | E. by S. | Clear | 8 0 | 26 0 | — | 79 0 | 30 7 | | |
| 22 | E. by S. | Cloudy | 9 8 | 26 4 | — | 79 0 | 30 9 | — | Saw a Noddy. |
| 23 | E by N. | Rainy | 10 4 | 26 0 | — | 75 0 | 30 13 | — | { Heavy showers; saw two Grampuses. |
| 24 | E. by S. | Cloudy | 11 52 | 26 3 | — | 77 0 | 30 17 | — | { Strong breezes, as the day before. |

| | | | | | | | | | Remarks |
|---|---|---|---|---|---|---|---|---|---|
| 25 | E. S. E. | Cloudy | 13 29 | 26 13 | — | 76 0 | 30 20 | 0 0 3 44 W. | Ditto weather. |
| 26 | E. by S. | Cloudy | 15 18 | 26 41 | 29 34 W. | 75 0 | 30 2 | — | { Saw flying-fish with double fins. |
| 27 | E. S. E. | Showers | 16 36 | 27 12 | — | 73 0 | 30 20 | — | { Unsettled weather; swell from the eastward. |
| 28 | E. S. E. | Cloudy | 18 13 | 28 2 | — | 73 0 | 30 22 | — | Fresh breezes. |
| 29 | East | Clear | 19 36 | 29 38 | — | 72 0 | 30 24 | 0 0 1 30 E. | { Pleasant weather. Looking for Trinidada. |
| 30 | N.E.byE. | Cloudy | 20 41 | 30 50 | — | 72 0 | 30 26 | | |
| 31 | N.E.byE. | Clear | 21 48 | 32 5 | — | 75 0 | 30 26 | 5 47 E. 5 24 | Pleasant dry weather. |

## AUGUST 1787.

| Days. | Winds. | Weather. | Latitude in | Long. in | Longitude per Time-keeper, and Lunar Ob. | Therm. | Barom. | Variation per Az. and Am. | REMARKS. |
|---|---|---|---|---|---|---|---|---|---|
| 1 | N. E. | Clear | °  '<br>22 39 S. | °  '<br>33 24 W. | — | 75 0 | 30 17 | — | Pleasant weather. |
| 2 | N. E. | Clear | 23 3 | — | — | 73 0 | — | — | Saw the coast of Brazil. |
| 3 | Variable | Hazy | 23 12 | — | — | 72 0 | — | — | { In sight of Rio de Janeiro Sugar Loaf. |
| 4 | Variable | Hazy | 23 14 | — | — | 69 0 | — | — | |
| 5 | Variable | Hazy | 23 6 | — | — | 71 0 | — | — | { Saw many Whales and Porpoises. |
| 6 | Variable | Clear | — | — | — | 72 0 | — | — | Anchored out side of Rio bar. |
| 7 | Calm | Clear | — | — | — | 72 0 | — | — | { Anchored in Rio de Janeiro Harbour. |

| Day | Wind | Weather | | | | Therm. | | | Remarks |
|---|---|---|---|---|---|---|---|---|---|
| 8 | Calm | Dark | — | — | — | 74° | — | — | A visit of ceremony by all the Officers paid the Vice-King. |
| 9 | — | Rain | — | — | — | 65° | — | — | At anchor in Rio de Janeiro Harbour. |
| 10 | — | Cloudy | — | — | — | 70° | — | — | |
| 11 | Calm | Clear | — | — | — | 77° | — | — | |
| 12 | Calm | Clear | — | — | — | 76° | — | — | |
| 13 | Calm | Clear | — | — | — | 75° | — | — | |
| 14 | Calm | Clear | — | — | — | 76° | — | — | |
| 15 | Calm | Clear | — | — | — | 75° | — | — | |
| 16 | Calm | Clear | — | — | — | 76° | — | — | |

## A U G U S T  1787.

| Days. | Winds. | Weather. | Latitude in | Long. in | Longitude per Time-keeper, and Lunar Ob. | Therm. | Barom. | Variation per Az. and Am. | REMARKS. |
|---|---|---|---|---|---|---|---|---|---|
| 17 | Variable | Rain | — | — | — | 69° | — | — | |
| 18 | Variable | Dark | — | — | — | 69° | — | — | At anchor in Rio de Janeiro Harbour. |
| 19 | Variable | Dark | — | — | — | 72° | — | — | |
| 20 | Variable | Cloudy | — | — | — | 74° | — | — | |
| 21 | Variable | Clear | — | — | — | 75° | — | — | Prince of Brazils birth-day; paid compliments to the Vice-King. |
| 22 | Calm | Clear | — | — | — | 76° | — | — | At anchor in Rio de Janeiro Harbour. |
| 23 | Calm | Hazy | — | — | — | 76° | — | — | |

| | | | | | | | | | Remarks |
|---|---|---|---|---|---|---|---|---|---|
| 24 | Variable | Hazy | — | — | 74° | — | — | — | |
| 25 | Calm | Clear | — | — | 72° | — | — | — | |
| 26 | Variable | Clear | — | — | 70° | — | — | — | |
| 27 | Variable | Cloudy | — | — | 72° | — | — | — | At anchor in Rio de Janeiro Harbour, |
| 28 | Variable | Clear | — | — | 76° | — | — | — | |
| 29 | Calm | Clear | — | — | 78° | — | — | — | |
| 30 | Variable | Clear | — | — | 74° | — | — | — | |
| 31 | Calm | Clear | — | — | 75° | — | — | — | |

## SEPTEMBER 1787.

| Days. | Winds. | Weather. | Latitude in | Long. in | Longitude per Time-keeper, and Lunar Ob. | Therm. | Barom. | Variation per Az. and Am. | REMARKS. |
|---|---|---|---|---|---|---|---|---|---|
| 1 | Calm | Clear | — | — | — | 78 ° | — | — | { All the Officers took leave of the Vice-King. |
| 2 | Calm | Cloudy | — | — | — | 72 ° | — | — | } Still in Rio harbour. |
| 3 | Calm | Dark | — | — | — | 72 ° | — | — | |
| 4 | Variable | Clear | — | — | — | 76 ° | — | — | { Sailed for the Cape of Good Hope. |
| 5 | Variable | Cloudy | — | — | — | 71 ° | — | — | Rio Sugar Loaf in sight. |
| 6 | N. E. | Cloudy | 24 33 S. | 42 32 W. | — | 72 ° | 30 2 | — | |
| 7 | N. N. E. | Dark | 25 47 | 40 52 | — | 73 ° | 30 28 | — | At night heavy rain. |

| No. | Wind | Weather | | | | | | | Remarks |
|---|---|---|---|---|---|---|---|---|---|
| 8 | S. by E. | Cloudy | 25 54 S. | 39 47 W. | 39 39 W. | 68 0 | 30 21 | — | Showery at times. |
| 9 | S. ½ E. | Clear | 26 6 | 38 25 | 38 9 | 67 30 | 30 23 | — | Fine dry weather. |
| 10 | S. S. E. | Clear | 25 55 | 37 15 | 37 7 | 63 0 | 30 22 | 4 30 E. 0 0 |  |
| 11 | E. N. E. | Cloudy | 27 6 | 37 18 | — | 68 0 | 30 16 | — | Strong breezes, with squalls. |
| 12 | E. N. E. | Rainy | 28 40 | 36 8 | — | 67 0 | 30 14 | — | { Ditto weather, with heavy rain. |
| 13 | N. by E. | Rainy | 29 52 | 34 7 | — | 64 0 | 30 14 | — | Ditto weather. |
| 14 | S. by E. | Dark | 30 28 | 32 26 | — | 66 0 | 30 12 | — | Light airs. |
| 15 | South | Cloudy | 30 37 | 32 11 | 31 39 | 68 0 | 30 20 | — | Caught a Shark. |
| 16 | N. by E. | Cloudy | 30 54 | 31 21 | — | 67 0 | 30 25 | — | Damp moist air. |

## SEPTEMBER 1787.

| Days. | Winds. | Weather. | Latitude in | Long, in | Longitude per Time-keeper, and Lunar Ob. | Therm. | Barom. | Variation per Az. and Am. | REMARKS. |
|---|---|---|---|---|---|---|---|---|---|
| 17 | E. by N. | Cloudy | ° ′ 31 36 S. | ° ′ 28 56 W. | 31 34 W. | 66 0 | 30 17 | — | Damp moist air. |
| 18 | N. N. E. | Dark | 32 17 | 26 20 | — | 63 0 | 30 14 | — | { Rain. Saw several Albatrosses and Pintado Birds. |
| 19 | South | Cloudy | 32 10 | 24 14 | 24 30 | 57 0 | 30 15 | — | A Convict lost overboard. |
| 20 | S.E. byE. | Cloudy | 31 54 | 22 26 | — | 58 0 | 30 12 | — | { Albatrosses and Pintado Birds about the ship. |
| 21 | S. E. | Clear | 32 7 | 22 24 | 22 45 | 58 30 | 30 15 | — | |
| 22 | N. E. | Cloudy | 33 4 | 22 4 | — | 59 0 | 30 38 | — | Cold dry weather. |
| 23 | N. N. E. | Dark | 33 54 | 19 28 | — | 59 0 | 29 96 | — | Strong squalls. |

| | Wind | Weather | Latitude | Longitude | | Therm. | Barom. | | Remarks |
|---|---|---|---|---|---|---|---|---|---|
| 24 | S. S. W. | Cloudy | 34 9 | 16 37 | — | 54 0 | 29 94 | — | Cold weather; high sea. |
| 25 | W. by N. | Squally | 34 25 | 13 24 | — | 54 0 | 29 84 | — | Strong gales, with some hail, and a high sea. |
| 26 | West | Clear | 34 19 | 10 10 | — | 53 0 | 30 20 | — | Many birds about the ship. |
| 27 | West | Cloudy | 34 25 | 7 13 | — | — | 30 36 | — | |
| 28 | W. N. W. | Cloudy | 34 36 | 3 59 | — | 61 0 | 29 96 | — | Unsettled weather. |
| 29 | S. S. E. | Squally | 34 20 | 1 56 | — | 59 0 | 30 1 | — | Cold, wet, unpleasant weather. |
| 30 | Variable | Clear | 33 55 S. | 1 8 W. | 3 10 W. | 56 0 | 30 4 | 6 0 W. | Inclinable to calm. |

## OCTOBER 1787.

| Days. | Winds. | Weather. | Latitude in | Long. in | Longitude per Time-keeper, and Lunar Ob. | Therm. | Barom. | Variation per Az. and Am. | REMARKS. |
|---|---|---|---|---|---|---|---|---|---|
| 1 | N. N. W | Dark | 34 42 S. | 1 10 E. | — | 60 7 | 29 19 | — | { Saw a great many birds of different kinds. |
| 2 | N. W. | Clear | 35 9 | 2 49 E. | 0 36 E. | 60 4 | 30 17 | — | Pleasant weather. |
| 3 | N E. | Cloudy | 35 20 | 3 17 | — | 62 0 | 30 22 | 12 8 W. | Light air, and small rain. |
| 4 | N. by W. | Foggy | 35 35 | 4 56 | — | 63 6 | 30 14 | — | Moderate weather; some rain. |
| 5 | — | Foggy | 35 39 | 5 57 | — | 62 9 | 30 22 | — | Cloudy, damp weather. |
| 6 | E. by N. | Clear | 36 18 | 6 9 | — | 63 4 | 30 8 | — | { Light air, and pleasant weather. |
| 7 | N. E. | Dark | 36 51 | 6 37 | 5 52 E. | 61 5 | 29 93 | 16 30 W. | Damp, moderate weather. |

| | | | | | | | | | Remarks |
|---|---|---|---|---|---|---|---|---|---|
| 8 | N. W. | Clear | 36 59 | 8 35 | 7 55 | 60 0 | 29 97 | — | Air damp, although clear. |
| 9 | W. by N. | Clear | 36 28 | 10 39 | — | 60 3 | 30 0 | 16 40 W. / 10 54 W. | Flocks of Oceanic Birds. |
| 10 | W. by N. | Clear | 35 27 | 13 37 | — | 57 8 | 30 36 | — | { Flying clouds; many birds about. |
| 11 | West | Cloudy | 35 0 | 15 49 | — | 60 1 | 30 3¹ | — | Saw some Peterels. |
| 12 | South | Cloudy | 34 28 S. | 17 24 E. | — | 60 4 | 30 20 | 21 10 W. / 18 45 | A swell from the S. E. |
| 13 | W. S. W. | Hazy | — | — | — | — | — | — | { Anchored in Table Bay, Cape of Good Hope. |
| 14 | — | — | — | — | — | — | — | — | |
| 15 | — | — | — | — | — | — | — | — | } At anchor. |
| 16 | — | — | — | — | — | — | — | — | |

## OCTOBER 1787.

| Days. | Winds. | Weather. | Latitude in | Long. in | Longitude per Time-keeper, and Lunar Ob. | Therm. | Barom. | Variation per Az. and Am. | REMARKS. |
|---|---|---|---|---|---|---|---|---|---|
| 17 | — | — | — | — | — | — | — | — | |
| 18 | — | — | — | — | — | — | — | — | |
| 19 | — | — | — | — | — | — | — | — | |
| 20 | — | — | — | — | — | — | — | — | At anchor: my living on shore for the recovery of my health prevented me from filling up this blank. |
| 21 | — | — | — | — | — | — | — | — | |
| 22 | — | — | — | — | — | — | — | — | |
| 23 | — | — | — | — | — | — | — | — | |

# A P P E N D I X.

Still at anchor at the Cape of Good Hope.

| 24 | 25 | 26 | 27 | 28 | 29 | 30 | 31 |
|----|----|----|----|----|----|----|----|
| I | I | I | I | I | I | I | I |
| I | I | I | I | I | I | I | I |
| I | I | I | I | I | I | I | I |
| I | I | I | I | I | I | I | I |
| I | I | I | I | I | I | I | I |
| I | I | I | I | I | I | I | I |
| I | I | I | I | I | I | I | I |
| I | I | I | I | I | I | I | I |

## NOVEMBER 1787.

| Days. | Winds. | Weather. | Latitude in | Long. in | Longitude per Time-keeper, and Lunar Ob. | Therm. | Barom. | Variation per Az. and Am. | REMARKS. |
|---|---|---|---|---|---|---|---|---|---|
| 1 | | | | | | | | | |
| 2 | | | | | | | | | |
| 3 | | | | | | | | | Still at anchor at the Cape of Good Hope. |
| 4 | | | | | | | | | |
| 5 | | | | | | | | | |
| 6 | | | | | | | | | |
| 7 | | | | | | | | | |

| No. | | | | | | | Remarks |
|---|---|---|---|---|---|---|---|
| 8 | — | — | — | — | — | — | |
| 9 | — | — | — | — | — | — | |
| 10 | — | — | — | — | — | — | Still at anchor at the Cape of Good Hope. |
| 11 | — | — | — | — | — | — | |
| 12 | — | — | — | — | — | — | |
| 13 | S. by E. | Clear | — | — | — | 63 0 | 30 40 | Sailed from the Cape of Good Hope. |
| 14 | S. by E. | Clear | 35 12 S. | 16 2 E. | 15 7 E. | 63 0 | 30 30 | |
| 15 | S. by W. | Clear | 35 23 | 15 4 | 13 29 | 62 30 | 30 53 | |
| 16 | Variable | Hazy | 34 44 | 14 56 | 12 37 | 63 45 | 30 25 | A dysentery made its appearance. |

## N O V E M B E R   1787.

| Days. | Winds. | Weather. | Latitude in | Long. in | Longitude per Time-keeper, and Lunar Ob. | Therm. | Barom. | Variation per Az. and Am. | REMARKS. |
|---|---|---|---|---|---|---|---|---|---|
| 17 | South | Squally | 36 40 S. | 14 10 E. | 11 42 E. | 61 15 | 30 14 | — | Rain. |
| 18 | South | Cloudy | 37 13 | 14 26 | 10 43 | 61 30 | 30 32 | 21 99 W. | |
| 19 | Variable | Hazy | 37 40 | 13 58 | 10 29 | 62 45 | 30 8 | 20 54 | Inclinable to calm. |
| 20 | Calm | Hazy | 37 38 | 13 50 | 10 21 | 64 15 | 29 99 | 21 18 | |
| 21 | N. N. E. | Clear | 38 39 | 16 37 | 12 57 | 65 0 | 29 88 | — | Saw some Whales. |
| 22 | N. N. W. | Clear | 39 0 | 20 5 | — | 65 0 | 29 91 | 20 4 | |
| 23 | West | Cloudy | 39 8 | 22 49 | — | 65 30 | 29 95 | — | Prince of Wales lost a Sailor overboard. |

| | | | | | | | | | Remarks |
|---|---|---|---|---|---|---|---|---|---|
| 24 | S. S. W. | Cloudy | 39 5 | 25 3 | — | 63 30 | 30 7 | — | Saw a great number of birds. |
| 25 | Variable | Cloudy | 38 48 | 24 34 | 20 49 | 61 30 | 31 1 | — | Heavy rain, with squalls. |
| 26 | S.W. | Clear | 38 8 | 25 31 | — | 62 0 | 30 20 | — | |
| 27 | E. S. E. | Clear | 38 31 | 26 17 | — | 61 30 | 30 20 | — | |
| 28 | E. N. E. | Hazy | 39 10 | 28 5 | — | 62 0 | 29 8 | 27 0 / 27 30 | Strong gales, with drizzling rain. |
| 29 | W. S. W. | Hazy | 39 56 | 30 12 | — | 63 30 | 29 30 | — | Moderate weather; damp air. |
| 30 | Variable | Clear | 40 0 | 31 22 | — | 66 30 | 30 9 | 28 30 W. | Heavy rain. |

## DECEMBER 1787.

| Days. | Winds. | Weather. | Latitude in | Long. in | Longitude per Time-keeper, and Lunar Ob. | Therm. | Barom. | Variation per Az. and Am. | REMARKS. |
|---|---|---|---|---|---|---|---|---|---|
| 1 | W. S. W. | Clear | 40 4 S. | 33 53 E. | — | 62 0 | 29 8 | 26 54 W. | Moderate, pleasant weather. |
| 2 | S.W.by W. | Clear | 40 3 | 35 10 | 36 45 | 61 30 | 29 30 | 29 20 / 28 30 | Saw many birds. |
| 3 | North | Clear | 40 18 | 38 44 | 41 1 | 61 45 | 29 87 | 30 42 / 31 20 | |
| 4 | N. N. W. | Cloudy | 40 36 | 42 40 | — | 60 30 | 29 8 | — | Strong gales; wet, unpleasant weather, and high sea. |
| 5 | Calm | Hazy | 40 15 | 44 20 | — | 58 0 | 29 8 | 31 10 | A great swell in the evening; wind at E. N. E. |
| 6 | N.W.byW | Clear | 40 49 | 45 54 | — | 60 0 | 29 62 | | |
| 7 | W. N.W | Clear | 40 34 | 48 11 | — | 61 30 | 29 77 | 29 58 | |

| | Wind | Weather | Lat. | | | | | | Remarks |
|---|---|---|---|---|---|---|---|---|---|
| 8 | West | Clear | 40 19 | 50 21 | — | — | — | 31 0 | |
| 9 | N. N. E. | Rain | 40 21 | 53 20 | — | 61 30 | 29 77 | 32 12 | Moderate breezes. |
| 10 | W. S. W. | Clear | 41 12 | 56 20 | — | 59 30 | 29 81 | — | Cold, moderate weather. |
| 11 | West | Cloudy | 40 56 | 58 34 | | | | | |
| 12 | N. N. E. | Clear | 40 56 | 61 50 | — | 62 30 | 30 0 | 29 9 / 30 30 | |
| 13 | W. S. W. | Hazy | 40 57 | 65 40 | — | 62 30 | 29 6 | — | { Squally at times, with small rain. |
| 14 | S. W. | Clear | 41 2 | 68 50 | — | 60 0 | 30 33 | 28 33 W. / 27 30 | Moderate, light winds. |
| 15 | N. N. W. | Clear | 40 56 | 71 8 | — | 61 0 | 29 85 | 23 30 / 25 0 | Saw some large Whales. |
| 16 | W. N. W. | Clear | 41 6 | 74 54 | — | 61 30 | 30 16 | 22 16 / 23 50 | { Saw a Seal, some rock-weed, and many birds of the Petrel kind. |

## DECEMBER 1787.

| Days. | Winds. | Weather. | Latitude in | Long. in | Longitude per Time-keeper, and Lunar Ob. | Therm. | Barom. | Variation per Az. and Am. | REMARKS. |
|---|---|---|---|---|---|---|---|---|---|
| 17 | N. N. W. | Dark | 41° 10′ S. | 77 37 E. | — | — | — | — | Saw fome Gulls in the evening. |
| 18 | S. by W. | Cloudy | 41 6 | 79 47 | — | 55 30 | 30 6 | — | Cold weather; faw fome Whales. |
| 19 | Variable | Dark | 41 5 | 82 29 | — | 55 30 | 30 8 | — | Cold weather. The fcurvy broke out on board the Prince of Wales. |
| 20 | Variable | Cloudy | 41 4 | 84 29 | — | 55 30 | 29 96 | 19 0 | |
| 21 | S. W. | Dark | 41 4 | 86 47 | — | 57 0 | 29 80 | — | Rain. Saw fome fea-weed. |
| 22 | W. N. W. | Hazy | 41 21 | 90 7 | — | 59 0 | 29 82 | — | Freſh breezes, with fmall rain. |
| 23 | W. by N. | Hazy | 41 34 | 93 27 | — | 59 0 | 30 7 | | |

| | | | | | | | | | Remarks |
|---|---|---|---|---|---|---|---|---|---|
| 24 | W. by N. | Cloudy | 41 44 | 95 49 | — | 53 30 | 30 10 | 17 40 / 18 0 | { Moderate weather; many birds about the ship. |
| 25 | N.W.byN. | Hazy | 42 9 | 99 33 | — | 61 30 | 29 98 | — | Drizzling rain. |
| 26 | W. S W. | Clear | 42 20 | 102 6 | — | 57 0 | 30 2 | 14 30 | |
| 27 | W. N. W. | Hazy | 42 40 | 105 36 | — | — | — | — | Saw more sea-weed. |
| 28 | W. N. W. | Hazy | 42 59 | 109 14 | — | 58 30 | 30 11 | — | { Saw several Albatrosses and Gulls. |
| 29 | N. W. | Hazy | 43 35 | 113 29 | — | — | — | 15 20 | High following sea. |
| 30 | W. S. W. | Clear | 43 51 | 116 32 | — | 55 30 | 29 67 | — | Some Whales about the ship. |
| 31 | N. N. W. | Cloudy | 43 53 S. | 120 39 E | — | — | — | — | { Dark gloomy weather, with rain and squalls. |

## JANUARY 1788.

| Days. | Winds. | Weather. | Latitude in | Long. in | Longitude per Time-keeper, and Lunar Ob. | Therm. | Barom. | Variation per Az. and Am. | REMARKS. |
|---|---|---|---|---|---|---|---|---|---|
| 1 | N. by W. | Clear | ° ′ <br> 44 4 S. | ° ′ <br> 123 48 E. | — | — | — | — | Heavy gales, with fudden fqualls; at night the wind N. by E. |
| 2 | W. N. W. | Cloudy | 43 34 | 126 48 | — | 59 0 | 29 62 | — | Unpleafant, unfettled weather; many birds about the fhip. |
| 3 | W. N. W. | Rain | 43 48 | 130 40 | — | 56 30 | 29 96 | — | Saw fome Seals, and many Albatroffes. |
| 4 | W. N. W. | Cloudy | 44 0 | 134 15 | 135 30 | 57 45 | 30 0 | 1 22 W. <br> 1 0 | Some Mother Carey's chickens about the fhip. |
| 5 | N. W. | Clear | 44 2 | 137 50 | — | 55 0 | 29 88 | 1 0 E. | Cold weather; paffed fome fea-weed. |
| 6 | Weft | Cloudy | 44 4 | 141 5 | — | 56 0 | 29 88 | — | Some fqualls, with rain. |
| 7 | N. N. W. | Cloudy | 44 4 | 144 48 | — | 62 0 | 29 90 | — | Saw the S. W. Cape of New Holland. |

| No. | Wind | Weather | | | | | | | Remarks |
|---|---|---|---|---|---|---|---|---|---|
| 8 | Variable | — | — | — | — | 63 45 | 29 92 | — | |
| 9 | Variable | Squally | 44 15 | — | — | 66 30 | 29 96 | 5 30 | { Dark, damp weather, with thunder and lightning. |
| 10 | Variable | Dark | 42 28 | — | — | 61 40 | 29 1 | 7 24 | Strong, fudden fqualls. |
| 11 | Variable | Cloudy | 41 15 | — | — | 65 0 | 29 77 | 8 50 | { Squally, Birds and Seals about the Ship. |
| 12 | S. S. W. | Clear | 40 1 | — | — | 62 30 | 29 31 | 9 40 | { Whales and birds about the fhip. |
| 13 | Variable | Hazy | — | — | — | 66 30 | 29 70 | 10 50 / 10 52 | |
| 14 | W. S. W. | Hazy | 37 39 | — | — | 66 30 | 29 79 | 10 30 | Warm moift air. |
| 15 | Variable | Dark | 37 39 | — | 151 30 | 74 30 | 30 29 | — | { Ditto weather, with ftrong breezes. |
| 16 | North | Hazy | 37 22 | — | 151 40 | 75 15 | 29 66 | — | { Ditto weather; at night thunder and lightning. |

## J A N U A R Y  1788.

| Days. | Winds. | Weather. | Latitude in | Long. in | Longitude per Time-keeper, and Lunar Ob. | Therm. | Barom. | Variation per Az. and Am. | REMARKS. |
|---|---|---|---|---|---|---|---|---|---|
| 17 | Variable | Clear | 35 48 S. | — | 151 36 | 74 15 | 29 6 | 9 40 E. | Inclinable to calm. |
| 18 | S. S. E. | Cloudy | 34 30 | — | — | 72 30 | 29 96 | — | { Pleafant weather. Saw the land over Red Point. |
| 19 | Variable. | Cloudy | — | — | — | 70 30 | 30 33 | — | { In the morning faw the land near Botany Bay. |
| 20 | — | Clear | — | 34 0 E. | 151 23 E. | 74 45 | 30 20 | — | Anchored in Botany Bay. |
| 21 | — | Clear | — | — | — | 75 0 | 30 21 | — | |
| 22 | — | — | — | — | — | 74 30 | 30 21 | — | |
| 23 | — | — | — | — | — | 75 0 | 30 17 | — | |

> This day I had the misfortune to break the only thermometer I had left of fix, and my barometer, on taking them on fhore, to determine the difference between it and the air on board a fhip.

| | | | | | | | |
|---|---|---|---|---|---|---|---|
| — | — | — | — | — | — | — | — |
| 75 0 29 97 | 70 0 29 98 | — | — | — | — | — | — |
| — | — | — | — | — | — | — | — |
| — | — | — | — | — | — | — | — |
| — | — | — | — | — | — | — | — |
| — | — | — | — | — | — | — | — |
| — | — | — | — | — | — | — | — |
| 24 | 25 | 26 | 27 | 28 | 29 | 30 | 31 |

# Physician Travelers

AN ARNO PRESS/NEW YORK TIMES COLLECTION

Abel, Clarke.
**Narrative of a Journey in the Interior of China.** 1818.

Bancroft, Edward.
**An Essay on the Natural History of Guiana.** 1769.

Bell, John.
**Observations on Italy.** 1825.

Brown, Edward.
**Account of Some Travels.** 1673-1677.

Granville, Augustus Bozzi.
**St. Petersburgh: Travels to and From That Capital.** 1828.
(2 volumes)

Hamilton, Alexander.
**Itinerarium.** 1907.

Hodgkin, Thomas.
**Narrative of a Journey to Morocco.** 1866.

Holland, Henry.
**Travels in the Ionian Isles, Albania, Thessaly, Macedonia, etc.** 1815.

Holmes, Oliver Wendell.
**Our Hundred Days in Europe.** 1887.

Jeffries, John.
**A Narrative of Two Aerial Voyages.** 1786.

Kane, Elisha Kent.
**Arctic Explorations in 1853, 1854, 1855.** 1856. (2 volumes)

Linnaeus, Carl.
**A Tour in Lapland.** 1811.

Lister, Martin.
**A Journey to Paris in 1698.** 1698.

Park, Mungo.
**Travels in the Interior Districts of Africa.** 1799.

White, John.
**Journal of a Voyage to New South Wales.** 1790.

Wilde, William.
**Lough Corrib: Its Shores and Islands.** 1867.

Wittman, William.
**Travels in Turkey, Asia Minor, Syria and Egypt.** 1803.

Wurdeman, John G. F.
**Notes on Cuba.** 1844.